(Un)Settled Sojourners in Cities

Temporary migration is a human response to uncertain economic, ecological, political and socio-cultural environments. This book provides an important contribution to the literature on the rights, lived experiences and trajectories of temporary migrants. It focuses on the precarity of temporary migrants at different scales in urban settings, varying from the household, institution, and neighbourhood to the city. Temporary migrants experience oscillations in precarity that vary with their categorization as skilled (professionals with valued skill sets, international students) or unskilled (domestic workers, labourers), their ambiguous legal status and the locales in which they reside and work. Individual chapters use case studies from around the world (USA, Canada, Ireland, Turkey, Singapore, China) to show how temporal and scalar precarity intersect and are mediated by national and local policies, civil society, as well as the personal and social attributes of migrants themselves such as gender, race, and country of origin. Although often overlooked due to their transitory status, the chapters demonstrate how temporary migrants are embedded in urban life and resist their categorization as disposable through individual and collective efforts. This book will be of interest to researchers and advanced students of Sociology, Politics, Human Geography, Urban Studies, and Social and Cultural Anthropology. It was originally published as a special issue of the *Journal of Ethnic and Migration Studies*.

Elizabeth Chacko is Professor of Geography and International Affairs at George Washington University, USA. She has conducted research in the United States, India, Ethiopia, and Singapore on the flows of people, capital and ideas, and their impacts on economic, cultural, and social geographies in cities.

Marie Price is Professor of Geography and International Affairs at George Washington University, USA. She is interested in how cities and civil society respond to immigrants as well as how immigrants influence these localities through their own agency and networks. Most of her work focuses upon the Americas.

Research in Ethnic and Migration Studies

Series editor: **Paul Statham**, *Director, Sussex Centre for Migration Research (SCMR), University of Sussex, UK*

The *Research in Ethnic and Migration Studies* series publishes the results of high-quality, cutting-edge research that addresses key questions relating to ethnic relations, diversity and migration. The series is open to a range of disciplines and brings together research collaborations on specific defined topics on all aspects of migration and its consequences, including migration processes, migrants and their experiences, ethnic relations, discrimination, integration, racism, transnationalism, citizenship, identity and cultural diversity. Contributions are especially welcome when they are the result of comparative research, either across countries, cities or groups. All articles have previously been published in the *Journal of Ethnic and Migration Studies (JEMS)*, which has a rigorous peer review system. Collective volumes in this series are either the product of Special Issues published in the journal or published articles that the Editor has selected from individual submissions.

Thai-Western Mobilities and Migration
Intimacy within Cross-Border Connections
Edited by Paul Statham, Sarah Scuzzarello, Sirijit Sunanta and Alexander Trupp

Migration and Marriage in Asian Contexts
Edited by Zheng Mu and Wei-Jun Jean Yeung

New Theoretical Dialogues on Migration in China
Edited by Hong Zhu and Junxi Qian

(Un)Settled Sojourners in Cities
Challenges of "Temporariness" among Migrants and Asylum Seekers
Edited by Elizabeth Chacko and Marie Price

The Spiralling of the Securitization of Migration in the European Union
Edited by Valeria Bello and Sarah Léonard

The Question of Skill in Cross-Border Labour Mobilities
Edited by Gracia Liu-Farrer, Brenda S.A. Yeoh and Michiel Baas

For more information about this series, please visit:
www.routledge.com/Research-in-Ethnic-and-Migration-Studies/book-series/REMS

© Elizabeth Chacko. Photo of a couple participating in a protest organised by a group of temporary migrants from Central America outside the White House in Washington, DC in March 2022, demanding permanent resident status. The sign reads, “We are thousands of essential workers. Residence for all!”

(Un)Settled Sojourners in Cities

Challenges of "Temporariness" among Migrants and Asylum Seekers

Edited by
Elizabeth Chacko and Marie Price

Routledge
Taylor & Francis Group
LONDON AND NEW YORK

First published 2023
by Routledge
4 Park Square, Milton Park, Abingdon, Oxon OX14 4RN

and by Routledge
605 Third Avenue, New York, NY 10158

Routledge is an imprint of the Taylor & Francis Group, an informa business

British Library Cataloguing in Publication Data
A catalogue record for this book is available from the British Library

ISBN13: 978-1-032-43381-3 (hbk)
ISBN13: 978-1-032-43382-0 (pbk)
ISBN13: 978-1-003-36705-5 (ebk)

DOI: 10.4324/9781003367055

Typeset in Minion Pro
by Newgen Publishing UK

Publisher's Note
The publisher accepts responsibility for any inconsistencies that may have arisen during the conversion of this book from journal articles to book chapters, namely the inclusion of journal terminology.

Contents

Citation Information

The chapters in this book were originally published in the *Journal of Ethnic and Migration Studies*, volume 47, issue 20 (2021). When citing this material, please use the original page numbering for each article, as follows:

Chapter 1

Introduction—(Un)settled sojourners in cities: the scalar and temporal dimensions of migrant precarity
Elizabeth Chacko and Marie Price
Journal of Ethnic and Migration Studies, volume 47, issue 20 (2021), pp. 4597–4614

Chapter 2

The uneven geography of asylum and humanitarian relief: place-based precarity for Central American migrant youth in the United States judicial system
Sarah A. Blue, Alisa Hartsell, Rebecca Torres and Paul Flynn
Journal of Ethnic and Migration Studies, volume 47, issue 20 (2021), pp. 4631–4650

Chapter 3

Precarity of refugees: the case of Basmane-İzmir, Turkey
Asli Ceylan Oner, Bahar Durmaz-Drinkwater and Richard J. Grant
Journal of Ethnic and Migration Studies, volume 47, issue 20 (2021), pp. 4651–4670

Chapter 4

Soft violence: migrant domestic worker precarity and the management of unfree labour in Singapore
Rhacel Salazar Parreñas, Krittiya Kantachote and Rachel Silvey
Journal of Ethnic and Migration Studies, volume 47, issue 20 (2021), pp. 4671–4687

Chapter 5

Temporary migrants and public space: a case study of Dongguan, China
Yining Tan
Journal of Ethnic and Migration Studies, volume 47, issue 20 (2021), pp. 4688–4704

Chapter 6

Consuming the neighbourhood? Temporary highly skilled migrants in Montreal's Mile End
Gabrielle Désilets
Journal of Ethnic and Migration Studies, volume 47, issue 20 (2021), pp. 4705–4722

Chapter 7

Promising precarity: the lives of Dublin's international students
Mary Gilmartin, Pablo Rojas Coppari and Dean Phelan
Journal of Ethnic and Migration Studies, volume 47, issue 20 (2021), pp. 4723–4740

Chapter 8

Emerging precarity among international students in Singapore: experiences, understandings and responses
Elizabeth Chacko
Journal of Ethnic and Migration Studies, volume 47, issue 20 (2021), pp. 4741–4757

Chapter 9

The ordinary lives and uneven precarity of the DACAmented: visualising migrant precarity in metropolitan Washington
Marie Price and Giancarla Rojas
Journal of Ethnic and Migration Studies, volume 47, issue 20 (2021), pp. 4758–4778

Notes on Contributors

Sarah A. Blue, Department of Geography, Texas State University, San Marcos, TX, USA.

Elizabeth Chacko, Department of Geography, George Washington University, Washington, DC, USA.

Pablo Rojas Coppari, Department of Sociology, Maynooth University, Maynooth, Ireland.

Gabrielle Désilets, Institut national de santé publique du Québec, Montreal, Canada.

Bahar Durmaz-Drinkwater, Department of Architecture, İzmir University of Economics, Balçova-İzmir, Turkey.

Paul Flynn, Sail Internet, Palo Alto, CA. USA.

Mary Gilmartin, Department of Geography, Maynooth University, Maynooth, Ireland.

Richard J. Grant, Department of Geography and Regional Studies, University of Miami, Coral Gables, FL, USA; School of Tourism and Hospitality, College of Business and Economics, University of Johannesburg, Johannesburg, South Africa.

Alisa Hartsell, Department of Geography, Texas State University, San Marcos, TX, USA.

Krittiya Kantachote, Srinakharinwirot University, Bangkok, Thailand.

Asli Ceylan Oner, Department of Architecture, İzmir University of Economics, Balçova-İzmir, Turkey.

Rhacel Salazar Parreñas, University of Southern California, Los Angeles, CA, USA.

Dean Phelan, School of Geography, Archaeology and Irish Studies, University of Galway, Galway, Ireland.

Marie Price, Department of Geography, George Washington University, Washington, DC, USA.

Giancarla Rojas, Washington, DC, USA.

Rachel Silvey, University of Toronto, Toronto, Canada.

Yining Tan, School of Geography, Development & Environment, University of Arizona, Tucson, AZ, USA.

Rebecca Torres, Department of Geography and the Environment, University of Texas at Austin, Austin, TX, USA.

Introduction—(Un)settled sojourners in cities: the scalar and temporal dimensions of migrant precarity

Elizabeth Chacko and Marie Price

ABSTRACT

In this volume, we focus on temporary migrants as an important and often overlooked demographic in urban areas around the world. We demonstrate through empirical evidence that these migrants experience oscillations in precarity over time and that these fluctuations are mediated and better understood through a sensitivity to different scales and scalar processes. Most migration policies are created by national governments that privilege certain categories of migrants (such as high-skilled professionals or international students) over others (such as low-skilled or asylum seekers). However, the lived experience of many temporary migrants plays out in the households, neighbourhoods, and cities in which they reside and work. Temporary migrant precarity is also influenced by policies and practices shaped by local urban governments and civil society. Thus, temporary migrants are subject to intersecting and varied levels of temporal and scalar precarity, often compounded by personal and social attributes. Finally, we demonstrate that many temporary migrants employ individual and collective agency to resist their categorisation as disposable and transitory workers.

> We are the precarious, the flexible, the temporary, the mobile. We're the people that live on a tightrope, in a precarious balance, we're the restructured and outsourced, those who lack a stable job, and those who are overexploited ... We're just like you: contortionists of flexibility.[1]

This book is concerned with the precarity of temporary migrants and how this precarity intersects with urban life and space. Precarity is characterised by a status that is temporary, uncertain, and restrictive in terms of mobility and benefits (Anderson 2010; Standing 2011; Hira-Friesen 2018; Strauss and McGrath 2017). It can also result in exploitative employment conditions (Anderson 2010; Butler 2012). Precarity is not a fixed status, and most migrants experience oscillations in their levels of precarity over time and through space. Migrants themselves find ways to manage their precarity, and as the opening quote suggests, may become 'contortionists of flexibility' in doing so. As one contributor to this volume argues 'Heterogeneous and multidirectional flows mean people move in increasingly diverse ways, migration is no longer conceived as a one-way linear flow leading to settlement and integration' (Désilets 2021).

We, therefore, investigate the scalar and temporal aspects of precarity as experienced by a wide range of temporary urban migrants: from low to high-skilled, international students, asylum seekers and refugees to name a few. Cities receive the majority of the world's migrants (Bravo 2018), either through internal migration or international migration. These urban settings are not mere backdrops but generative spaces that influence levels of precarity (Nicholls and Uitermark 2016). The contributors in this volume, however, have strategically used distinct scales of analysis (such as a household, neighbourhood, or judicial boundary) to better understand migrant precarity. Cities are also the settings where multiple forms and levels of precarity intersect and overlap; where migrants engage in place-based citizenship (denizenship) through residence and localised economic, social, cultural and political contributions even when they are not considered permanent settlers or citizens (Komine 2014; Collins 2018). Discrete spaces within cities such as neighbourhoods, plazas, university campuses, schools, places of work, worship, and play are all possible settings of contact between migrants and native-born. It is in such spaces and localities that conflict about who belongs in the city and under what conditions, may erupt into a discourse of crisis and/or practices of intentional inclusion. Nina Glick Schiller and Ayse Caglar contend that the migration literature says very little 'about the relationship of migrants and cities' which is a gap that the essays in this volume engage with regards to temporary migrants (2011, 2).

In an era when many countries are turning to work arrangements that preclude long-term settlement and citizenship, precarity among temporary migrants is an urgent concern for the migrants themselves as well as the localities in which they settle. As Cooke, Wright, and Ellis (2018) argue in a recent perspective on the mobility transition concept,

> unskilled immigrant workers, and perhaps the skilled too, may find their mobilities and rights of residence in destination countries even more tightly constrained going forward as states aim to expand temporary visa guest-worker programmes as substitutes for their growing reluctance to accept permanent migration (2018, 519)

especially from certain countries of origin. Trends toward temporariness are happening at a time when the global estimate of migrant stock is at an all time high (272 million in 2019) and refugee populations (29 million) are also at record levels (United Nations Population Division 2019).[2] Ironically, various temporary statuses are proliferating even when the need for labour (both low- and high-skilled) is on the rise due to aging populations and labour niches that are regularly filled by migrants. We contend there is a renewed emphasis on *permanent temporariness* which allows urban localities to meet their labour demands while only ceding minimal rights to the migrants themselves (Bailey et al. 2002; Collins 2011; Price and Benton-Short 2008). This insistence on temporariness leads to heightened precarity.

Temporariness begins with the terms of entry, conditions that assert the length of stay, kinds of work and even mobility from job to job. Yet temporariness as a label has pernicious social consequences, categorising large groups of urban dwellers as less attached to a locality due to the 'termed' conditions of their stay (Anderson 2010). Temporal concerns are also influenced by the age of the migrants, especially the distinctions between children, youth, and adults and how the receiving destination processes and receives such newcomers based on their age and gender. Temporality also illuminates the time of day or week that migrants engage with urban spaces and other residents in more or less restricted ways. These ephemeral moments can lead to a heightened sense of freeing or belonging as well as confinement and exclusion (Lobo 2021; Tan 2021).

We contend that a sensitivity to different scales and scalar processes lends itself to a more nuanced understanding of migrant precarity. Precarity is experienced at the intimate scale of the human body but also it is influenced by policies determined by the nation-state or supranational entities such as the European Union, MercoSur or the United Nations. At the same time, there are divergent strategies between local and national governments as to the implementation of policies towards migrants, with ramifications for reception, inclusion/exclusion, integration and precarity. Consideration of diverse scales grounds the temporary migrant experience and underscores the localised interactions and encounters newcomers experience, the landscapes they help create and the institutions they interact with.

As argued by Panizzon and van Riemsdijk (2019), at times a crisis mentality towards migration leads to complex governance dynamics in which 'levels of policy-making interact, conflict, or disengage' in ways that require deeper exploration (2019, 2). Such conflicts in governance are readily highlighted in urban settings, where the *de facto* experience of inclusion and livelihood comes into conflict with the *de jure* reality of conditional status imposed by other levels of governance.

In terms of global governance, the United Nations endorsed the Global Compact for Safe, Orderly and Regular Migration in 2018 with the intention of improving the governance of migration, reducing migrant vulnerability, and strengthening the potential for migrants' contributions to sustainable development (United Nations 2018). With specific regard to cities, the New Urban Agenda (NUA) endorsed in 2016 by the United Nations underscores the relationship between cities, migrants, and human rights (United Nations 2017). A key objective of the NUA is to reduce various forms of discrimination experienced by all categories of urban migrants, regardless of their migration status. Discrimination, which may be in the form of limited access to housing, legal employment, health care and education, is intertwined with the precarity that temporary migrants face. This stated normative goal, however, is difficult to achieve due to enforcement challenges at various scales.

Acknowledging that all those living within a city are vital to its social reproduction and fabric echo earlier concerns embedded in the rights to the city and social justice literatures (Fainstein 2011; Harvey 2009; Mitchell 2003; Wills et al. 2010; Glick Schiller and Caglar 2011). We recognise that urban migrants are imbricated in a complex web of legal policies and socio-economic processes that operate at various scales. But migrants are also actors who exercise agency in shaping a diverse range of social practices and spaces in cities.

Four research questions guide this exploration of the intersection of precarity, temporary migrant status and cities. The essays in this volume collectively explore these questions, although any individual contribution may not address all of them.

(1) *How does precarity inform our understanding of temporary migration and its effects on cities and the migrants themselves?*
(2) *How does migrant precarity shift through space and across multiple scales?*
(3) *How do conditions of entry and particular migrant characteristics impact the experience of precarity over time?*
(4) *How do cities influence precarity and how does precarity influence cities?*

Precarity and temporary migrants

Development scholar Standing (2011) defined the precariat as populations who rely on money wages, often from temporary or flexible work, without any non-wage benefits or income security. He noted the relationship between present-day migration regimes and the creation of precarious labour, including low-skilled temporary migrant workers. Immigration policies and labour laws in migrant receiving countries, coupled with the worker's immigration status often allow for the systemic exploitation of temporary migrant workers (Anderson 2010; Lewis et al. 2015). Butler (2012) underscores the idea that precarity is not self-determined but an imposed condition of insecurity in both life and work. The precarisation of labour, which has been associated with neoliberal economic policies, leads to uncertainty of employment and the increasing normalisation of this unpredictability (Rachwal 2017). Lorey (2015) notes that flexibility of labour, although often couched in terms of increasing freedoms, often leads to new cycles of exploitation, with effects in economic, social, cultural and corporeal realms. Thus precarity is experienced not simply in economic terms, but results in other kinds of vulnerabilities as well.

The most vulnerable among the precariat are migrants lacking a recognised legal status in the countries in which they live. Referred to as 'un-citizens' (Nash 2009), even when they are able to obtain work, these migrants are often subjected to substandard working conditions, exploitation by employers who underpay or withhold wages, forced overtime as well as long and erratic working hours. These migrants are also more likely to be exposed to occupational hazards that have impacts on long term physical, mental and emotional health (Preibisch and Otero 2014).

Since the 1990s, according to Donato and Gabaccia, '… women travelling as part of temporary labour recruitment schemes (have) become more common' (Donato and Gabaccia 2015, 113). In particular, the number of females (both married and unmarried) migrating to do reproductive work in domestic and institutional settings increased even in the context of more restrictive migration environments (Donato and Gabaccia 2015). Women employed as overseas contract workers, may be subject to 'triple discrimination' when their statuses as temporary migrants, as females and as precarious workers intersect. Those who work in unregulated low-skill sectors such as domestic work, elder and child care, and commercial sex work are especially vulnerable, and could additionally face restrictions in their spatial mobility in the cities in which they live (Piper 2009; Vosko 2010; Yeoh and Huang 2010). There is even a growing literature that recognises the particular vulnerabilities of children and youth as part of these irregular and/or temporary migrant populations in cities (Allterton 2018; Menjívar and Perreira 2019).

Countries increasingly rely on temporary (and irregular) migrants to meet labour needs, offering temporary work visas over permanent residence even for highly skilled labour (Boese and Macdonald 2017). Thus, high-skilled migrant workers may find themselves subjected to precarious employment or become involved in 'gig work' that is uncertain both in terms of tenure and income. Their precarity may be witnessed in uncertain employment prospects, the quality of the jobs they take, their earnings and lack of job security. In her study of high-skilled immigrants in Canada, Hira-Friesen (2018) notes that recent immigrants are more likely to be engaged in temporary and involuntary part-time work than their Canadian-born counterparts or even more established immigrants. Even asylum seekers, who are often highly skilled, live in extremely precarious states, and may be in limbo for years before their cases are decided, even though they can add much to the economies of the urban areas in which they live (Jacobsen 2006). Viewing migrants as 'temporary guests' rather than as future citizens may offer economic benefits to urban jurisdictions but this also incurs social challenges in terms of how cities functionally include individuals who are labelled temporary but are, in fact, long-term urban residents (Price and Benton-Short 2008; Price and Chacko 2012).

Growing numbers of international students also make up the increase in temporary migrants. According to UNESCO (2019), about 5.3 million students were enrolled in institutions of tertiary education outside their country of citizenship. International students may experience 'extended precarity' as they seek to convert their tenuous student visa status into a more stable position that allows them to live and work in a country after the completion of their studies. In many Western countries, students may obtain practical training for a limited period of time after their course of study and even be absorbed into the workforce if they have the requisite skills and training, while in other countries they are required to leave shortly after graduation. However, the desire for a more permanent legal standing also makes students more vulnerable to labour exploitation in receiving countries (Robertson 2015; Thomas 2017; Maury 2017). Student experiences in the country, city and the wider community outside of campus may be constrained by visa status, resources, fluency in the culture and language of the host country, and limited avenues for inclusion (Chacko and Sojo 2016).

The urge to control migration has led to a proliferation of migration classifications in terms of entry and stay, many of which are predicated on the idea of temporariness. In the United States since the 1990s, new categories of temporary migrants have expanded and include H1-B (skilled worker) visas, Temporary Protected Status (TPS), Deferred Action for Childhood Arrivals (DACA) and Unaccompanied Migrant Children (UMC). Labels such a TPS, DACA and UMC may confer quasi-legal non-immigrant status but seldom provide a path to citizenship, resulting in an unstable situation of 'liminal legality' (Menjivar 2006), a state of legal limbo that could be unevenly applied to different family members and that could be overturned by new administrations. For example, in September 2017, U.S. President Donald Trump and Attorney General Jeff Sessions announced that the U.S. government would rescind the DACA programme. This effectively reversed a programme that had been in existence for five years and gave undocumented youth the right to work legally, as well as safeguards from deportation. Similarly, since 1990, the U.S. government offered Temporary Protected Status (TPS) to migrants from certain countries who were fleeing war and armed conflict, environmental disaster and other extenuating conditions. TPS allowed these persons to reside and work in the United States until it was safe for them to return. In 2018, however, the U.S. Department of Homeland Security ended TPS for migrants from El Salvador, Haiti, Nicaragua and Sudan, making them ineligible to stay legally beyond deadlines given by the government despite many of them having lived in the United States for decades (USCIS 2019).

We acknowledge that immigration has become an especially divisive issue, as highlighted in 2016 by the United Kingdom 'Brexit' vote to leave the European Union and the election of Donald Trump in the United States. In both election campaigns, anti-immigrant sentiments were pervasive in the political discourse. In particular, the Trump Administration's policy of wall-building, zero-tolerance, reduced legal migration, and bans on particular origin countries and refugees have been some of the most strident anti-immigration policies in nearly a century (Chishti, Pierce and O'Connor 2019). The politicalisation of migration and migrants into a discourse of 'crisis' is driving many countries away from policies that offer permanent residence or citizenship to newcomers and towards policies of temporariness, precarity or outright exclusion. Examples of this are numerous and from a wide range of countries. From the building of a wall between India and Bangladesh, denaturalising Haitians in the Dominican Republic, Australia's Operation Sovereign Borders, or challenging the citizenship of the Windrush generation of Caribbean settlers in the United Kingdom. Exclusionary regimes based on resistance to settlement and/or citizenry, and limitation of movement for those allowed to enter, pose serious challenges to the basic human right of mobility and increase the level of precarity in the lives of all migrants.

Scalar and temporal dimensions of precarity

Scale and time have profound impacts on the migrant experience, and as such are fundamental when investigating precarity. Collectively, we understand scale as socially constructed and we concur with Marston's (2000) argument for the need to consider the demands of social reproduction and consumption when addressing the socio-political impacts of scale on migration. When one considers temporary migrants engaged in domestic labour, the linkages to social reproduction are obvious. Yet at the intimate level of the household, where migrants engage in 'care work' and may even be considered part of the family, limits to their spatial mobility are regularly imposed as to where they can sleep, places they can visit, or even if they can leave the house at all.

Our intent is to unpack the interconnecting spatialities of scale in the lives of migrants living in cities. We are not limited to a singular scale; rather, we share the view of Jones et al. (2017) that processes of scalar production are central to complex spatial differentiations that temporary migrants experience. In this sense, scalar (as opposed to a fixed scale) suggests not simply a hierarchical continuum but also the possibility of jumping scale (Smith 1992), for example, from the household to the state, as in the case of many contracted migrant labourers. Most migration events involve movement across multiple scales that are interconnected. It is telescoping nature of scale that is socially constructed and embedded with power relations that informs our understanding of migrant precarity.

The contributors to this volume were asked to consider how scalar dimensions affect the temporary migrant experience. At some scales (such as a recreation centre or park) migrants express feelings of wholeness, belonging or inclusivity. Yet shifting to another scale, experiences of displacement or vulnerability may intensify. Experiences of refugees and asylum seekers oscillate between precarity and freedom depending upon scale and/or locality. Locating the sites and scales of precariousness and highlighting ways in which these uncertainties are addressed or mitigated via grass-roots initiatives, humanitarian organisations, and advocacy groups is an important contribution of the essays in this volume.

Exploring the neighbourhood scale, provides an opportunity to appreciate the role of migrants in remaking neighbourhoods such as Montreal's Mile End (Désilets 2021) or the Basmane neighbourhood in Izmir, Turkey (Oner, Durmaz-Drinkwater and Grant 2021). In these dynamic neighbourhoods, researchers observe competing scales of governance interacting with local institutions and individuals. In the case of the high-skilled migrants in Montreal's Mile End, they are key actors in the remaking of this multicultural hub of high tech professionals into a gentrified hipster zone of consumption (Désilets 2021). The differentiation of scale by the migrants themselves is also acute, especially when their status is highly precarious. Undocumented youth in the U.S. with DACA described areas that felt more secure and less secure in their daily commutes (Price and Rojas 2021). In Dongguan, China, a destination for many temporary workers, Tan (2021) elaborates on the vitality of the public square for migrants' sense of belonging and engagement. Similarly, Chacko (2021) notes that international students studying for a bachelor's degree in Singapore feel a sense of belonging to the university campus but have a more tenuous connection to other parts of the city.

Scalar divisions can be meaningful, arbitrary or insignificant when considering migrant precarity but this volume underscores the often overlooked role of scale in the migrant experience. In much migration literature, the territorial state is the scale of convenience with a focus on immigrants crossing state boundaries (Castles, de Haas, and Miller 2014). Governments of sovereign states have a vested interest in governing borders and deciding who should enter, yet the assumption that the same set of laws and selection processes are uniformly applied throughout the territorial state for different migrant types is readily challenged (Mountz 2010; Lobo 2016; Williams and Mountz 2018; Caponio and Jones-Correa 2018; Agnew 2019). When considering sub-state jurisdictions – neighbourhoods, cities, towns, counties – it becomes clear that particular scalar units impact migrants differently (Walker and Leitner 2013; Walker 2014). Consider the practice of granting asylum to unaccompanied minors in the United States (Blue et al. 2021). The authors demonstrate that a determining factor in receiving asylum is the federal court district to which a case was assigned, with California and especially San Francisco being far more generous than courts in Texas or states in the southern U.S. Similar regional variations were observed when federal deportation decisions were compared (Price and Breese 2016). This underscores the idea that if different scales are not considered, then these differentiations of precarity go unnoticed.

Figure 1 suggests ways in which scale may affect migrant precarity. At the household level, a temporary migrant may feel relatively safe and secure, and thus experience low precarity. Yet if a migrant works in a household where employer abuse occurs, then precarity could be quite high. Similarly, in neighbourhoods where immigrant populations are concentrated and social networks are dense, daily precarity could be low. However, in neighbourhoods where there are heightened tensions between native born and migrants, or a particular migrant group is singled out on account of their race, religion or country of origin, then precarity increases. Cities and entire metropolitan areas also influence migrant precarity. There are cities that actively develop policies aimed at inclusion, in which case precarity is lessened as seen in sanctuary cities in the United States (Delgado 2018). There are also unwelcoming cities, in which migrant services are limited or migrant populations are aggressively policed.

Probably more common are mixed practices of inclusion and exclusion, as geographers Walker and Leitner (2013) demonstrated in their analysis of the variegated landscape of inclusionary practices in metropolitan Washington DC. Policies of sub-state jurisdictions, such as departments, provinces, and various administrative units may also impact precarity. In the United States, individual states differ in their interpretation of immigration

Figure 1. Examples of high and low precarity at different scales.

enforcement and the extension of rights to individuals who are not authorised to remain in the U.S. but may have resided in a state for decades (Mathema 2018). These policy differences are pronounced and directly influence levels of precarity, as Blue et al. (2021) demonstrate.

In addition to scalar considerations, most migrants experience oscillations in their levels of precarity over time. Migrant precarity fluctuates as a result of legal status, policy changes, age, physical abilities, and crisis-driven events that may produce waves of migrants. In particular, policy changes surrounding the conditions of entry or residence can increase or decrease precarity. For example, a contract labourer may legally work in a country for many years experiencing modest precarity, but if that worker becomes injured or pregnant, precarity is heightened if the contract is terminated and the migrant is told or forced to leave (Hennebry and Williams 2015; Yeoh 2006).

Considering precarity over time, in addition to scalar sensitivities, provides a more comprehensive understanding of the issues faced by temporary migrants. Figure 2

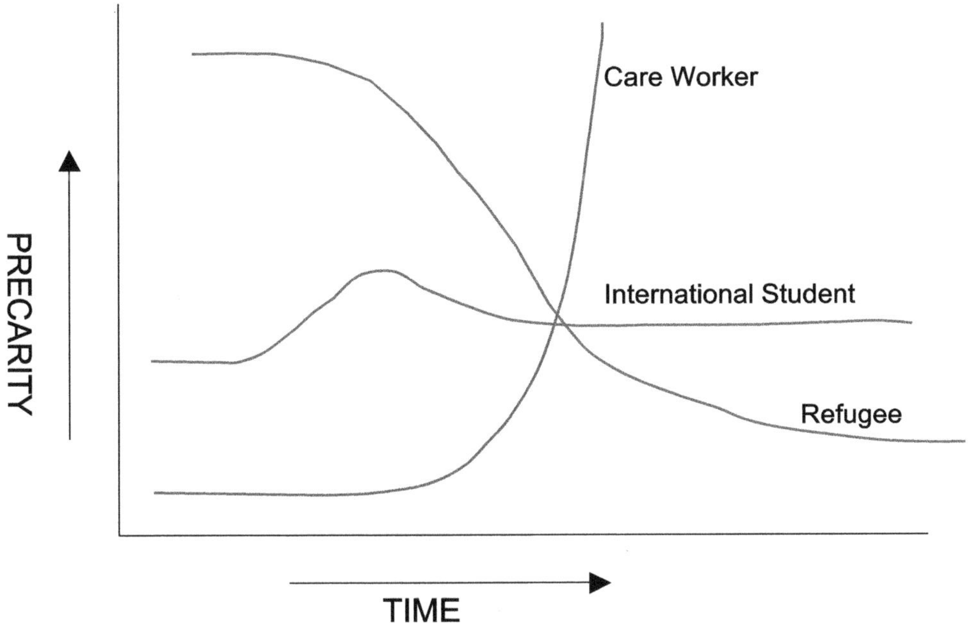

Figure 2. A hypothetical illustration of the shifting intensity of precarity over time by three migrant types.

illustrates possible scenarios of how three temporary migrants – an asylum seeker, international student and care worker – might encounter precarity over time. A migrant might enter a city with extremely high precarity as an asylum seeker and attempt to transition to a permanent status. If asylum is granted, then precarity could markedly decline but if asylum is rejected, precarity increases. In contrast, an international student may begin her studies with moderate precarity because of the conditional aspects of her visa tied to one school, a time frame, and continued academic progress. Upon graduation, precarity might increase as the student seeks to find employment and/or transition to another type of visa. Precarity may then decline if the student's migration status is adjusted or if she returns to her country of origin. Lastly, a care worker placed in a setting where she is treated well by her employer may enter with relatively low precarity, although if her physical condition changes (such as through pregnancy) then her precarity could markedly increase, leading to her removal from the job and even the country.

The world's sovereign states create categories of migrant entry and temporariness that can be hostile, indifferent, or provide protection. Depending on the country in question, these laws can result in higher or lower precarity for particular migrant groups as well as migrants in general. Lastly, intergovernmental bodies such as the United Nations or the International Organisation for Migration (IOM) endorse the universal declaration of human rights which acknowledges the human right to move within one's territorial state, to leave one's territorial state, and the right to seek asylum from persecution in another country. In theory, such universal rights exist to lower the precarity of migrants but they are difficult to enforce. These same international bodies are also criticised for reinforcing precarity by aligning themselves with the interests and agendas of migrant-receiving developed states who are often their financial sponsors (Geiger and Pécoud 2014; Pécoud 2018).

The intersection of cities, precarity and migrants

This volume explores how cities influence the precarity of temporary migrants and how precarity among temporary residents influences cities. Cities, particularly global cities, are characterised by inequality and precarity not just in the economic realm, but also in access to housing and social benefits (Jordan 2017). Collins (2011) review of migration in the Asia-Pacific cities of Singapore, Taipei, Tokyo and Seoul notes an increasing reliance on temporary migration regimes that aim to 'use and discard' migrant labour while prohibiting the development of social roots. He observes, 'the presence of significant numbers of temporary migrants also has significance for housing, transport and public spaces, and their presence can lead to both passing and more long-term transformations of the urban built environment' (Collins 2011, 322).

What does it mean for a city to have large numbers of temporary migrants in various states of precarity? Some extreme examples are found in the gleaming and rapidly growing Persian Gulf cities of Dubai, Doha, Riyadh, and Kuwait City where the majority of the urban residents are temporary migrants with minimal rights and limited inclusion or integration. Low skilled temporary workers often live in labour camps in cramped conditions and have little if any interaction with the city beyond their places of work and stay. Temporary migrants who received the lowest pay also faced the greatest deprivations in terms of basic amenities and personal mobility, their precarity heightened because employers often confiscate and hold on to their passports for the entirety of their stay (Gardner et al. 2013). In such cities, temporary migrants are fundamental to the economic growth and development of urban localities but they are intentionally not considered as belonging to these settings in any meaningful way. Such urban denizens are excluded from political participation (such as voting, protesting, or organising) and are often banned from access to forms of education, housing, and pensions that are available to citizens.

The level of precarity experienced by migrants living in large urban centres, even within the same country, may vary considerably. In a study of worker precarity in seven Chinese regional urban centres, migrants working in Shanghai (a global city) were found to suffer less precarity than their counterparts in other regional urban centres such as Guangzhou, Wuhan and Harbin, indicating perhaps that globalisation allowed for greater institutionalisation and standardisation of inclusive labour regulations and practices (Sun and Chen 2017). However, even within global cities in China, the educational qualifications of the migrants could influence degrees of precarity, with high skilled migrants being less vulnerable than the low skilled (Sun and Chen 2017; Wang, Li, and Deng 2017). In Singapore, the presence of temporary workers on their day off in public spaces such as parks, open air spaces in ethnic enclaves and cultural conservation districts masks the lack of structural integration in the city. Additionally, the country's laws distinguish between different kinds of temporary low-skilled workers. Singapore's Employment Act lays down standard rules that govern the employment of male temporary workers who often work in construction and landscaping, but this protection does not extend to domestic workers, who are primarily female, thereby increasing the latter's precarity within their workplace, the household (Yeoh 2006). In the United States measures to establish sanctuary cities or provide municipal forms of identification, such as the IDNYC for all residents in New York City, allows for inclusion and protection of migrants with irregular status in some cities but not others (Price 2015).

Chapters in this volume

The contributors to this volume use a range of theoretical frameworks and empirical approaches to examine and analyse the scalar and temporal ramifications of precarity for temporary urban migrants. They investigate how precarity is experienced by individuals and groups in different urban settings, all the while aware of broader national contexts and global economic shifts. The localities considered include: Singapore, Dublin, Montreal, Dongguan (China), Izmir (Turkey), Washington DC, and federal immigrant court boundaries within the United States (which vary in size from a single metropolitan area to several bordering states). The papers are grouped into three broad and overlapping categories based upon the status of these temporary migrants: (1) asylum seekers and refugees, (2) low skilled migrants, and (3) high skilled migrants (including international students). Each status group experiences varying degrees of precarity and integration, which change across scales and over time. By investigating how temporariness is embedded in migration regimes in a wide range of urban areas, we intentionally avoid specious distinctions between cities of the Global North and South.

Refugees and Asylum seekers often arrive in urban areas with varying levels of precarity. Asylum seekers experience high precarity due to limited rights and privileges and a tenuous legal status. Refugees arrive with permanent resident status, and therefore, less precarity, but even their experience of, and connections to the cities in which they live can be fraught with estrangement, marginalisation and exclusion if they are not formally resettled in a host community. Although these temporary migrants are disadvantaged in their socio-economic status, and are often unemployed or underemployed due to their limited right to work, they experience fleeting moments of freedom and connectedness.

Asli Ceylan Oner, Bahar Durmaz-Drinkwater and Richard J. Grant in their study of Syrian refugees living in the Basmane district of the city of Izmir in Turkey seek to understand how refugees negotiate and transform the built and cultural environments of the neighbourhoods in which they reside. These researchers use direct observation and media analysis to understand the lived experiences of precarity among refugees who have few rights and privileges. Despite their (un)settled lives, Syrian refugees built social ties with the city of Izmir through interactions with civil society, participation in the informal economy, and by making efforts to learn the local language and culture, thus making claims to urban space. The authors concentrate on the intra-relationships among place, refugees, and locals, seeking to contribute to the debate of how refugees produce differential pathways for adaptation and experiences of precarity. They conclude that a longer-term framework would facilitate the adaptation of refugees and their inclusion and integration in cities and city spaces.

Migrant youth from Central America crossing through Mexico to the United States face unusually dangerous circumstances during their journey as well as precarity when they request asylum in the United States of America. The contribution of **Sarah Blue, Alisa Hartsell, Rebecca Torres and Paul Flynn** considers how unaccompanied minors are processed in a federal system in which disparate outcomes are explained by strong place effects. Using administrative case data from over 232,000 unaccompanied migrant cases, the authors demonstrate that the location of the U.S. immigration court, as well as if a minor has legal representation, greatly influenced whether or not an unaccompanied minor received asylum. This regional disparity, and the increased role of local politics, produces uneven outcomes in which federal law fractures along the jurisdictional boundaries of immigration courts which are boundaries that are drawn for administrative purposes and should not influence outcomes. In terms of cities, certain courts located in major immigrant gateways such as San Francisco and New York City had much more favourable outcomes for asylum seekers.

Low skilled migrants often experience high levels of precarity and exploitation. Two papers that address low-skilled labour examine the social and spatial precarity of these migrants. Parreñas, Kantachote, and Silvey (2021) offer a penetrating analysis of migrant domestic workers in Singapore; arguing that the temporary and restrictive conditions of entry are akin to indentureship and that such labour regimes would be better understood as 'un-free' rather than 'free' labour. They also introduce the concept 'soft violence', which is the practice of cloaking the unequal relationship in domestic work via the cultivation of a relationship of 'personalism' while simultaneously amplifying employers' control of domestic workers. Empirically they draw from semi-structured interviews of employers, which reveal a range of attitudes but underscore the daily precarity and term-based restrictions these workers face. Singapore (as a city and a state) has created regulations to reduce the exploitation of household domestics, yet the researchers illustrate how precarity is amplified by restricted mobility within the household and across the city, along with debt bondage associated with financing the migrant's travel from overseas. They conclude that many middle class families in cities around the world have become reliant upon temporary migrant labour to sustain household reproduction and living standards, all the while turning a blind eye to the subordinate, isolating, and precarious conditions of these same household residents.

Yining Tan offers a case study from Dongguan, China, where temporary migrant workers from the interior provinces are the economic backbone of this industrial city along the Guangzhou-Shenzhen economic corridor. In Dongguan, where most of the residents are registered as 'temporary' migrants under the hukou system, newcomers struggle for economic, social and spatial inclusion in a system that refuses to recognise permanence. Through participant observation and semi-structured interviews, Tan documents the spatial restrictions on these migrants as well as the significance of the public square in shaping social belonging and claiming urban space. Such spaces serve to integrate all residents of the city, and as the number and proportion of the city's residents classified as temporary grows, research at this scale shows how temporary migrants are claiming certain 'public' urban spaces as their own.

Highly skilled migrants and international students are of interest to this research because the assumption is that they make up a population that is highly mobile and well educated and thus live less precarious lives as migrants. **Gabrielle Désilets** explores the concentration of high-tech temporary migrants in Montreal's Mile End neighbourhood. Mile End attracts IT workers for the gaming, film, and AI industries who are drawn to this 'hip' neighbourhood that has been repurposed for the needs of the tech industry and the consumption patterns of its workers. Using an ethnographic approach, Désilets describes the experience temporary 'middling migrants' who often begin their migration journeys as college students, and then develop the skills and the desire to relocate globally as part of a skilled but middle-class workforce. In addition to exploring landscape changes brought by these newcomers, she addresses the tensions inherent between the needs for local civic engagement and place-based belonging in contrast with the transnational urban lifestyle that many of these migrants pursue. She questions the structure of global labour in which these temporary migrants are embedded. A structure marked by temporarily forcing migrants to live 'in-between' places, sometimes for several years. Never fully recognised, nor acting as political agents in the country of departure or of arrival, this migration has notable effects on urban local communities and on migrant's perception of 'integration' and forms of identification.

Two of the articles in the volume investigate precarity as experienced by international students who are in training to be high skilled workers. **Mary Gilmartin, Pablo Rojas Coppari, and Dean Phelan** examine the intersections of legal, economic and personal precarisation and precarity among international students who are in Dublin, Ireland, to study language or obtain a degree. They find that the embodied experiences of precarity for this temporary migrant group, although laced with anxiety due to uncertain legal status and unclear future employment, is somewhat assuaged by hopes and promise. According to the authors, the 'promising precarity' that the students simultaneously experience along with anxiety stems from small acts of resistance, organised activism and their full lives as social beings living in Ireland and strategising to stay on permanently in the country.

In her study of international students of Chinese and Indian descent majoring in STEM fields in baccalaureate programmes at a leading university in Singapore, **Elizabeth Chacko** investigates how these students' emerging precarity affects their subjective well being and how they counter ideas of their inherent inassimilability through narratives of cultural belonging. Focus group discussions and structured interviews with the students reveal that as migrants who believe they are poised to enter the workforce in the receiving country, students experience precarity that emanates from an uncertain legal status as they finish their courses of study, which has ramifications for employability and employment. While uncertainty of prolonged stay often deters students from developing roots in the city, they have developed an affection for spaces (such as the university campus) within it and exhibit agency in diminishing their perceived precarity by positioning themselves as 'locals' with an intimate knowledge of the city and Singaporean culture, and therefore, exemplars of future workers, permanent residents and even citizens.

Marie Price and Giancarla Rojas explore how college students with DACA status understand and navigate the built environment of metropolitan Washington in the context of oscillating precarity for themselves and their families. They position

DACAmented college students as skilled migrants, because with DACA these undocumented youth attend college with in-state tuition and legally work. To understand the experience of temporariness they employ a spatial and visual approach, having six DACA holders engage in a participatory photo project as a means to visualise everyday life with and without DACA status. The photos underscore the ordinariness of their daily lives as well as strategic locations of safety and areas of avoidance. Given the uncertainty of retaining DACA status, these college students expressed a heightened sense of fear, even though they have felt safe for most of their lives within their suburban neighbourhoods.

Conclusion

By using case studies from East and Southeast Asia, North America, the Middle East, and Europe, the articles in this volume provide empirical evidence of how precarity is experienced by temporary migrants in urban spaces at discrete and overlapping scales. There are different categories of temporary migrants, yet in each study, the precarity of migrant lives oscillates through time, across scale, and in particular localities. Precarity, as experienced by these migrants, is influenced by macro level factors such as fluctuating national regulations and policies, the vicissitudes of labour markets, changes in nuances of popular discourse on migration and migrants as well as personal and social characteristics such as age, gender, socio-economic class and even race/ethnicity and cultural characteristics in local settings. It is this attention to the temporal and scalar dimensions of precarity that ties the papers in this volume together. Migrant precarity is dynamic, and to fully understand the experiences of temporary migrants one needs to consider the nuanced effects of scale and time in addition to national policies and labour markets.

This book contributes to the literature on precarity in three important ways. Firstly, the issue explores the spatial and scalar dimensions of precarity for temporary migrants. The articles demonstrate that in any given urban space, different migrant populations may have access to varying localised sets of resources and are subject to distinct policies, and therefore, experience precarity in dissimilar ways. The papers also highlight variations of precarity at different scales within cities, ranging from the household and neighbourhood to the municipality or city. Secondly, the settings where these studies occur are also subjects of inquiry as these urban places provide the socio-political contexts for the migrant experience where local and national policies overlap and intersect. It is important to remember that cities are also being shaped, in ephemeral and enduring ways, by these (un)settled sojourners through their work and daily engagements. Thirdly, the research demonstrates how temporary migrants are employing individual and collective agency to resist their categorisation as disposable and transitory workers whose services are easy to cut and who are not worthy of being considered permanent residents or citizens. Many, including refugees and asylum seekers who are typically perceived as highly vulnerable, are able to create formal and informal spaces of inclusion within cities. Others offer new nomenclatures and classifications that demonstrate that they are denizens, fully immersed in the cities in which they live, study, and work.

While most studies of migrant precarity focus on legal precarity and its ramifications for temporary migrants, by demonstrating that precarity can shadow the status of all categories of temporary migrants, including the highly skilled, who are typically considered protected and secure, this volume underscores the ways in which temporary migrants' status is always in an uneasy state of ambiguity. Also, as the prevalence of temporary migrants grows throughout the world, this collection offers a more nuanced and empirically driven investigation of the consequences temporariness imposes across scales, over time and upon cities.

Notes

1. 'Mayday, Mayday! Les precàries i precaris es rebel.len', Manifiesto convocatoria Barcelona EuroMayDay 2004 https://marceloexposito.net/pdf/mayday_periodico.pdf
2. The United Nations Migrant Stock totals do not distinguish between temporary and more permanent conditions of migration. Yet many national policies and bilateral agreements stipulate temporary arrangements, especially the proliferation of temporary work visas for high skilled and low skilled migrants.

Disclosure statement

No potential conflict of interest was reported by the author(s).

References

Agnew, John. 2019. "Spatial Uncertainties of Contemporary Governance." *Territory, Politics, Governance* 7 (4): 435–437.

Allterton, Catherine. 2018. "Impossible Children: Illegality and Excluded Belonging Among Children of Migrants in Sabah, East Malaysia." *Journal of Ethnic and Migration Studies* 44 (7): 1081–1097.

Anderson, Bridget. 2010. "Migration, Immigration Controls and the Fashioning of Precarious Workers." *Work, Employment and Society* 24 (2): 300–317.

Bailey, Adrian, Richard Wright, Alison Mountz, and Ines Miyares. 2002. "(Re)producing Salvadoran Transnational Geographies." *Annals of the Association of American Geographers* 92: 125–144.

Blue, Sarah A., Alisa Hartsell, Rebecca Torres, and Paul Flynn. 2021. "The Uneven Geography of Asylum and Humanitarian Relief: Place-Based Precarity for Central American Migrant Youth in the United States Judicial System." *Journal of Ethnic and Migration Studies* 47 (20): 4631–4650. doi:10.1080/1369183X.2020.1732588.

Boese, Martina, and Kate Macdonald. 2017. "Restricted Entitlement for Skilled Temporary Migrants: The Limits of Migrant Consent." *Journal of Ethnic and Migration Studies* 43 (9): 1472–1489.

Bravo, Jorge. 2018. *Sustainable Cities, Human Mobility and International Migration*. Report of the Secretary-General for the 51st session of the Commission on Population and Development (E/CN.9/2018/2).

Butler, Judith. 2012. "Precarious Life, Vulnerability and the Ethics of Cohabitation." *Journal of Speculative Philosophy* 26 (2): 134–151.

Caponio, Tiziana, and Michael Jones-Correa. 2018. "Theorising Migration Policy in Multi-Level States: The Multi-Level Governance Perspective." *Jounral of Ethnic and Migration Studies* 44 (10): 1995–2010.

Castles, Stephen, Hein de Haas, and Mark J. Miller. 2014. *The Age of Migration: International Population Movements in the Modern World*. 5th ed. New York: Guilford Press.

Chacko, Elizabeth. 2021. "Emerging Precarity Among International Students in Singapore: Experiences, Understandings and Responses." *Journal of Ethnic and Migration Studies* 47 (20): 4741–4757. doi:10.1080/1369183X.2020.1732618.

Chacko, Elizabeth, and Gloriana Sojo. 2016. "Spaces of Integration: International Students in a Global City." In *Chap. 22 in Race, Ethnicity and Place in a Changing America*, edited by J. W. Frazier, E. L. Tettey-Fio, and N. F. Henry, Vol. 3, 335–343. Albany: SUNY Press.
Chishti, Muzzafar, Sarah Pierce, and Allison O'Connor. 2019. *Despite Flurry of Actions, Trump Administration Faces Constraints in Achieving Its Immigration Agenda*. Policy Beat, April 25, 2019. Washington, DC: Migration Policy Institute.
Collins, Francis L. 2011. "Transnational Mobilities and Urban Spatialities: Notes From the Asia-Pacific." *Progress in Human Geography* 36 (3): 316–335.
Collins, Francis L. 2018. "Desire as a Theory for Migration Studies: Temporality, Assemblage and Becoming in the Narratives of Migrants." *Journal of Ethnic and Migration Studies* 44 (6): 964–980.
Cooke, Thomas J., Richard Wright, and Mark Ellis. 2018. "A Prospective on Zelinsky's Hypothesis of the Mobility Transition." *Geographical Review* 108 (4): 503–522.
Delgado, Melvin. 2018. *Sanctuary Cities, Communities and Organizations: A Nation at the Crossroads*. New York: Oxford University Press.
Désilets, Gabrielle. 2021. "Consuming the Neighbourhood? Temporary Highly Skilled Migrants in Montreal's Mile End." *Journal of Ethnic and Migration Studies* 47 (20): 4705–4722. doi:10.1080/1369183X.2020.1732616.
Donato, Katharine M., and Donna Gabaccia. 2015. *Gender and International Migration*. New York: Russell Sage Foundation.
Fainstein, Susan. 2011. *The Just City*. Ithaca, NY: Cornell University Press.
Gardner, Andrew, Silvia Pessoa, Abdoulaye Diop, Kaltham Al-Ghanim, Kien Le Trung, and Laura Harkness. 2013. "A Portrait of Low-Income Migrants in Contemporary Qatar." *Journal of Arabian Studies* 3 (1): 1–17.
Geiger, Martin, and Antoine Pécoud. 2014. "International Organisations and the Politics of Migration." *Journal of Ethnic and Migration Studies* 40 (6): 865–887.
Gilmartin, Mary, Pablo Rojas Coppari, and Dean Phelan. 2021. "Promising Precarity: The Lives of Dublin's International Students." *Journal of Ethnic and Migration Studies* 47 (20): 4723–4740. doi:10.1080/1369183X.2020.1732617.
Glick Schiller, Nina, and Ayse Caglar. 2011. *Locating Migration: Rescaling Cities and Migrants*. Ithaca, NY: Cornell University Press.
Harvey, David. 2009. *Social Justice and the City*. Athens: The University of Georgia Press.
Hennebry, Jenna, and Gabriel Williams. 2015. "Making Vulnerability Visible: Medical Repatriation and Canada's Migrant Agricultural Workers." *Canadian Medical Association Journal* 187 (6): 391–392.
Hira-Friesen, Parvinder. 2018. "Immigrants and Precarious Work in Canada: Trends, 2006–2012." *Journal of International Migration and Integration* 19 (1): 35–57.
Jacobsen, Karen. 2006. "Refugees and Asylum Seekers in Urban Areas: A Livelihoods Perspective." *Journal of Refugee Studies* 19 (3): 273–287.
Jones, I. I. I., John Paul, Helga Leitner, Sallie A. Marston, and Eric Sheppard. 2017. "Neil Smith's Scale." *Antipode* 49 (S1): 138–152.
Jordan, Lucy. 2017. Introduction: Understanding Migrants' Economic Precarity in Global Cities." *Urban Geography* 38 (10): 1455–1458.
Komine, Ayako. 2014. "When Migrants Became Denizens: Understanding Japan as a Reactive Immigration Country." *Contemporary Japan* 26 (2): 197–222.
Lewis, Hannah, Peter Dwyer, Stuart Hodkinson, and Louise Waite. 2015. "Hyper-precarious Lives: Migrants, Work and Forced Labour in the Global North." *Progress in Human Geography* 39 (5): 580–600.
Lobo, Michele. 2016. "Geopower in Public Spaces of Darwin, Australia: Exploring Forces That Unsettle Phenotypical Racism." *Ethnic and Racial Studies* 39 (1): 68–86.
Lorey, Isabell. 2015. *States of Insecurity: Government of the Precarious*. London: Verso.

Marston, Sallie. 2000. "The Social Construction of Scale." *Progress in Human Geography* 24 (2): 219–242.
Mathema, Silva. 2018. *What DACA Recipients Stands to Lose–and What States Can Do About It.* Washington, DC: Center for American Progress.
Maury, Olivia. 2017. "Student-migrant Workers." *Nordic Journal of Migration Research* 7 (4): 224–232.
Menjivar, Cecilia. 2006. "Liminal Legality: Salvadoran and Guatemalan Immigrants' Lives in the United States." *The American Journal of Sociology* 111 (4): 999–1010.
Menjívar, Cecilia, and Krista M. Perreira. 2019. "Undocumented and Unaccompanied: Children of Migration in the European Union and the United States." *Journal of Ethnic and Migration Studies* 45 (2): 197–217.
Mitchell, Don. 2003. *The Right to the City: Social Justice and the Fight for Public Space.* New York: The Guilford Press.
Mountz, Alison. 2010. *Seeking Asylum: Human Smuggling and Bureaucracy at the Border.* Minneapolis: University of Minnesota Press.
Nash, Kate. 2009. "Between Citizenship and Human Rights." *Sociology* 43: 1067–1083.
Nicholls, Walter J., and Justus Uitermark. 2016. "Migrant Cities: Place, Power and Voice in the Era of Super Diversity." *Journal of Ethnic and Migration Studies* 42 (6): 877–892.
Oner, Asli Ceylan, Bahar Durmaz-Drinkwater, and Richard J. Grant. 2021. "Precarity of Refugees: The Case of Basmane-İzmir, Turkey." *Journal of Ethnic and Migration Studies* 47 (20): 4651–4670. doi:10.1080/1369183X.2020.1732591.
Panizzon, Marion, and Micheline van Riemsdijk. 2019. "Introduction to Special Issue: 'Migration Governance in an Era of Large Movements: A Multi-Level Approach." *Journal of Ethnic and Migration Studies* 45 (8): 1225–1241.
Parreñas, Rhacel Salazar, Krittiya Kantachote, and Rachel Silvey. 2021. "Soft Violence: Migrant Domestic Worker Precarity and the Management of Unfree Labour in Singapore." *Journal of Ethnic and Migration Studies* 47 (20): 4671–4687. doi:10.1080/1369183X.2020.1732614.
Pécoud, Antoine. 2018. "What Do We Know About the International Organization for Migration?" *Journal of Ethnic and Migration Studies* 44 (10): 1621–1638.
Piper, Nicola. 2009. "Feminisation of Migration and the Social Dimensions of Development: the Asian Case." *Third World Quarterly* 29 (7): 1287–1303.
Preibisch, Kerry, and Gerardo Otero. 2014. "Does Citizenship Status Matter in Canadian Agriculture? Workplace Health and Safety for Migrant and Immigrant Laborers." *Rural Sociology* 79 (2): 174–199.
Price, Marie. 2015. *Cities Welcoming Immigrants: Local Strategies to Attract and Retain Immigrants in U.S. Metropolitan Areas in World Migration Report: Migrants and Cities: New Partnerships to Manage Mobility*. Geneva: International Organization for Migration.
Price, Marie, and Lisa Benton-Short. 2008. *Migrants to the Metropolis: The Rise of Immigrant Gateway Cities*. Syracuse, NY: Syracuse University Press.
Price, Marie, and Derek Breese. 2016. "Unintended Return: U.S. Deportations and the Fractious Politics of Mobility for Latinos." *Annals of the American Association of Geographers* 106 (2): 366–376.
Price, Marie, and Elizabeth Chacko. 2012. "Migrant inclusion in cities: Innovative urban Policies and Practices." Paper prepared for UN-Habitat and UNESCO.
Price, Marie, and Giancarla Rojas. 2021. "The Ordinary Lives and Uneven Precarity of the DACAmented: Visualising Migrant Precarity in Metropolitan Washington." *Journal of Ethnic and Migration Studies* 47 (20): 4758–4778. doi:10.1080/1369183X.2020.1732619.
Rachwal, Tadeusz. 2017. *Precarity and Loss: On Certain and Uncertain Properties of Life and Work.* Weisbaden: Springer Fachmedian Wiesbaden.
Robertson, Shanthi. 2015. "Contractualization, Depoliticization and the Limits of Solidarity: Noncitizens in Contemporary Australia." *Citizenship Studies* 19 (8): 936–950.
Smith, Neil. 1992. "Contours of Spatialized Politics: Homeless Vehicles and the Production of Geographical Scale." *Social Text* 33: 55–81.
Standing, Guy. 2011. *The Precariat: The New Dangerous Class.* London: Bloomsbury Academic.

Strauss, Kendra, and Siobhán McGrath. 2017. "Temporary Migration, Precarious Employment and Unfree Labour Relations: Exploring the 'Continuum of Exploitation' in Canada's Temporary Foreign Worker Program." *Geoforum; Journal of Physical, Human, and Regional Geosciences* 78: 199–208.

Sun, Zhongwei, and Jia Chen. 2017. "Global City and Precarious Work of Migrants in China: A Survey of Seven Cities." *Ûrban Geography* 38 (10): 1479–1496.

Tan, Yaning. 2021. "Temporary Migrants and Public Space: A Case Study of Dongguan, China." *Journal of Ethnic and Migration Studies* 47 (20): 4688–4704. doi:10.1080/1369183X.2020.1732615.

Thomas, Susan. 2017. "The Precarious Path of Student Migrants: Education, Debt, and Transnational Migration among Indian Youth." *Journal of Ethnic and Migration Studies* 43 (11): 1873–1889.

UNESCO. 2019. *International Students – Migration Data Portal.* https://migrationdataportal.org/themes/international-students.

United Nations. 2017. *New Urban Agenda, Habitat III.* Quito: United Nations.

United Nations. 2018. *Global Compact for Migration.* Accessed September 30, 2019. https://refugeesmigrants.un.org/migration-compact.

United Nations Population Division. 2019. Workbook UN Migrant Stock. https://www.un.org/en/development/desa/population/migration/data/estimates2/estimates19.asp.

United States Citizenship and Immigration Services (USCIS). 2019. https://www.uscis.gov/humanitarian/temporary-protected-status.

Vosko, Leah. 2010. *Managing the Margins: Gender, Citizenship, and the International Regulation of Precarious Employment.* Oxford: Oxford University Press.

Walker, Kyle. 2014. "The Role of Geographic Context in the Local Politics of US Immigration." *Journal of Ethnic and Migration Studies* 40 (7): 1040–1059.

Walker, Kyle, and Helga Leitner. 2013. "The Variegated Landscape of Local Immigration Policies in the US." *Urban Geography* 32 (2): 156–178.

Wang, Hao, Wei Li, and Yu Deng. 2017. "Precarity Among Highly Educated Migrants: College Graduates in Beijing, China." *Urban Geography* 38 (10): 1497–1516.

Williams, Kira, and Alison Mountz. 2018. "Between Enforcement and Precarity: Externalization and Migrant Deaths at Sea." *International Migration* 56 (5): 74–89.

Wills, Jane, Kavita Datta, Yara Evans, Joanna Herbert, Jon May, and Cathy McIlwaine. 2010. *Global Cities at Work: New Migrant Divisions of Labour.* London: Pluto Press.

Yeoh, Brenda S.A. 2006. "Bifurcated Labour: The Unequal Incorporation of Transmigrants in Singapore." *Tijdchrift Voor Economische en Sociale Geografie* 97 (1): 26–37.

Yeoh, Brenda, and Shirlena Huang. 2010. "Transnational Domestic Workers and the Negotiation of Mobility and Work Practices in Singapore's Home-Spaces." *Mobilities* 5 (2): 219–236.

The uneven geography of asylum and humanitarian relief: place-based precarity for Central American migrant youth in the United States judicial system

Sarah A. Blue, Alisa Hartsell, Rebecca Torres and Paul Flynn

ABSTRACT

The rising number of unaccompanied migrant children (UMC) crossing the U.S.-Mexico border received intense media attention during 2014 and remains significant. Unaccompanied minors seeking relief through the immigration court system is at a record high. A crisis of legal representation and of disparity in granting asylum or other humanitarian relief across Department of Justice (DOJ) immigration courts and among individual judges creates an unequal geographical landscape of justice for young migrants/asylum-seekers. This study uses empirical data from over 232,000 UMC cases to analyse the effect that place of residence has on access to a fair court hearing. This research adds to previous studies by emphasising the importance of place for unaccompanied minors who have been released to sponsors across the United States. Given that court adjudications vary considerably from judge to judge and across courts; and that access to legal resources differs from city to city and across regions – where a UMC resides has a major impact on the likelihood of a fair hearing. This finding has major implications for understanding how locality impacts unaccompanied minor migrant youth precarity.

Introduction

Children making the journey across national borders in search of safety is a global phenomenon. According to the United Nations High Commissioner for Refugees (UNHCR), in 2018 there were approximately 138,000 unaccompanied or separated children in the world, of which only a fifth were able to seek asylum (UNHCR 2019). The migration of unaccompanied migrant children (UMC) from Central America and Mexico to the United States – more than 242,000 between October 2009 and January 2016 – captured international attention and became a U.S. immigration policy flashpoint (Johnson 2016).

A report by the Congressional Research Service (Kandel 2017) indicated that the 'surge' in UMC migration was, in fact, an incremental (albeit uneven) rise over the last several years; from 16,067 in FY 2011 to the sensationalised 68,500 UMC arriving in FY 2014. The numbers of UMC presenting themselves at the southern U.S. border have fluctuated significantly since then, dropping to 39,970 in FY 2015 (Kandel 2017) and then reaching 48,325 in FY 2018 (U.S. Customs and Border Protection 2019). The persistent number of UMC arrivals from year to year evidence a sustained humanitarian crisis, in part, as a result of significant increase in Mexican border enforcement (Swanson et al. 2015). In a major reversal, Central American rather than Mexican migrants now account for the majority of unaccompanied children and family arrivals. In 2009, Mexicans comprised 82 per cent and Central Americans 17 per cent of UMC (Kandel 2017); while in 2018 along the southwest border 79 per cent of UMC were Central American and only 21 per cent were from Mexico (U.S. Customs and Border Protection 2019).

After these young migrants and asylum-seekers cross the border, they often approach immigration agents, requesting help.[1] Under anti-trafficking legislation protections, unaccompanied minors children from non-contiguous countries such as Central America must be released from detention and turned over to the Office of Refugee Resettlement (ORR) within 72 hours. The ORR – the U.S. agency responsible for sheltering the UMC until they can safely be placed with a sponsor living in the U.S. – releases the minors with orders to appear in a Department of Justice (DOJ) immigration court.[2] Without regard to individual circumstances, each UMC is placed in formal removal proceedings for deportation. The required hearing in front of a DOJ immigration judge is often their only opportunity to argue for asylum or another form of legal relief. Most UMC do not have access to an attorney, which significantly lowers their likelihood of obtaining humanitarian relief. Because of the large geographical variation in how judges in different immigration courts rule on UMC cases, where the UMC's sponsor lives has an outsised influence on whether or not the child is able to remain in the United States.

The immigration court hearing decides a young migrant's fate – determining whether they will remain in the United States. In many cases, it is a matter of life or death – deciding whether they will be returned to the dangerous environments from which they recently fled. However, large variations in asylum adjudication across regional immigration courts and among individual judges in a single court means that the chances of being able to remain in the United States is ultimately a game of chance (Ramji-Nogales, Schoenholtz, and Schrag 2011). This is contrary to the promise of equal justice before the law as promised in the U.S. court system. The problem of geographic asylum disparities is not unique to the U.S. with significant asymmetries documented in Canada, the U.K. and Australia, among others (Luker 2013; Ramji-Nogales, Schoenholtz, and Schrag 2011). In the U.S. court system, UMC are assigned to courts in DOJ immigration jurisdictions based on their sponsors' residence upon release. From October 2013 through May 2017, almost 170,000 UMC were released to sponsors in every state in the United States (ORR 2017). While the majority reside in the large immigrant states of California, Texas, Florida and New York; there is also a disproportionately high number of UMC in 'new destination' states including Maryland, Virginia, New Jersey, Louisiana, Nebraska, Delaware, Rhode Island and the District of Colombia (Washington DC). Massachusetts and the southern states of Georgia, Tennessee, Alabama, and North Carolina also have a higher proportion of UMC than the rest of the country (ORR 2017).

This study examines the problem of unequal access to fair proceedings in immigration courts through a spatial analysis of the settlement patterns of UMC and the immigration courts and jurisdictions to which they are assigned. Mapping the location and adjudication outcomes for all of the DOJ immigration courts highlights the great distances between some UMCs' hearings and their assigned DOJ immigration courts (and to major cities that have more legal advocacy resources). It also allows a closer analysis of the extent of geographical disparity underlying asylum adjudication for UMC in the United States and the potential consequences of disparity for UMC and their families. Drawing attention to these local disparities aligns with the theme of this special issue addressing migrant precarity across scale and over time (Chacko and Price, 2021).

This paper is structured as follows: we first provide an overview of the increased number of Central American UMC, their possibilities for immigration relief in or deportation from the United States and the legal process they encounter upon arrival. We draw on two bodies of literature to contextualise the geographic disparity in asylum adjudication: geographic scholarship on the politics of scale in local enforcement of federal immigration policies and jurisprudence literature focusing on the crisis of legal representation for unauthorised immigrants in removal proceedings. After a brief discussion of data and methods, we present results from an analysis of court locations, UMC residences and court outcomes for this vulnerable population. We conclude that distance from courts and large cities with specialised legal aid and regional unequal case adjudication, leads to an unfair system. Geographic disparities in deportation and/or relief result in a system in which justice is not necessarily based on individual merits of a case but on the availability and access to local resources given where the migrant's case is assigned and decided.

Avenues of potential migration relief for unaccompanied minors

The Homeland Security Act (HSA) of 2002 transferred responsibility of minors to the Department of Health and Human Services (HHS) and created a definition for unaccompanied children as

> a child who has no lawful immigration status in the United States, has not attained 18 years of age, and who has no parent or legal guardian in the United States, or no parent or legal guardian in the United States available to provide care and physical custody. (HSA 2002 §462)

Adults who were either apprehended by ICE or presented themselves at the border are often held in detention while awaiting hearings. As stipulated by the Trafficking Victims Protection Reauthorization Act (TVPRA) of 2008, UMC are released to sponsors while waiting for their immigration hearing and have the right to have their claim heard in the 'non-adversarial' environment of the asylum office (Center for Gender and Refugee Studies 2015).[3] The child has the burden of proof to establish their asylum claim, a complex labyrinth of paperwork that is virtually impossible for a young person to navigate alone (KIND 2015; Roubein 2014). Central American UMC processed at the border are placed in removal proceedings and assigned to a DOJ immigration court (even if applying for asylum through the asylum office (USCIS)). If the asylum office (USCIS) interview is unsuccessful, the UMC has a second chance to plead their case for asylum in the DOJ immigration court. The immigration court is an overtly adversarial space, where the UMC must defend themselves against a government lawyer who argues for the child's deportation (AIC 2015).

In addition to seeking asylum, there are other possible ways that UMC can seek humanitarian relief in the United States. Unaccompanied minors may qualify for relief provided under U.S. law for victims of trafficking and crime (T and U visas) or for children who have been abused, abandoned or neglected (SIJS). Children may also apply for withholding of removal and protection from removal based on the United Nations Convention Against Torture (CAT). Prior to the Trump administration's specific instructions to discourage the practice, a growing number of immigration lawyers were securing legal status for UMC through Special Immigrant Juvenile Status (SIJS) (Einbinder 2018; Hlass 2017). SJIS is a unique immigration protection available solely to children who cannot be reunited with at least one parent due to abuse, abandonment and/or neglect. It is based on state law definitions of abuse, abandonment and/or neglect, which introduces another level of place-based precarity. Highlighting the need for legal representation, SJIS must be approved by state family courts before proceeding to federal immigration courts. If these conditions are proven in family court, the applicant may file a SIJS petition with the U.S. Citizen and Immigration Services (USCIS). Surveys of UMC screened upon arrival estimated that 40 per cent (2010 study) and 60 per cent (2014 study) were eligible for some form of humanitarian relief (Byrne and Miller 2012); though far fewer were granted protection. The challenges of determining whether children qualify for some form of protection given their age, complexity of claims, and trauma is a time-consuming process (AIC 2015). The majority of UMC do not have access to an attorney, which significantly lowers their chances of obtaining humanitarian relief. Almost 90 per cent of unrepresented children in immigration court from 2014 to 2016 were given removal orders (KIND 2017). Representation rates have fluctuated dramatically since the increase of UMC from Central America, amid the changing geopolitical climate surrounding immigration and refugees. In 2013, 38 per cent of represented children were allowed to remain. That number increased to 54 per cent in 2015 but plummeted to 23 per cent in 2016 (TRAC 2017b). Clearly, having legal representation, while not guaranteed, is critical to securing protection.

The devolution of immigration policy

Geographers have emphasised the politics of scale and variation in local enforcement of federal immigration policies (Coleman 2009; Ellis 2006; Price and Breese 2016; Varsanyi 2008a, 2008b; Walker and Leitner 2011; Wells 2004). While the federal government sets national immigration policy, including priorities and target numbers for removal of undocumented immigrants; how these policies are implemented varies at state, county and municipal scales. Similarly, mid-1990s immigration legislation shifted responsibilities for the policing and well-being of immigrants to lower tiers of government through the Illegal Immigration Reform and Immigrant Responsibility Act (IIRIRA) of 1996. This 'devolution' of immigrant policy has made state and local government increasingly responsible for both enforcement and providing services to immigrants (Coleman 2009; Varsanyi 2008a, 2008b; Wells 2004). Legal scholars have contributed empirical and qualitative evidence detailing and explaining UMCs' uneven access to legal representation (Eagly and Shafer 2016; Hlass 2014, 2017).

While the federal government maintains the right to determine entry and exit of immigrants at a national level, increasingly state, county and municipal scale legislation adversely affects unauthorised immigrants' security and livelihoods. The DOJ immigration courts are not part of the U.S. judicial system but rather directly under the supervision of the executive branch, so that the president and the attorney general issue directives on which cases to hear and even how judges should interpret the law (Ramji-Nogales, Schoenholtz, and Schrag 2011). Recently, the Trump administration initiated restrictions on the special protections outlined above that help unaccompanied minors secure legal relief, cut funding for the Justice AmeriCorps Program (detailed below) and rewrote judicial guidelines for UMC in deportation proceedings (Einbinder 2018). Thus, while federal policies such as TVPRA protect Central American UMC, expedited hearings and the targeting of certain groups for deportation by ICE are dictated at national level; the funding and provision of legal resources to aid immigrants has devolved to the state and local level. This is critical to understanding the geographic unevenness of outcomes for UMC, as where they reside influences the political climate of the assigned court as well as access to legal counsel.

Walker and Leitner (2011) systematically analysed implementation of immigration policies in different metropolitan areas according to characteristics such as immigrant population concentrations, pace of demographic change, homeownership rates and educational levels. The authors identified significant differences in regional implementation of immigration policy aimed at either protecting or rejecting unauthorised immigrants. Analysing 174 metro areas, they concluded that rural, suburban and exurban areas with rapid immigrant growth were more likely to adopt anti-immigrant resolutions. In contrast, inner cities with long-established immigrant populations, certain regions and states were consistently pro-immigrant. They found that almost two-thirds of central cities considered or implemented inclusionary policies, while three-quarters of suburban and rural municipalities introduced anti-immigration ordinances. The authors identified a 'patchwork' wherein local immigration policies vary by locality within the same metropolitan area, generally following the pattern of inclusionary central cities and inner-ring suburbs, and exclusionary outer-ring suburbs.

Legal scholar Laila Hlass has made invaluable contributions to understanding geographic differences in access to deportation relief through SIJS. Through analysis of UMC case data and interviews with attorneys, her research has focused on how variation in state laws, policies and resources affect eligibility and access to SIJS protection (Hlass 2014, 2017). Especially important were differences in state law that affects cut-off ages (18 vs. 21) for assigning guardianship necessary for the SIJS process and access to pro-bono legal aid. Moreover, in 'new destination' states such as Mississippi there were few non-profit organisations or pro-bono lawyers available to guide eligible UMC youth through the SIJS process. In contrast, in the large immigrant gateway jurisdictions of New York City and San Francisco, family courts are familiar with SIJS due to periodic trainings, standardised forms and guidance documents available. Some states are also 'resource-poor states' or 'resource-poor jurisdictions' with respect to 'nonprofit specialists' to represent UMC in state-level court proceedings (Hlass 2014).

Unequal justice

Jurisprudence literature has increasingly focused on the 'justice gap' – the lack of equality in an immigration and asylum system where quality representation is not available to vulnerable populations – resulting in a growing crisis of legal representation for the immigrant poor in removal proceedings. As public awareness increases regarding the crisis of unrepresented youth entering removal proceedings without legal advocates, the immigration law community has mobilised to serve vulnerable children and to increase funding through public-private partnerships (Hlass 2017; KIND 2017). An expanding network of pro bono providers are serving UMC and their sponsors, partly funded through a Justice AmeriCorps programme initiated in June 2014 to provide representation for unaccompanied children (Hlass 2017; Johnson 2016; KIND 2017).[4]

Syracuse University data indicate an increase in legal representation since 2014, especially for Central American youth (TRAC 2017b). With the significant rise in UMC beginning in 2014, by the end of that year, fewer than 20 per cent of UMC were represented in immigration court (TRAC 2014b). By 2019, still, only 47 per cent of the cases initiated had legal representation (TRAC 2019), as UMC are not provided government-appointed counsel (KIND 2017). If an UMC is unable to afford a private lawyer or secure pro bono counsel, they must appear before an immigration judge without an attorney. For the 232,121 UMC cases documented by Syracuse University from October 2004 through May 2017, 58 per cent had legal representation. Legal representation made a dramatic difference. Fifty-two per cent of the almost 97,000 young migrants without representation were ordered deported and only 7.5 per cent were allowed to remain in the United States. In contrast, only nine per cent of represented UMC cases ended in deportation and 47 per cent were allowed to stay (TRAC 2017b; see also KIND 2017). The remaining more than one-third of all cases were pending. As more unaccompanied youth go into their removal proceedings without representation, there is a growing movement in the immigration law community to protect vulnerable children and narrow the justice gap that results from lack of quality representation (Hlass 2017).

Geographic disparity exists across court jurisdictions also in the form of administrative pressure to expedite proceedings in response to an ever-growing backlog (Schoenholtz, Schrag, and Ramji-Nogales 2014; TRAC 2016c). Legal scholars and immigrant advocates have protested the imposition of 'speed at all costs policies' that began in 2007 and has worsened under the Trump administration (Baluarte et al. 2016; Einbinder 2018). Expedited proceedings lead to increased decision disparity among judges and across court jurisdictions by denying due process (Baluarte et al. 2016; TRAC 2016c). Variation within immigration courts and across jurisdictions are well-documented for adult populations (Ramji-Nogales, Schoenholtz, and Schrag 2011; Schoenholtz, Schrag, and Ramji-Nogales 2014). Adjudication disparity has increased over recent years, manifest in dramatically different rates at which judges grant or deny asylum to their random case assignments. Decision discrepancy points to the influence of judges' 'pre-existing predilections' rather than more uniform and apolitical decisions based on immigration law (Ramji-Nogales, Schoenholtz, and Schrag 2011; TRAC 2016a, 2016c).

Schoenholtz, Schrag, and Ramji-Nogales (2014) found extensive evidence of disparities in asylum granting across DOJ asylum offices and among asylum officers. When asked for their interpretation of the disparities across immigration courts, the asylum officers and supervisors indicated different cultures exist and are encouraged/enforced by supervisors. Other explanations included diverse legal standards across jurisdictions such as what case law serves as precedent. Another explanation is distinct patterns of application processes such as well-prepared attorneys accompanying clients to interviews versus paid preparers who provide boilerplate applications to lawyers unfamiliar with individual cases. Finally, there is variation in caseloads, i.e. in Houston, asylum officers spend most of their time deciding whether detained individuals who are slated for deportation have a case for asylum based on credible fear of persecution, giving them more of a law enforcement orientation than other officers whose sole responsibility is asylum adjudications. Baluarte et al. (2016) highlight a series of sub-regulatory practices that exist in courts in Houston and Dallas, TX; Charlotte, NC; and Las Vegas, NV that have led to these courts granting almost no asylum cases, leading to what the authors deem 'asylum-free zones'. These practices include denying asylum seekers' right to expert testimony, telephonic appearances, the right to present evidence, written orders, oral orders, and legal precedent, among others. Judges in these courts are primarily former prosecutors who enter asylum cases with a law-and-order mindset. Finally, with most asylum claims summarily denied, both private and pro bono attorneys are effectively discouraged from representing asylum applicants (Baluarte et al. 2016). Any combination of these factors led to large variations in grant rates across the asylum offices, with, for example, a 60 per cent approval rate in San Francisco compared to only 31 per cent in New York. Most UMC cases go to immigration court rather than determination by an asylum officer. However, the regional variations of different case precedents, diverse supervisory or administrative cultures and the prevalence of well-prepared versus generic and unsupportive legal aid are important to understand geographic disparities in deportation relief for UMC (Hlass 2014, 2017).

Central to the denial of justice for UMC is the systematic barrier to access to asylum procedure and other forms of humanitarian relief in the United States, particularly for Mexican and Central American youth (Campos and Friedland 2014; UNHCR 2014). Fleeing violence resulting from resistance to extortion or kidnapping does not fit neatly into increasingly narrow definitions of who qualifies for asylum. Central American and Mexican minors flee states that provide little to no protection for persecuted youth, yet they do not qualify under the restrictive parameters of an outdated refugee classification (Betts 2013; Dotson and Frydman 2017). Asylum seekers must prove they have suffered persecution due to race, religion, nationality, membership in a particular social group, or political opinion. In some instances, lawyers have successfully argued that young people, endangered by their refusal to join violent gangs, constitute a distinct 'social group' eligible for asylum, or that 'refusal to submit to extortion' should be considered a political view (Campos and Friedland 2014; Schoenholtz, Schrag, and Ramji-Nogales 2014). However, not all asylum officers or judges accept these definitions. Underscoring the temporal precarity of immigration relief, former U.S. Attorney General Jeff Sessions ruled in 2018 that fear of gangs and/or domestic violence no longer qualify as grounds for asylum (Smith 2019). For minors that can prove 'abuse, abandonment and/or neglect', relief has increasingly come through SIJS status (Hlass 2017). However, judge-to-judge and court-by-court disparities range dramatically on the extent to which these arguments result in a positive outcome for UMC, and Mexican UMC are often returned at the border by CBP without an opportunity to apply for humanitarian relief (Thompson et al. 2018; Cavendish and Cortazar 2011).

Data and methods

This study uses proximity analysis of the highest and lowest humanitarian relief-granting immigration courts by the number of judges, rates of denials, and distance from courts based on jurisdictions to determine access to high and low-granting DOJ immigration courts. This study draws on data from the Department of Justice (DOJ), U.S. Customs and Border Patrol (CBP), the Office of Refugee Resettlement (ORR), and Transactional Records Access Clearinghouse (TRAC) at Syracuse University. The DOJ releases the addresses for each court, including alternative locations for court appearances usually in the same city. Information pertaining to the number and names of judges assigned to each court is also available. Two types of immigration courts exist: immigration courts attached to detention centres, which rarely deal with unaccompanied juveniles, and immigration courts with geographic jurisdictions. Courts with attached detention centres attend to minors accompanied by a parent. Given our focus on unaccompanied migrant youth, the immigration courts attached to detention centres are excluded from this analysis.

Basic information for the court's jurisdictions is available on the DOJ website, however, the list of counties contained within the jurisdictions based on the Department of Homeland Security (DHS) field office service areas is only accessible through the DHS website. Jurisdictions are unevenly defined, ranging in organisation based on zip code, county lines, and state boundaries. The ORR releases the placement information of unaccompanied migrant children based on states and counties. The Transactional Records Access Clearinghouse (TRAC) at Syracuse University publishes data for asylum rates per court and per judge as well as UMC case information. For this analysis, we compared UMC case information with the court location data to assess if courts with greater average distance from UMC settlement counties have higher rates of removal orders, which may be due to non-appearance given distance from the court. Pending cases were also analysed to assess correlation between courts with high denial rates and pending cases.

Study data was organised in ArcGIS in a four-step process: geocoding the courts, creating polygons for the jurisdictions based on counties, inputting the county resettlement data, and conducting proximity analysis to determine distance between courts and county centres. The courts' data was added to visualise number of judges (Figure 1) and deportation and removal rates for UMC based on their decisions (Figure 2) (TRAC 2016c, 2017b). Only courts with geographic jurisdictions, not attached to detention centres, were included in this figure; and the denial rates are only for UMC cases. Denial rates were calculated using negative outcomes including 'removals', which are the judge's order to deport or exclude the UMC, either barring their return for a period of time or permanently; and 'voluntary departure', which requires a migrant to leave, but without a bar from returning. Positive outcomes include 'relief granted', which withholds removal; 'terminated', which dismisses a case due to 'no grounds for removal'; 'prosecutorial discretion', in which the government attorney drops the request for a removal order; and 'closures', by which the judge decides not to deport the child for other unspecified reasons, closes the case administratively (which is now exceedingly rare), or grants temporary protected status (TPS).

Second, the courts' jurisdictions polygons were created from DOJ data for DHS field offices. Jurisdictions vary in size and do not correspond to state boundaries. For

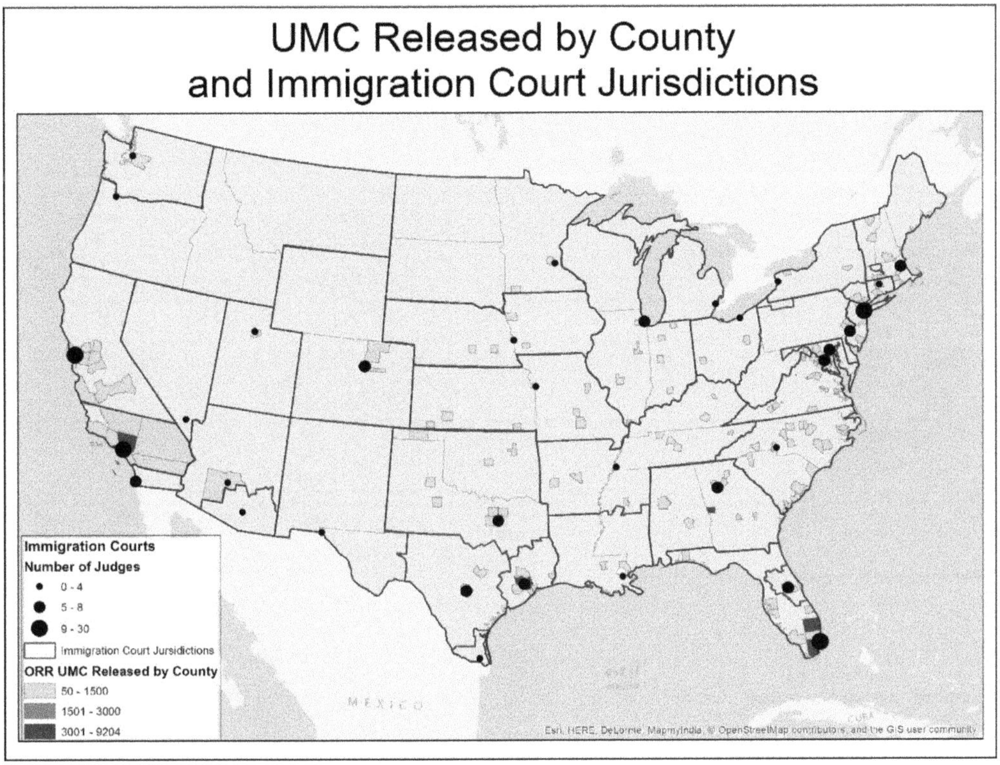

Figure 1. ORR UMC released by county between FY 2014 and 2016, by DOJ immigration court jurisdiction. Source: US DOJ 2017a, 2017b (color version available online).

example, the Bloomington Court Jurisdiction, located in Minnesota, also includes North and South Dakota. In more populous states like Texas, California, and New York the jurisdictions are smaller than the state and are divided by counties. For example, the San Diego court includes only two counties along the U.S.-Mexico border. The immigration court at El Paso includes a few Texas counties and all of New Mexico. Third, unaccompanied migrant children's settlement data based on county from ORR was added into ArcGIS to a county shape file from ESRI. Since the data refers to settlement at the county level, in order to determine distance from the courts we used the ArcGIS tool 'find county centers', creating points to examine distances with the Spatial Statistic Tool Mean Centre. Given that UMC's street addresses are not publicly available, distance to the courts is based on the county ORR designated and not actual distance.

Fourth, we used proximity analysis of county centroids to court locations to determine the distance to court. This analysis established the approximate distance children and their sponsors must travel to their assigned courts based on the counties' central points in the courts' geographic jurisdictions. Since this method only calculates Euclidean distance, it does not take into account delays based on traffic or transportation infrastructure that may further inhibit access. The geographic jurisdictions vary in size, especially in the western United States. This may represent a serious barrier to arriving in court or accessing legal aid, especially considering the limitations on undocumented populations' access to transportation.

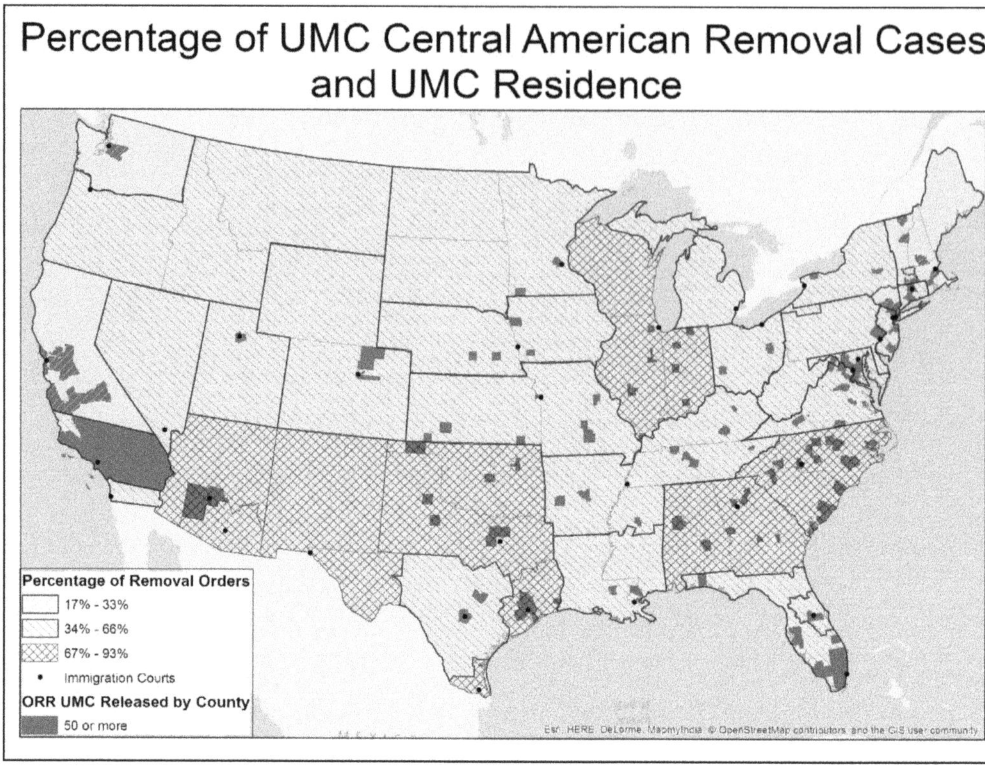

Figure 2. Percentage of negative immigration court case outcomes for Central American youth by court and UMC residence, October 2004 to May 2017. Source: TRAC 2017b; US DOJ 2017a, 2017b (color version available online).

Results and findings

To evaluate the geographical disparity underlying immigration relief and the backlog of pending cases for UMC in the United States, we first examine court locations, jurisdictions, and the residence of UMC awaiting court dates. This proximity analysis provides an overview of where the 35 DOJ immigration courts with regional jurisdictions are located in relation to where juvenile immigrants are living, revealing the distances they must travel to access resources and the court itself. Geographical incongruencies in adjudication for UMC cases across U.S. cities reflects uneven access to quality representation and disparity in receiving a fair hearing through the DOJ immigration court system. We apply three factors identified in secondary literature to explain disparities: the availability of specialised legal resources, access to those resources, and the local DOJ immigration court culture. Finally, a discussion of regional variation in pending cases provides insight into the growing problem of court backlogs that delay legal processes and prolong legal limbo.

Distance from immigration courts

A proximity analysis of immigration courts and the counties where UMC live highlights the difficult access to courts for many minors and their families, especially in Western

States (Figure 1). While the majority of UMC reside with sponsors or their families in large cities such as Los Angeles, Miami and Houston, Figure 1 illustrates that many counties with 50 or more UMC are not in large urban areas, but rather in rural 'new destinations' areas such as Nebraska, Arkansas, and North and South Carolina. The DOJ appoints judges to courts of diverse sizes ranging from those with only one or two regional judges to the largest courts with 28–30.

Travel distance to immigration courts is likely a barrier to immigration relief for UMC. Many UMC are too young to travel alone. Undocumented relatives have limited access to driver's licenses, dramatically increasing migrants' vulnerability and access to resources (Johnson 2004). Only 11 states and the District of Columbia currently allow undocumented residents to obtain a license (Mendoza 2016). Undocumented migrants have other distance-related constraints in accessing necessary resources, including well-established networks of pro bono legal aid concentrated in urban centres; insufficient funds to pay for travel and accommodations closer to legal counsel; and distant court or hearing location. Long travel times require adult sponsors to miss work, which is an economic strain for a population overrepresented among the working poor. Based on geographic jurisdictions, the Portland Court, which includes Oregon, Idaho, and Montana, had the longest average distance from counties to the court. This trip would take approximately four hours to complete via highway, however, many undocumented migrants do not have private transportation and the bus journey is much longer and costly. New York's immigration court had the shortest average travel distance for minors and their sponsors, at 28 miles, and with better public transportation options within the city. Many courts have alternative hearing locations conducted via teleconference at correctional facilities. Although accessing these facilities may be easier, technical difficulties and translation issues are frequent (Laird 2014). Without ready access to legal representation and the assigned court location, youth are more likely to miss their court date and receive in absentia removal orders or appear in court without attorneys (KIND 2017).

Disparities in adjudication outcomes

Geographic disparity in immigration court outcomes for UMC is clearly evident when comparing rates of removal and relief across jurisdictions. Analysis of TRAC data revealed that 49 per cent of non-detained UMC were granted relief from deportation, which roughly corresponds to studies that estimated 40–63 per cent of UMC would be eligible for some sort of humanitarian relief if provided legal representation (TRAC 2017b). Figure 2 shows the lowest, medium, and highest third removal adjudications of Central American UMC cases decided between October 2004 and May 2017, illustrating tremendous variation across regions of the United States. The immigration courts with the lowest removal rates were in the Western and Northeastern states, including the San Francisco, New York, Boston, and Seattle court jurisdictions, each with more than two-thirds of cases resulting in positive outcomes. San Francisco's immigration court, hearing a little over 9000 Central American UMC cases in this period (4.5 per cent of the total) had the lowest denial rate at 17 per cent. Court jurisdictions with higher removal rates were located in the South, with a few exceptions. Though they hear relatively low numbers of cases, El Paso, Harlingen, Tucson and Phoenix were among the highest removal courts, all with more than 75 per cent removal rate. The El Paso Court, in particular, stood out as the worst for juveniles facing removal. Of the approximately 1400 Central American UMC who had hearings at this court during 2004–2016 (0.7 per cent of total), 93 per cent were ordered to leave the United States. The court's overall rate of deportation was 97 per cent for adults and juveniles. The El Paso court is also difficult to access, considering that it encompasses far west Texas and all of New Mexico.

Of the courts hearing the largest number of Central American UMC cases, Houston stood out as having the highest denial rates (Table 1). The chances that a young person challenging a deportation order will receive a favourable ruling in Houston were less than half than in New York City. Atlanta, another court with a large jurisdiction, ordered removal adjudications for 76 per cent of the almost 9000 cases (four per cent of total) heard from FY 2005 to 2016. Although not among the top courts hearing Central American UMC cases, Chicago stood out in the Midwest as having high rates of removal. Of the almost 3600 Central American UMC with deportation orders in Illinois, Wisconsin, and Indiana, 68 per cent were given removal orders.

Although a migrant's chances of receiving a favourable ruling vary regionally by court jurisdiction, it is also important to recall the great disparity in individual judges' adjudications affects an individual's chance to receive a fair trial. TRAC data from 2010 to 2016 indicates the courts with highest removal rates also had the lowest range of decision disparity (Table 1). For example, of the seven judges in the Houston court, one judge's rulings ended either in 'removal' or 'voluntary departure' 96 per cent of the time, while the judge with the lowest removal rates still reached 67 per cent. With the exception of the Miami Court, those with more favourable rulings for Central American UMC had a wider range of decision disparity among judges. Whereas one judge in the San Francisco Court ordered removal 98 per cent of the time, another had only a 15 per cent removal rate.

Table 1. Decision disparity and denial rates for Central American UMC by immigration court. Source: TRAC 2016a, 2016c, 2017b.

Top 12 immigration courts hearing Central American UMC cases (and # of judges)	Decision disparity by judges total denial rates, FY 2010–2016			Central American UMC removal and voluntary departure cases, FY 2005–2016	
	Lowest	Highest	Range	Number of UMC cases adjudicated (and % of total)	Percentage of denial cases for Central American UMC High to low
Houston (7)	66.7	96	29.3	18433 (9.1%)	85%
Atlanta (6)	70.8	97.7	26.9	8779 (4.3%)	76%
Charlotte (3)	71.6	84.5	12.9	7667 (3.8%)	72%
Dallas (6)	69.3	93.2	23.9	7686 (3.8%)	69%
Baltimore (5)	2.6	58.2	55.6	11153 (5.5%)	51%
Memphis (4)	52.5	84.5	32	7653 (3.8%)	48%
Newark (8)	15.7	98.6	82.9	6719 (3.3%)	40%
Arlington (8)	17.4	88.5	71.1	15779 (7.8%)	38%
Los Angeles (30)	21.8	97.1	75.3	17211 (8.5%)	38%
Miami (18)	50.9	84.4	33.5	13019 (6.4%)	35%
New York (28)	2.2	59	56.8	20751 (10.2%)	32%
San Francisco (17)	15.3	97.7	75.3	9026 (4.5%)	17%
Central American UMC's national average (86% of all juvenile cases)				**202,722**	**51%**
Total national average for all cases					26%

Urban disparities and the uneven geography of legal outcomes

Our analysis suggests three factors that affect court outcomes for Central American UMC: legal representation, location of courts, and local political culture. As unaccompanied minors' chances of obtaining fair hearings are geographically rooted, so are the resources and conditions that are more likely to result in favourable outcomes. Much of the adjudication disparity aligns with variations in access to resources in large cities with well-established networks of legal assistance (Figure 2). Immigration courts located in Houston, Atlanta, Charlotte and Dallas stand out as having higher negative outcomes for Central American UMC, likely due to longer travel commutes to courts and more limited availability of legal counsel.

In the absence of a federal guarantee to legal counsel for asylum seekers, even children, a growing number of communities support free legal services for undocumented immigrants facing deportation through state and local government funding. However, shifting local politics continue to determine the availability of public funding, exacerbating the disparity in access to legal aid and fair court hearings across U.S. urban areas. Cities with the highest rates of deportation relief, San Francisco and New York City (Table 1), have long-established and well-funded pro bono networks that are not readily available to those living outside of the jurisdiction and assigned to other courts. For example, the nonprofit Vera Institute of Justice, using local public and private funding sources, has provided legal defense to all of New York City's eligible undocumented immigrants since 2013 (Blanco 2017).

Central American UMC with access to legal counsel gain higher rates of either asylum or, more commonly, another type of relief such as SIJS, than those without attorneys (KIND 2017; Hlass 2017). While adult asylum seekers from El Salvador, Honduras and Guatemala had the highest denial rates at 77–83 per cent (TRAC 2016a), Central American minors had greater success in recent years because of the growing network of pro bono legal providers who have come forward to represent UMC. For cases filed and heard in FY 2014 and 2015, 65 per cent of almost 87,500 UMC had legal representation. Of the minors who had legal representation, 88.5 per cent were allowed to stay in the United States while only 11.5 per cent were forced to leave. In contrast, during the same period, only 12.5 per cent of all unrepresented minors received a positive outcome while the great majority – 87.5 per cent – received a negative decision (KIND 2017). Furthermore, when negative outcomes are mapped across U.S. court jurisdictions geographic disparities in legal representation becomes clear (Figure 2).

A recent report by the American Immigration Council that analysed data from over 1.2 million deportation cases between 2007 and 2012 found great variation in legal representation by jurisdiction (Eagly and Shafer 2016). Of these cases, 66 per cent of non-detained immigrants secured legal representation. New York City had an 87 per cent representation rate for non-detained cases, while Atlanta and Kansas City's rate was only 47 per cent each. Legal representation for those in smaller city jurisdictions was even more grim: immigrants/asylum-seekers assigned to courts in small cities were more than four times less likely to obtain counsel than those assigned to large city courts (11 per cent in small cities versus 47 per cent in large cities) (Eagly and Shafer 2016). In small and medium-sized cities, fewer immigration attorneys specialising in UMC cases practice, there is more limited structural capacity to screen eligibility for different kinds of relief, and judges are often less familiar with country conditions or different types of humanitarian relief specific to UMC (Eagly and Shafer 2016; Hlass 2017). In smaller cities or rural areas, obtaining legal counsel for UMC is more costly and time consuming considering long travel distances to meet with attorneys, compile the evidence necessary for their case, and eventually attend court hearings (Eagly and Shafer 2016; Lee 2017).

Even major cities have varying capacity to serve UMC's legal needs. In July 2017, the DOJ's list of numbers of pro bono legal service providers revealed great disparities. The San Francisco and Miami courts listed ten providers each, while Chicago and Dallas courts listed three providers, and Tucson and Phoenix had one each (US DOJ 2017c). While large, well-established non-profits such as RAICES throughout Texas and The Door in New York City offer extensive and specialised services for UMC, many smaller providers are restricted in range of services and are able to serve only a limited number of clients – perhaps five to 10 cases at a time (Lee 2017). With the heightened number of UMC entering the U.S. in need of representation over the past several years, there are simply not enough nonprofit organisations, law school clinics, pro bono and 'low bono' attorneys to provide services to UMC and address the current representation gap (KIND 2017).

Another factor influencing negative outcomes is the local political culture, which affects both the availability of legal resources and the prevalent culture of practices in a given court. Unaccompanied minors living in Southern jurisdictions characterised by conservative political ideologies and a fast-growing immigrant population are more likely to be assigned to a court with high overall removal rates. The immigration courts located in Tucson, Phoenix, Atlanta and Houston are low-granting courts for Central American UMC. These cities are characterised by few legal resources for immigrants facing deportation (US DOJ 2017c); decidedly anti-immigrant state and county level policies restrict public funding for pro-bono legal representation. Tucson and Phoenix each had only one pro-bono legal resource available (one of which is a law clinic stating that it only holds consultations for six months of the year); the larger cities of Atlanta and Houston had only five and four agencies for their entire jurisdictions, respectively. Schoenholtz, Schrag, and Ramji-Nogales (2014) found that the Houston court had a local 'law and order' culture and less precedent for different forms of humanitarian relief. Explanations of significant distances to court and legal counsel, as well as a law enforcement court culture, are likely also true for courts located in the border cities of El Paso and Harlingen, Texas.

Pending cases

Geographic variation in pending cases is another indicator of unequal UMCs' experience as they await their hearings. Pending cases represent the active backlog in the DOJ immigration court system. As of May 2017, there were almost 600,000 pending immigration cases in the United States, including over a third of all UMC cases (84,218) (TRAC 2017a, 2017b). For Central American juveniles from Guatemala, El Salvador, and Honduras, the national percentage of pending cases was 38 per cent between 2009 to May 2017, slightly higher than the national percentage of all pending juvenile cases (36 per cent) (TRAC 2017b). The increasing and consistently high number of Central American unaccompanied minors over recent years has amplified the backlog that already existed due to intensified immigration enforcement without commensurate increases in judicial resources and infrastructure. While the legal community and popular media have drawn attention to the problem of chronic underfunding of the immigration courts and the lack of a right to court-appointed counsel (e.g. Eagly and Shafer 2016; Hlass 2014, 2017; Laird 2014; Lee 2017), the backlog's geographic unevenness has received less attention.

As evident in Figure 3, courts with half or more of their UMC cases pending include the smaller jurisdictions of Portland and Omaha, and the larger New York City court. Many of the larger courts that hear many Central American UMC cases have between 43 and 48 per cent of cases pending, including Boston, Baltimore, Houston and Arlington (Washington DC). The lowest number of pending cases is in Texas and Arizona, namely the border courts of Harlingen and El Paso (only five and nine per cent), Phoenix and Tucson (seven and 11 per cent) and the larger cities of San Antonio (14 per cent) and Dallas (23 per cent). With the exception of the Houston and California courts, the majority of UMC living in the south were less likely to have longer pending times for their cases to be heard. Courts that implement expedited hearings, such as Harlingen or El Paso, provide very little time for young migrants and their sponsors to obtain legal assistance.

Disparities in court backlogs across jurisdictions are another indicator of unequal spatial access to quality representation as well as temporal precarity for UMC. A low number of pending cases suggests courts that have more expedited UMC cases. In the

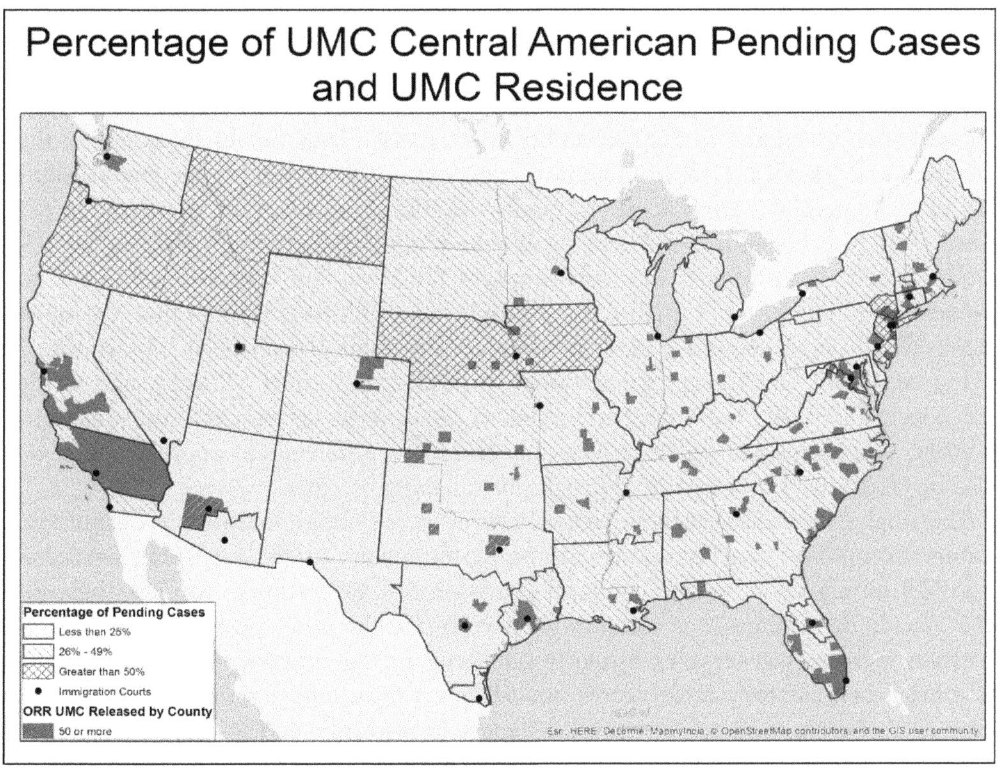

Figure 3. Percent of pending cases by court and UMC residence, FY 2009–May 2017. Source: TRAC 2017b; US DOJ 2017a, 2017b (color version available online).

expedited system, minors have only 21 days before their first hearing. This is insufficient time for attorneys to assemble a case for youth still traumatised from their journey, disoriented in their new environment (the ORR shelter) and confused that they were facing a deportation hearing (Laird 2014). Attorneys and judges have protested the constraints imposed by a lack of time and resources – in expedited courts, judges may hear as many as 50–70 petitions in a three- to four-hour period, which does not leave time to closely examine the particular circumstances of an individual case (Richey 2016). Court backlogs, in contrast, prolong the liminal status of minors and may jeopardise asylum cases, as situations shift and evidence becomes outdated (Laird 2014; Preston 2016). New cases may be assigned a hearing up to five or six years away. Greater backlogs, while not ideal, may suggest that judges are taking more time when evaluating cases and may indicate an administrative culture that is favourable to positive outcomes rather than one focused on expedited processing (Hlass 2017; Schoenholtz, Schrag, and Ramji-Nogales 2014; TRAC 2016b).

Conclusion

While previous studies have focused on the problem of decision disparity among judges in the DOJ immigration court system, this geographic analysis reinforces the problem of local inequities across U.S. cities in access to fair hearings for UMC. There is an uneven geography to deportation and granting humanitarian relief for unaccompanied migrant youth in the United States, which starkly contrasts with the basic principles of fairness on which the legal system is built, that underscores the precarity UMC face depending on where their case is adjudicated. Using empirical data from UMC cases, this study documents a clear geographical disparity underlying the granting of legal relief for UMC in the United States, as related to the availability of specialised legal resources, access to those resources and the local DOJ immigration court culture. It highlights the great distances that block some UMC from access to quality legal resources and the immigration court to which they are assigned, and also signals the temporal disparity in backlog for UMC awaiting their day in court. The consequences for UMC are dire: being released to a sponsor who lives far from quality legal resources or with little time to find appropriate and available legal counsel results in dramatically higher probability of deportation. Living near well-established legal resources or a favorable court culture– such as those that exist in cities like New York, San Francisco, Los Angeles, or San Antonio – in contrast to courts emphasising expedited processing and a law enforcement approach such as El Paso or Houston, translates into a geographic blessing or curse.

This analysis reveals that the increased role of local politics, manifest in devolution of immigration policy, directly influences geographic inequity in access to fair hearings in U.S. DOJ immigration courts. The local provision of legal resources (or lack thereof) to UMC facing deportation, has increasingly devolved to the state and local scale, thus dramatically increasing geographic disparities in accessing due process. The proximity analysis utilised in this study underscores how distance disadvantages those UMC living in more remote areas with greater travel distances to resources and to the court itself, and in regions without a solidified network of quality, youth-focused pro bono legal aid. State, county and municipal variation in public and private funding for legal defense are critical in the support and expansion of well-established pro bono legal resources.

Earlier studies emphasised how the decision disparities across courts and among judges within courts make deportation hearings a game of chance (Hlass 2014, 2017; Ramji-Nogales, Schoenholtz, and Schrag 2011; Schoenholtz, Schrag, and Ramji-Nogales 2014). However, comparing the residential location of UMC sponsors to court outcomes and the backlog of pending cases, much of the UMC case disparity evidenced in this proximity analysis can be attributed to access to resources in traditional gateway cities versus deficits in 'new gateway' and border cities.

These findings reinforce policy recommendations advocated in previous studies. The DOJ should provide greater resources and training for immigration judges to minimise adjudication disparities (Ramji-Nogales, Schoenholtz, and Schrag 2011). Immigration courts and the Board of Immigration Appeals should be moved out of the DOJ, thus granting these bodies greater independence from political influence (Ramji-Nogales, Schoenholtz, and Schrag 2011). More judges should be hired from diverse backgrounds that have the UMCs' best interests in mind, and the DOJ should advocate for an administrative environment that prioritises fair rulings and humanitarian relief for all who qualify (KIND 2017; Hlass 2017; Schoenholtz, Schrag, and Ramji-Nogales 2014). Sufficient time should be allowed for UMC to secure legal assistance and to prepare cases. Finally, all unaccompanied minors should be given access to the kind of legal resources and structures that have been increasingly effective in cities such as San Francisco, New York, Miami, and Los Angeles (Hlass 2014, 2017). These include better and standardised screening (federally required but provided at the state level) to determine eligibility for different forms of humanitarian relief; matching UMC with qualified legal representation; reinstating and extending public-private funding schemes (i.e. Justice AmeriCorps) that provide the most effective legal representation for UMC: and non-profit or pro bono organisations with attorneys who are familiar with both family and immigration law (Hlass 2014, 2017; KIND 2017). Geography should not determine access to fair due process, nor the legal outcomes or protections for minors seeking asylum and other forms of humanitarian relief in the United States justice system. The city in which a UMC lives should not determine the young migrant's fate.

Notes

1. While U.S. government entities and other organizations refer to "Unaccompanied Alien Children" (UAC), we reject this term as pejorative and instead use "Unaccompanied Migrant Children" (UMC). Many unaccompanied minors are asylum seekers or potentially qualify for other forms of legal relief to remain in the United States.
2. Underscoring the temporal precarity of UMC's situation, the legal rights granted to minors, including the protections under the Flores Agreement and the right to remain with their parents, has been under attack by the Trump administration.
3. TVPRA treats children from contiguous states of Mexico and Canada differently, requiring that they be screened within 48 hours by DHS. Screening is normally performed by CBP rather than asylum officers.
4. The Justice AmeriCorps program ended in September 2017 when its funding was not renewed by the Trump administration's Department of Justice (Einbinder 2018).

Disclosure statement

No potential conflict of interest was reported by the author(s).

References

AIC (American Immigration Council). 2015. *Special Report: A Guide to Children Arriving at the Border: Laws, Policies and Responses*. Accessed June 11, 2017. https://www.americanimmigrationcouncil.org/research/guide-children-arriving-border-laws-policies-and-responses.

Baluarte, David, Jeanne Atkinson, Michelle Mendez, Atenas Burrola, Lindsay Harris, Sarah Owings, Stephen Manning, and Blaine Bookey. 2016. "Before the Inter-American Commission on Human Rights: A Special Interest Hearing on the Human Rights of Asylum Seekers in the United States, Center for Gender & Refugee Studies, University of California Hastings College of the Law." Accessed May 1, 2018. http://cgrs.uchastings.edu/sites/default/files/Human%20Rights%20of%20Asylum%20Seekers%20in%20US%20%5BPetitioners%5D_1.pdf.

Betts, Alexander. 2013. *Survival Migration: Failed Governance and the Crisis of Displacement*. Ithaca, NY: Cornell University Press.

Blanco, Octavio. 2017. "New York to Provide Lawyers for Immigrants Facing Deportation." *CNN Money*, April 13. Accessed July 15, 2017. http://money.cnn.com/2017/04/13/news/economy/new-york-immigrant-legal-defense-fund/.

Byrne, Olga, and Elise Miller. 2012. *The Flow of Unaccompanied Children Through the Immigration System: A Resource for Practitioners, Policy Makers, and Researchers*. New York: Vera Institute of Justice.

Campos, Sara, and Joan Friedland. 2014. *Mexican and Central American Asylum and Credible Fear Claims: Background and Contexts*. Special Report. American Immigration Council.

Cavendish, Betsy, and Maru Cortazar. 2011. *Children at the Border: The Screening, Protection and Repatriation of Unaccompanied Mexican Minors*. Washington, DC: Appleseed.

Center for Gender and Refugee Studies, and Universidad Nacional De Lanus. 2015. *Childhood and Migration in Central and North America: Causes, Policies, Practices and Challenges*. San Francisco, CA: University of California Hastings College of the Law. https://cgrs.uchastings.edu/sites/default/files/Childhood_Migration_HumanRights_English_1.pdf.

Chacko, Elizabeth, and Marie Price. 2021. "(Un)Settled Sojourners in Cities: The Scalar and Temporal Dimensions of Migrant Precarity." *Journal of Ethnic and Migration Studies* 47 (20): 4597–4614. doi:10.1080/1369183X.2020.1731060.

Coleman, Mathew. 2009. "What Counts as the Politics and Practice of Security, and Where? Devolution and Immigrant Insecurity After 9/11." *Annals of the Association of American Geographers* 99 (5): 904–913.

Dotson, R., and L. Frydman. 2017. *Childhood Cut Short : Sexual and Gender-based Violence Against Central American Migrant and Refugee Children*.

Eagly, Ingrid, and Steven Shafer. 2016. *Access to Counsel in Immigration Court*. Special Report. American Immigration Council.

Einbinder, Nicole. 2018. "How the Trump Administration Is Rewriting the Rules for Unaccompanied Minors." PBS, Public Broadcasting Service. Accessed May 1, 2018. www.pbs.org/wgbh/frontline/article/how-the-trump-administration-is-rewriting-the-rules-for-unaccompanied-minors/.

Ellis, Mark. 2006. "Unsettling Immigrant Geographies: Us Immigration and the Politics of Scale." *Tijdschrift voor economische en sociale geografie* 97: 49–58.

Hlass, Laila L. 2014. *States and Status: A Study of Geographical Disparities for Immigrant Youth*, 46 *Columbia Human Rights Law Review* 266. Accessed June 17, 2017. http://papers.ssrn.com/sol3/papers.cfm?abstract_id=2577904.

Hlass, Laila L. 2017. *Minor Protections: Best Practices for Representing Child Migrants. 47 New Mexico Law Review 247*. Accessed June 17, 2017. http://ssrn.com/abstract=2986233.

Homeland Security Act of 2002. 2002. https://www.dhs.gov/homeland-security-act-2002.

Johnson, Kevin R. 2004. "Driver's Licenses and Undocumented Immigrants: The Future of Civil Rights Law?" *Nevada Law Journal* 5: 213–239.

Johnson, Jeh C. 2016. *Statement by Secretary Jeh C. Johnson on Southwest Border Security*. Department of Homeland Security Press Office. Accessed June 6, 2017. https://www.dhs.gov/news/2016/03/09/statement-secretary-jeh-c-johnson-southwest-border-security.

Kandel, William. 2017. *Unaccompanied Alien Children: An Overview*. Accessed June 17, 2017. https://fas.org/sgp/crs/homesec/R43599.pdf.

KIND (Kids in Need of Defense). 2015. "Asylum and Related Relief." Accessed July 12, 2017. https://supportkind.org/wp-content/uploads/2015/04/Chapter-5-Asylum-and-Related-Relief.pdf.

KIND (Kids in Need of Defense). 2017. "Unaccompanied Children: Ensuring Court Appearance & Fair Proceedings." Accessed July 8, 2017. http://lirs.org/wp-content/uploads/2017/01/Court-appearance-for-UACs-1.5.17.pdf.

Laird, Lorelei. 2014. "Lawyers and judges face hurdles in struggle to cope with influx of young immigrants." *Aba Journal*, December 14. Accessed July 15, 2017. http://www.abajournal.com/magazine/article/lawyers_and_judges_face_hurdles_in_struggle_to_cope_immigrants.

Lee, Patrick G. 2017. "Immigrants in Detention Centers Are Often Hundreds of Miles From Legal Help." *ProPublica*, May 16. Accessed July 15, 2017. https://www.propublica.org/article/immigrants-in-detention-centers-are-often-hundreds-of-miles-from-legal-help.

Luker, T. 2013. "Decision Making Conditioned by Radical Uncertainty: Credibility Assessment at the Australian Refugee Review Tribunal." *International Journal of Refugee Law* 25 (3): 502–534.

Mendoza, Gilberto. 2016. *States Offering Driver's Licenses to Immigrants*. National Council of State Legislators (NCSL). NCSL Immigrant Policy Project. Accessed July 4, 2017. http://www.ncsl.org/research/immigration/states-offering-driver-s-licenses-to-immigrants.aspx.

ORR (Office of Refugee Resettlement). 2017. *Unaccompanied Alien Children Released to Sponsors by State*. Accessed July 12, 2017. https://www.acf.hhs.gov/orr/resource/unaccompanied-alien-children-released-to-sponsors-by-state.

Preston, Julia. 2016. "Deluged Immigration Courts, Where Cases Stall for Years, Begin to Buckle." *New York Times*, December 1. Accessed July 6, 2017. https://www.nytimes.com/2016/12/01/us/deluged-immigration-courts-where-cases-stall-for-years-begin-to-buckle.html.

Price, Marie, and Derek Breese. 2016. "Unintended Return: U.S. Deportations and the Fractious Politics of Mobility for Latinos." *Annals of the Association of American Geographers* 106 (2): 366–376. doi:10.1080/00045608.2015.1120149.

Ramji-Nogales, Jaya, Andrew Ian Schoenholtz, and Philip G Schrag. 2011. *Refugee Roulette: Disparities in Asylum Adjudication and Proposals for Reform*. New York: New York University Press.

Richey, Warren. 2016. "Alejandra, Age 7, Is Facing A Judge Alone. Is That Due Process?" *The Christian Science Monitor*, November 1. Accessed July 15, 2017. https://www.csmonitor.com/USA/Politics/2016/1101/Alejandra-age-7-is-facing-a-judge-alone.-Is-that-due-process.

Roubein, Rachel. 2014. "Here's How Hard It Is for Unaccompanied Minors to Get Asylum." *The Atlantic*, July 15. Accessed July 12, 2017. https://www.theatlantic.com/politics/archive/2014/07/heres-how-hard-it-is-for-unaccompanied-minors-to-get-asylum/456267/.

Schoenholtz, Andrew I., Philip G. Schrag, and Jaya Ramji-Nogales. 2014. *Lives in the Balance: Asylum Adjudication by the Department of Homeland Security*. New York: New York University Press.

Smith, Hillel R. 2019. "Asylum and Related Protections for Aliens Who Fear Gang and Domestic Violence." *Congressional Legal Research Legal Sidebar*. Accessed October 8, 2019. https://fas.org/sgp/crs/homesec/LSB10207.pdf.

Swanson, Kate, Rebecca M. Torres, Amy Thompson, Sarah A. Blue, and Oscar Misael Hernandez Herandez. 2015. *A Year After Obama Declared a "Humanitarian Situation" at the Border, Child Migration Continues*. NACLA Report on the Americas. Accessed August 27, 2015.

Thompson, Amy, Rebecca Torres, Kate Swanson, Sarah A. Blue, and Óscar Misael Hernández Hernández. 2018. "Re-Conceptualising Agency in Migrant Children From Central America and Mexico." *Journal of Ethnic and Migration Studies*. doi:10.1080/1369183X.2017.1404258.

TRAC. 2014b. *Representation for Unaccompanied Children in Immigration Court*. Accessed June 22, 2017. http://trac.syr.edu/immigration/reports/371/include/timeseriesG.html.

TRAC. 2016a. *Judge Asylum Denial rate figures*. Accessed June 22, 2017. http://trac.syr.edu/immigration/reports/447/include/denialrates.html.

TRAC. 2016b. *Immigration Backlog Still Rising Despite New Judge Investitures.* Accessed July 4, 2017. http://trac.syr.edu/immigration/reports/429/.

TRAC. 2016c. *Asylum Outcome Increasingly Depends on Judge Assigned.* Accessed July 4, 2017. http://trac.syr.edu/immigration/reports/447/.

TRAC. 2017a. *Backlog of Pending Cases in Immigration Courts as of May 2017.* Accessed July 7, 2017. http://trac.syr.edu/phptools/immigration/court_backlog/apprep_backlog.php.

TRAC. 2017b. *Juveniles - Immigration Court Deportation Proceedings.* Accessed July 7, 2017. http://trac.syr.edu/phptools/immigration/juvenile/.

TRAC. 2019. *Juveniles — Immigration Court Deportation Proceedings.* Accessed October 13, 2019. https://trac.syr.edu/phptools/immigration/juvenile/.

UN High Commissioner for Refugees (UNHCR). 2014. *Children on the Run: Unaccompanied Children Leaving Central America and Mexico and the need for International Protection.* Accessed July 6, 2017. http://www.unhcr.org/56fc266f4.html.

UN High Commissioner for Refugees (UNHCR). 2019. *Global Trends: Forced Displacement in 2018.* Accessed September 27, 2019. https://www.unhcr.org/globaltrends2018/.

United States Customs and Border Protection. 2019. *U.S. Border Patrol Southwest Border Apprehensions by Sector FY2018.* Accessed October 8, 2019. https://www.cbp.gov/newsroom/stats/usbp-sw-border-apprehensions.

United States Department of Justice. 2017a. *EOIR Immigration Court Listing: Administrative Control List.* Accessed July 13, 2017. https://www.justice.gov/eoir/immigration-court-administrative-control-list.

United States Department of Justice. 2017b. *EOIR Immigration Court Listing.* Accessed July 13, 2017https://www.justice.gov/eoir/eoir-immigration-court-listing.

United States Department of Justice. 2017c. *List of Pro Bono Legal Service Providers.* Accessed July 15, 2017. https://www.justice.gov/eoir/list-pro-bono-legal-service-providers.

Varsanyi, Monica W. 2008a. "Immigration Policing Through The Backdoor: City Ordinances, the "Right To The City," and the Exclusion of Undocumented Day Laborers." *Urban Geography* 29: 29–52.

Varsanyi, Monica W. 2008b. "Rescaling the "Alien," Rescaling Personhood: Neoliberalism, Immigration, and the State." *Annals of the Association of American Geographers* 98: 877–896.

Walker, Kyle E., and Helga Leitner. 2011. "The Variegated Landscape of Local Immigration Policies in the United States." *Urban Geography* 32 (2): 156–178.

Wells, Miriam J. 2004. "The Grassroots Reconfiguration of U.S. Immigration Policy." *The International Migration Review* 38 (4): 1308–1347.

Precarity of refugees: the case of Basmane-İzmir, Turkey

Asli Ceylan Oner, Bahar Durmaz-Drinkwater and Richard J. Grant

ABSTRACT

Over the last decade, the precarity of refugees and temporary migrants and its associated ambiguities is an increasing focus of scholarly inquiry and policy debate. In particular, the Syrian conflict since 2011 has led to dramatic refugee crises especially in terms of the number of people displaced into neighbouring countries, including Turkey, Lebanon, Jordan and Iraq, with Turkey hosting the largest refugee population in the world.

Within Turkey, Syrian refugees are concentrated in camps, border towns, major cities and particular urban neighbourhoods. The Basmane neighbourhood, an old inner city quarter of İzmir, Turkey, is a special case, and we directly observe and detail various dimensions of the precarity of Syrian immigrants there at the apex of the refugee flow, and assess how temporary migration affected İzmir's permanent residents. Focusing on physical and social transformations in Basmane, we concentrate on the intra-relationships among place, refugees, and locals and seek to contribute to the debate of how (un)settled situations of refugees produce differential pathways for adaptation and experiences of precarity. The research indicates that socio-spatial dynamics in Basmane contributes to the adaptation of refugees and affects their precarity as the hub for temporary immigrants in İzmir.

Introduction

The Syrian civil war that commenced in 2011 spiralled into a massive humanitarian crisis and resulted in the largest refugee exodus of this century. As of September 2019, approximately 5.6 million Syrian refugees were registered in Egypt, Lebanon, Iraq, Jordan and Turkey (UNHCR 2019a). United Nations High Commission for Refugees (UNHCR 2019b) reports that a further 6.2 million people are displaced in Syria, the largest number of internally displaced in any country of the world. From the onset, Turkey established an 'open-door policy', welcoming Syrian refugees under the assumption that they would return after the war. By 2015, Turkey had risen to the second largest contributor to humanitarian relief in the world (Global Humanitarian Assistance Report 2016). However, in October 2015, the Turkish government decided to close its border with

Syria, except for seriously injured Syrian asylum seekers, and subsequently (January 2016) introduced visa requirements for Syrians arriving from third countries. Turkey now shelters the largest number of Syrian refugees of any country in the world (UNHCR 2019a), an (un)settled population of over 3.6 million people. Among this population, 98 per cent is dispersed in high concentrations in border cities of the south and southeast provinces of Turkey as well as in major metropolitan areas (e.g. Istanbul shelters 550,000 refugees, while İzmir gives refuge to 147,000 Syrians (UNCHR 2019c)). In late 2019, approximately 2% remain in refugee camps. (Multeciler 2019).

Given that many Syrians in Turkey qualify as 'protracted refugees' (according to Crisp's [2003] definition as refugees who have lived in exile for more than 5 years), society in general has to now grapple with the transition from needs-based (charity) to rights-based service provision; encompassing more demanding challenges of welfare and inclusion within a host community (Mackreath and Sagnic 2017). In Turkey, several cities and towns, especially on the west coast, shelter those who hitherto intended to cross the border predominantly into the European Union (EU), via proximate Greek islands. These coastal places became especially important as transient sites. One of these major cities, İzmir and its coastal hinterland (including Çeşme, Foça, Karaburun, Ayvalık, Kuşadası, Bodrum), has received much media attention (e.g. Hubbard 2015) as a hub for refugees in transit, but the conditions of those who remained are understudied.

Shedding light on the physical and social adaptation of refugees, we uncover diverse and disparate human pathways. Combined, the presence of refugees has been a catalyst for neighbourhood change, co-producing an ethnic enclave of sorts. Basmane, an old inner-city quarter of İzmir, may be an extreme example of an area's transformation, involving co-existence of diverse trajectories, enmeshing subjects and objects and peoples encounter with one another. Ilcan, Rygiel, and Baban (2018) suggest three forms of precarity in terms of refugees: precarity of status, precarity of space and precarity of movement. In terms of the refugees in Basmane, there is a precarity of status due to withholding of formal protection embodied in citizenship rights, so refugees become precarious sojourners forced to rely on an unclear and ambivalent regime of human rights, generally in the form of international conventions, highly abstract from their everyday realities. Precarity also encompasses socio-spatial dimensions in Basmane in the sense that the spaces of refugees are given meaning through the precarious experience of everyday living. There is also a precarity of movement whereby refugees respond to their predicament through both organising with NGOs and/or self-organising to campaign for their rights while others yearn for a physical move to the EU in the hope of better protections but after the 2016 agreement between the EU and Turkey, have to contend with their stay in Turkey.

Our research approach follows in the tradition of Mazurana, Jacobsen, and Gale (2013) with an assessment of refugees in urban places in post-conflict situations from below as opposed to most of the literature (Banki 2013; Basok et al. 2015; Castillo 2016) that focuses either on the national/international policy management arena and/or on camps and border zones (Baban, Ilcan, and Rygiel 2017). Focusing on the neighbourhood scale, we unearth new networks among marginalised spaces and note a precarious social reordering (Chacko and Price 2021). We use participant observation, extensive site reconnaissance of the urban built environment and repeat site visits, and draw on the grey literature, brochures and websites of various civil society organisations to document the evolving dimensions of precarity especially after the EU-Turkey agreement on March 2016.

Our paper proceeds in five sections. Following the introduction, we situate the refugee influx into the city in terms of precarity (Waite 2009; Manjikian 2010; Banki 2014) and combine this with theoretical insights from Michael De Certeau (1984) on everyday tactics as practices of the subordinate population, which enable them to have a sense of belonging, juxtaposed against the strategies of the powerful (Lobo, 201X). Our third section sketches the national context of evolution of Turkey's emergency response to Syrian refugees; the fourth section presents a finer grained neighbourhood case study of Basmane, İzmir. In the case study, we focus on the physical and social transformation of Basmane, a historic inner-city, low-income migrant area of İzmir that gained worldwide notoriety (Hubbard 2015) during the peak of humanitarian crisis when refugees desired to cross the Aegean Sea to reach the EU borders. We examine everyday practices and tactics of belonging with illustrations from the cultural realm of inclusion mediated in cooperation with civic organisations and Turkish citizens. In conclusion, we discuss the findings from the case study within the conceptual framework of precarity in terms of the socio-spatial context of Basmane.

Precarity and tactics of belonging of refugees

Scholars (e.g. Purcell 2002; Bauder 2016) have raised ethical questions about the urban habitation of refugees, which includes (among other rights) a right to access and use of physical and social space in the city. Such a lens throws light on how refugees contribute to the production of the space of daily life and how the temporariness of their political condition is reflected against the permanence of the built urban environment and its citizenry (Chacko and Price 2021). To survive in this state of uncertainty, refugees appropriate various spaces such as parks, meeting places, streets and neighbourhoods (Melara et al. 2013). They self-organise to adapt to their new environments, and engage with/in tactics to gain a sense of belonging. For example, geographic clustering enables a sense of familiarity in an unfamiliar environment (Thompson 2016). These result in a moment and a site that engenders both connectedness and social inclusion as well as various resistances (Manjikian 2010; Banki 2014; Thompson and Grant 2015). (Un) settled moments can also alternate between tactics of concentrating and/or dispersing in different times and in particular places (Grant and Thompson 2015; Levine-Rasky 2016). We explain the tactics of Syrians in Izmir to create a sense of belonging and their efforts at making a living to exemplify various realms of precarity from a socio-spatial perspective. We are especially interested in the notion of precarity in terms of migration/movement and urban space.

The contemporary roots of the term precarity date back to the 1960s, and the term was employed to understand conditions of labourers, related to insecurity and uncertainty related to the rise of post-fordism (Kasmir 2018; Waite 2009). First coined in France by Bourdieu (1963), precarity distinguished casual workers (*the precarite*) from permanent workers. The term has been extensively employed and debated in Europe and entered the English academic domain at the turn of the twenty-first century when insecurity (as opposed to employment) became the defining feature of many societies. Waite (2009, 426) defines *'precarity' as referring to life worlds characterised by uncertainty and insecurity that are either thought to originate from a generalised societal malaise, or as a result of particular experiences derived from neo-liberal labour markets.* Waite (2009) emphasises that precarity refers to a condition of life and/or mobilisation among based on precarious experiences. The term is associated with the absence of comfort, predictability, material or psychological welfare and is related to temporality, uncertainty, ambiguity, insecurity, risk, and vulnerability (Ilcan, Rygiel, and Baban 2018; Waite 2009). People who experience those situations could be labourers, students, migrants, or refugees. Standing (2011) posits that the *precariat* constitute a new form of social class.

Different forms and degrees of precarity exist and the situational context can vary internationally in time and space. An emerging scholarship on Syrian refugees in Turkey (Senses 2016; Baban, Ilcan, and Rygiel 2017; Ilcan, Rygiel, and Baban 2018) applies the term to explain several dimensions of precarity. We build on this literature and contribute to the spatial and scalar dimensions of precarity of Syrian refugees in Basmane, and introduce an urban perspective to the conditions and processes of mobilisation and habitation of refugees.

Research on migrants and precarity also emphasises the dynamic unforeseen, uncertain and insecure contexts (Waite 2009; Hodge 2015; Baban, Ilcan, and Rygiel 2017; Gavanas and Calzada 2017; Ilcan, Rygiel, and Baban 2018). Refugees have to navigate their place in the city, their social rights, and access to humanitarian assistance and protection and urban services. Leaving home for unfamiliar locations in search for a better security also entails different uncertainty, risk and new ambiguities, often inserting refugees into an in-between situation, between home and new home-making. This context portends a backdrop of precarity and the structural inequities that the 'wounded' find themselves located within and the proactive ways in which they negotiate and engage in home-making. As Ilcan, Rygiel, and Baban (2018) claim, the condition of precarity is not stable and is subject to constant changes due to the policies, practices and actors that produce and govern precarity.

As noted earlier, the precarity of Syrian refugees in Turkey defines their partial but contested residency rights, their rights to work, but also frequent engagement with informal economies, their heavy dependence on state and civic organisations for assistance (Baban, Ilcan, and Rygiel, 2017), language barriers, and their haphazard involvement in place-making in neglected spaces like downgraded historic neighbourhoods (Melara et al. 2013). This in-betweenness is deeply connected to social and spatial contexts (Manjikian 2010; Thompson 2016), is negotiated in particular places and is heavily contingent on unofficial arrangements (Banki 2013). Participation and engagement within specific social networks can minimise some of the effects of precarity, and it can also open up possibilities for proactive mobilisation to respond to conditions.

The people without power, such as refugees, have to strategise ways to navigate their insecure environments and reduce uncertainties. De Certeau (1984) makes a critical distinction between the strategies of the powerful and the tactics of the powerless to reveal the dynamics of power and coalitions that emerge in instances such as refugees' attempts to make homes in host societies. A tactic is defined as 'a calculated action determined by the absence of a proper locus: it has no spaces of autonomy and is characterised by decision-making with the context of spaces dominated by others' (De Certeau 1984, 37). Rather than situating tactics within the interstices of securitised space of the governmental and the organised camps for refugees, studies employing De Certeau's framework

Figure 1. Location of Basmane and nearby historic environment (Source: Google Maps 2019).

show that the city viewed from above – mapped, planned, produced – differs from the city experienced on the streets, where refugees walk through unplanned paths, appropriate spaces, and use time in unplanned and unforeseen ways (Grant and Thompson 2015). It is the everyday city life and areas where the Syrian refugees are concentrated such as Basmane that we focus as a case study in this paper (see Figure 1).

Refugees employ tactics to decrease the negative side effects of precarity and to establish a life, to settle, to make a living in a new and unfamiliar environment where they try to make a living away from home. These tactics are explained in detail in the Basmane section from a socio-spatial perspective.

Turkey's emergency response to Syrian refugees

By 2016, Turkey hosted over 3.6 million Syrian refugees, of which 98% inhabited urban centres; thus urban adaptation is paramount for these massive flows of people. The western cities in Turkey were initially perceived as transit locations by refugees who wished to reach the EU borders (UNHCR 2016). During 2015 and 2016, approximately 550,000 Syrians entered Europe via the sea route from Turkey to Greece (International Organisation for Migration (IOM) 2017). However, in March 2016, the EU and Turkey concluded a Joint Action Plan to control this migrant inflow and to remove incentives to seek irregular routes to the EU. This EU-Turkey accord announced that all new irregular migrants crossing from Turkey to the Greek islands would be returned to Turkey, and it also included a one-for-one refugee return, meaning that for every Syrian refugee returned to Turkey, another Syrian would be resettled in the EU (Baban, Ilcan, and Rygiel, 2017). In addition, Turkey would receive financial compensation (a 3 billion Euros allocation to be supplemented with an additional 3 billion Euros up to the end of 2018), visa-free travel would be introduced, and forward progress would be made in its EU membership negotiations (İçduygu and Şimşek 2016). This agreement affected the

Syrian population in İzmir, which began to seek ways of settling in the city instead of crossing borders.

Officially, the Turkish government recognises Syrian refugees not as asylum seekers but as 'guests' hosted by Turkey and under a 'temporary protection' regime (Akgündüz, Berg, and Hassink, 2015; Heck and Hess, 2017). According to Akgündüz, Berg, and Hassink (2015, 4), this designation has several important implications: they cannot apply for asylum in a third country, hindering opportunities to participate in further international migration, while with their 'guest status', they can be internally relocated by the Turkish government. In general, the government takes a service-based humanitarian approach for Syrian refugees. Syrian refugees can benefit from free basic health care, education, and social assistance, but researchers (Yıldız and Uzgören 2016; Baban, Ilcan, and Rygiel, 2017; Mackreath and Sagnic 2017) highlight major obstacles to accessing these services in practice.

Initially, the local population in different cities in Turkey had a positive attitude, helping Syrian 'wounded guests' obtain shelter, medical attention, food, and clothing, but perceptions began to shift as some 'guests' showed no signs of wanting to leave (Kirişçi 2014). As the population of Syrian refugees rose, urban life became more challenging in terms of housing, wages, and the capacity of existing physical infrastructure (ORSAM 2015). While tolerance among the hosts has, for the most part, prevailed, fears about an anti-Syrian reaction remain, practices of exclusion are becoming embedded, and the employment of Syrians at below minimum wage engenders hostility from Turkish workers who find themselves replaced by cheaper labour (Kirişçi 2014). According to Demir (2015, 7) the majority of Turkish people (81.7%) strongly disapprove granting citizenship to refugees, and only 'one-in-five' believes that refugees can integrate. On the positive side, the number of criminal cases directly involving refugees is very low, and although integration problems between locals and refugees exist, grassroots organisations engage Syrians, contributing to a social peace (ORSAM 2015).

The national temporary protection regime necessitates that to access social services, Syrians must register with the Turkish government's Disaster and Emergency Management Agency (AFAD) in their city of residence to receive an identity card, *kimlik* (in Turkish) (Baban, Ilcan, and Rygiel, 2017). Some Syrians view this card as geographically restricting, as it is location specific; to relocate within Turkey, they must inform the authorities in advance, cancel their current kimlik, and subsequently re-register in the new location (UNHCR 2017). The system might present delays or challenges in receiving a new kimlik, so aid workers and civil society organisations provide for basic needs in such cases. Largely because of the perceived mobility restrictions, Syrians feel the precariousness of their situation and are hesitant to register in cities, especially in coastal cities like İzmir, where there may be a small possibility of crossing EU borders at some future time (Baban, Ilcan, and Rygiel, 2017). Many, therefore, live on the edge.

Given the scale and scope of the refugee challenge in Turkey, international humanitarian organisations are conspicuously absent. The total number of international organisations actively working with Syrians in Turkey numbered only 42 in 2015 (Mackreath and Sagnic 2017). Consequently, civil society and Turkish individuals become hugely important in facilitating local inclusion. Civil society space in Turkey is occupied by organisations that depend on international funders and organisations that rely on access to funding through the government, private donors, and faith-based organisations.

Kuzmanovic (2016) emphasises that civil society is in a nascent state of development in Turkey and suffers from a lack of visibility, making it harder for Syrians to locate assistance. Faith-based civic organisations are known not to advertise well, not wanting to draw too much attention to their accomplishments and thereby operating in accordance with Islamic humility (Mackreath and Sagnic 2017). However, an assessment at the sub-city area level creates a window into civil society organisations that engage with new culturally mediated spaces, particularly with regard to inclusion; this is similar to what Michele Lobo found in her work with refugees in Darwin, Australia (Lobo, 201X).

Case study: Basmane and Syrian refugees

İzmir, a port city, is the third most populous city of Turkey, with a population of 4.3 million (Turkish Statistical Institute (TUIK) 2017). Since the 1980s, the city has received internal migrants, and it also has been a destination for international migrants from Afghanistan and Iraq, as well as Asia and Africa. The city's population diversity plays an influential role in attracting Syrian refugees, often arriving via migration chains of relatives and friends.

Syrians are found in a patchwork pattern across İzmir, encompassing differences in socio-economic background, gender, age, religion, access to familial or other support networks, health, aptitude for integration, and level of engagement with civil society. Some of the wealthy have retreated into private spaces, and less wealthy population have dispersed away from the central areas of the city after finding a place in the informal economy (Karadağ 2015). As Belanger and Saracoglu (2018)'s findings also suggest, Syrian refugees are dispersed around İzmir where they can find job opportunities in centrally located districts such as Basmane and Kadifekale, and relatively more peripheral locations of Çimentepe, Buca, and Yeşildere (Figure 2) (Yıldız and Uzgören 2016).

İzmir has been immersed in refugee flows in three ways. First, it served as a major transit point for those making their way across the Mediterranean Sea from coastal towns such as Ayvalık, Çeşme, Kuşadası, and Bodrum to reach the Greek islands of Chios (7 km from Çeşme), Lesvos (10 km from Ayvalık), Samos (2 km from Kuşadası), and Kos (5 km from Bodrum). Basmane Train Station plays a major role in connecting these places to the south-eastern region of Turkey via İzmir. Second, it is a hub for those wanting to settle and, third, it is a base for those needing to spend an intermediate period to accumulate enough funds to finance an onward journey (Yıldız and Uzgören 2016) and/or a possible future return for a few. Yıldız and Uzgören (2016) reported 74,000 registered Syrians in İzmir in 2015, the registered population rose to 98,000 in 2017 (Erdoğan 2017) and currently the official population has exceeded well above 146,000 people (Multeciler 2019). İzmir's urban life, therefore, exhibits multiple realities of acceptance, adaptation, and estrangement, for both refugees and residents, but certain alliances can foster pathways of agency and engagement, as opposed to reproducing patterns of marginalisation and exclusion.

Despite İzmir functioning as a migrant hub, tourist destination, and, arguably, one of the most politically liberal cities in Turkey, Syrians experience alienation and otherness. Child labour, informal work, low wages or non-remuneration for work, discrimination in wages and de-qualification of professional experiences, accompanied by abject conditions of shelter, health, education and other social services as well as general discrimination exist (Senses 2016; Ilcan, Rygiel and Baban 2018; Saracoglu and Belanger 2018).

Figure 2. Major locations of Syrians in central İzmir (Source: Google Maps 2019).

Negative opinions frame the refugee population as potential social risk generators, as job-takers in the informal economy due to their willingness to work for lower wages without social protection, and as an economic burden on the state. Some İzmirians complain that particular central city neighbourhoods became overcrowded since the Syrians arrived, and rents increased five-fold, because Syrians cover exploitative rents by overcrowding and sharing floor space (Karadağ 2015).

The İzmir municipality walks a fine line among humanitarian relief, non-interference, and control but leaves much of the engagement with Syrians to civil society. For example, responding to the pressure of civil society organisations for better refugee infrastructure, the municipality installed temporary public toilets around parts of the city, but at the same time they attempted to close off access to various parks at certain times (e.g. Kültürpark to Syrians) to prevent people sleeping there (Karşıyakahaber 2015). Importantly, the İzmir municipality does not want to alienate voters by spending large sums of money on refugees, and authorities also want to protect the image of the city as a tourist destination. On the other hand, the recently elected mayor has also declared that the Syrian refugees are the guests of the city and until there is a more permanent solution at the national level, the people of İzmir need to show hospitality to these guests (İlkses Gazetesi 2019).

Despite the precarity of their situation due to the lack of status, employment, limited access to resources, and circumscribed mobility, refugees have engaged in proactive tactics to settle, to belong and integrate into the physical and social context of the city as discussed below.

Tactics of belonging through the built environment

Basmane is one of the oldest areas in İzmir that has been accommodating migrants, refugees and new-comers through the ages. Wissink, Düvell, and van Eerdewijk (2013) define it as a transit migration hub located in the heart of the city, surrounded by public space, archaeological sites, affordable spaces and job opportunities in various sectors such as textiles, wedding and fashion industries, leather and electronics, which are clustered in and around Basmane. The main street, Anafartalar Street (1800 m long), is mainly a pedestrian street, extending from Basmane Train Station to Konak Square. The street connects the district with the Kemeraltı Historic Bazaar, seaside and Konak Square, hence providing an important connection between the train station and the city's commercial and tourist areas. Konak Square, a landmark historic public square redesigned in 2002 is particularly important since it is possible to see many Syrians relaxing there or selling items on adjoining streets. Furthermore, Hatuniye Square and the mosque located along Anafartalar Street also act as social networking sites for Syrians. Being located between the two important transportation hubs of Konak Square and Basmane Train Station, and surrounded by areas offering job opportunities, affordable living and public space, Basmane's built environment offers refugees many short-term and long-term possibilities to adapt and make a living. Furthermore, the central park of Izmir, Kültürpark, is located just 5 min' walk away from Basmane, which hosted many immigrants during the immigrant influx in 2015. We observed many Syrians sleeping rough in the park and temporarily camping there when they first arrived in Basmane.

As well as location, the scale of Basmane offers possibilities to integrate the tactics of belonging. Basmane's main roads have an enclosing effect as does its topography, since one of the city's edges is bordered by a hill, Kadifekale. Small-scale ground floor premises in the area increase the visibility of products and services from the street and contribute to accessibility and a sense of belonging. Here, store fronts displaying Arabic signs contribute to the image of the area as a 'Syrian Enclave' or 'Little Syria'.

Historically, Basmane was a multi-ethnic area with residential neighbourhoods, mosques, churches and synagogues. This multicultural diversity is still visible within the historic built environment. Kortejo, a special building typology, consists of private rooms built along a corridor overlooking a central courtyard, with common spaces like a kitchen and bathroom. These Kortejos were designed to accommodate the Jewish population that migrated from Spain in the 15th century, and are unique to Basmane (Beşikçi, 2016). Several Kortejos spread across Basmane are used as affordable hotels or textile ateliers. However, the manager of one of the Kortejo hotels recently stated that they are no longer accepting refugees.

Traces of past historical importance are evident in the built form and spatial layout, whether the buildings are abandoned or maintained and renovated. A large number of buildings fell into disuse and are in various states of disrepair, often due to their old age. Many structures are over 100 years old and require extensive and expensive repairs (beyond neglect and wear and tear, humidity, roofing issues, deficient sanitary infrastructure, electrical issues, and occasionally structural issues are often involved). The area's twenty-first-century reputation (prior to the Syrian influxes) stemmed from its marginalised low-income population and their associated social and employment challenges, diminishing the area's attractiveness to locals and tourists alike. Decades of sheltering internal migrants from south-eastern Turkey has resulted in the area being associated with 'outsiders', in spite of its local historical significance. Many İzmirians avoid Basmane for safety reasons because of the negative image, which has also led many long-standing residents to move to more stable neighbourhoods. In addition, investors have tended to overlook Basmane. As the city expanded and new areas emerged, Basmane became a deteriorating inner city location. We argue that as well as the importance of location and scale, its deteriorated built environment with abandoned empty spaces is one of the factors contributing to the precarious situation of refugees here.

Nevertheless, the area contains many historic İzmir houses, many of which have been transformed into hotels and museums and for a while these were vibrant establishments. Among the important buildings is Uşakizade Mansion, belonging to the family of Latife Uşşaki, wife of Mustafa Kemal Ataturk, the founder of the Republic of Turkey. Until quite recently, this building had been used as a hotel (Sadıkbey Hotel) but is now abandoned. Other classic hotels in the area include Cihan Palas (The Emniyet Hotel) on Anafartalar Street, one of the oldest buildings, which was in the heart of the entertainment area during the early twentieth century (Figure 3). Today, its ground floor functions as a café where Syrians also visit, but the upper floors have fallen into disuse.

The Basmane area has had recent adaptive reuse projects. For example, an old İzmir house functioned in 2014 as İzmir Women's Museum, the first of its kind in Turkey, and another old house was converted into the Radio and Democracy Museum. The most important adaptive reuse project was an entire street of hotels. This 'Hotel Street' was renovated in the early 2000s, during which the exterior building façades and infrastructure were renovated (Kayın 2004). This street initiative won the Urban Transformation Award in 2005 from the Union of Historical Towns (Figure 4).

Beginning in 2011, these affordable hotels began accommodating the first wave of Syrian refugees. Hotels offered transit individuals floor space for around US$10 per night. In addition, Basmane's abandoned houses provided a temporary shelter to refugees. This episode of warehousing transit individuals was not foreseen, and even rundown, unsafe buildings became occupied and accidents and fires were recorded.

Figure 3. Historic Basmane: Uşakizade Mansion and Cihan Palas Hotel.

Figure 4. Hotel Street in the beginning of 2000s after renovation (Source: Kayın 2010).

The refugee influx into disused buildings and affordable hotels was to be a temporary phenomenon, and their presence in the district illustrated the untapped potential for reuse, repurposing, and rediscovery of past glories. At its peak, the intensive presence of Syrian refugees in the area led to a new phase of urban downgrading (Figure 5) (Melera et al. 2013). Worried about the rapid deterioration and overuse of premises, hotel managers who were interviewed revealed that, after 2015, establishments along Hotel Street and in Basmane in general were no longer willing to accommodate Syrian refugees.

The aftermath of the EU-Turkey accord witnessed a different spatial imprint on Basmane. After the large Syrian outflows to other İzmir locations from early 2016 onwards, Basmane became a Syrian 'home' instead of 'pit-stop', and the ancillary economy changed accordingly (Özerim and Crawley 2016). As Syrians settled in the area, quieter streets housed many refugees, and the hotel district transitioned to a different user group. A form of entrepreneurship by young and highly educated people emerged, providing affordable accommodation to cater to a new clientele (i.e. backpackers, researchers, and tourists). Stylish, modern, and eclectic boutique hotels, such as the Lotus Garden Hostel, a uniquely renovated 1939 wooden

Figure 5. Hotel Street in 2017.

building, came into being. TripAdvisor (2017) rates this establishment among the top five budget accommodations in İzmir, and Basmane may be on its way to becoming a trendy, affordable place for budget-conscious visitors.

The area now demonstrates novel and interesting place-making through the merging of diverse populations in buildings from different periods. Syrians have become more embedded in the fabric of the neighbourhood's streets and economy. A good example of this everyday place-making is 1297 Street, where Syrians mix with a population from south-eastern Turkey; children play on the streets, and women sit outside on the steps and chat with their neighbours (Figure 6). The vibrancy of the streets is considered a positive factor by locals, tourists, and investors. Nevertheless, there is a need to protect Basmane's historical houses as important examples of architecture from the nineteenth and twentieth centuries, and there is a concern that trendy developments and capital influxes could convert many buildings with little regard for historical preservation. Poor past record-keeping and a culture of enabling irregular conversions need to be curbed.

Since the first influx of refugees, a large shadow economy (Schneider and Enste 2013) and a space of difference formed around Basmane. During the peak of the illegal passages across the Aegean Sea, the district served as a principal point for people-smuggling operations. This illegal economy was centred around the vicinity of the Çorakkapı Mosque area (Özerim and Crawley 2016), the nearby coffee houses, Anafartalar Street and Hatuniye Square (Figure 7). It was very common to see shops selling life jackets and necessary supplies for the journey across the Aegean. Basmane had clearly demarcated focal points within the shadow economy. We recently observed that those shops still sell life-jackets and related infrastructure.

During the peak of the refugee crisis, refugees made their way in a 'daily crush' along the thoroughfares to be transported to Greece, paying US$1000 per person to cross the Aegean Sea (Weise 2016). During 'intended short stays', Basmane restaurants functioned as local food stops for the transit refugees that craved home-cooked meals; middlemen and

Figure 6. 1297 Street and some of the houses that Syrians and population from South-eastern Turkey live.

Figure 7. Places of social interaction and network in Basmane.

their touts funnelled refugees into cafés and meeting spots to conclude deals; shops along Anafartalar Street or Fevzipaşa Boulevard sold life-vests, and money exchange shops converted funds into Euros.

After the EU-Turkey deal, Basmane also experienced outflows of Syrians to other areas of the city closer to jobs, and the function and perceptions of Basmane inhabitants changed accordingly. Some Basmane streets had high concentrations of Syrian refugees who wanted to settle in the area, and the vicinity of Anafartalar Street has matured into a node of Syrians, developing into a 'Little Syria'. Several restaurants specialise in Syrian cuisine and almost all retail establishments now display bilingual Turkish and Arabic signboards. Anafartalar Street has a daily life centred around Syrians with retrofitted affordable accommodations, cafés, small food stores, phone card shops, barber shops, bakeries specialising in Syrian desserts, and markets and stalls that extend to the sidewalks and streets, impeding vehicular and pedestrian flows. Typically, signage on shop windows is either in Arabic or in both Arabic and Turkish. Anafartalar Street is always busy, and its ivy canopy gives a feeling of enclosure and security (Figure 8). This economy that was formed in and around Basmane eased the adaptation of Syrians. They work, use the services provided and in some cases they own and manage these places (Izmir Büyükşehir Belediyesi Akdeniz Akademisi 2018). The Basmane area has transitioned into more normalised functions, serving as the central node for (un)settled Syrians' daily retail and social networking activities as these residents become more embedded into the fabric of the neighbourhood's streets and economy.

Figure 8. Local Shops along Anafartalar Street.

The physical characteristics of built environment, such as centrality, location, adaptability, locality, historic built heritage, image, affordability, proximity, public spaces, scale are the factors that has positively contributed to the adaptation of Syrians by providing opportunities and space to integrate their tactics of belonging together with their social support networks and solidarity mechanisms, which are explained in the next section.

Tactics of belonging through the social environment

Mackreath and Sagnic (2017) report that Syrians are shunning host organisations, and retreating into highly dependent networks based on hometown and religious and ethnic communities, which might be expected as precarity becomes an enduring condition and as cultural organisations have a limited appeal. In addition, there is a distinct social space online (examples include Facebook groups in Arabic and Turkish such as Syrians in İzmir and Syrian Community in İzmir, translated from Arabic), which is very important for information sharing and emotional support, including information on how to engage with formal NGOs. These informal networks act within the sphere of the household and can facilitate civil society, especially by operating to some extent as prerequisites for refugee NGOs (office-based or neighbourhood outreach), which otherwise would have to invest resources continually in establishing contact with Syrian refugees (Tan 2016). Those who can afford to access this social space are the better off, younger, and technologically savvy refugees (Tan 2016). Crowdfunding campaigns to support Syrians stuck in İzmir also raise money to assist refugees (e.g. a YouCaring campaign in early 2017 raised almost US$2500 (YouCaring 2017)). Marginalised groups appear to have the greatest level of insecurity and far fewer means to become self-securing; they are heavily dependent on outreach help. Tan (2016, 84) notes that many Syrian refugees have no contact with any organisation and rely on self-help, family, and kinship networks.

In terms of the national social context, the government grants Syrians rights to access social services, and Syrian children are awarded identical rights with local counterparts, including the right to a free education in a local school. When Syrian children do attend school, many experience language-related problems. The Society of Syrians in İzmir, the City Governorship, the Directorate for National Education, and NGOs made a combined attempt to open a school with Arabic instruction; however, this endeavour collapsed at the last minute (Karadağ 2015). Beyond education, there are well-documented issues with regard to Syrians accessing social services. Karadağ (2015) notes that even when Syrians can access hospitals, there are some problems related to their Arabic identity cards, which cannot be understood by the local hospital staff. Thus, language is a major barrier in all environments of social life.

Everyday realities mean that Syrians have to be proactive in strategising for daily survival, and many focus on the immediate home environment, their social networks, and civil society to survive. Often, marginalised Syrian families cannot afford school uniforms and transportation costs (Baban, Ilcan, and Rygiel, 2017), and consequently they are forced to obtain employment for themselves and/or their children (some parents have health and/or disability issues as a consequence of war) in nearby textile factories and in informal work settings. While the government provides some health care and access to education, civil society organisations play a major role in the care of Syrians at the neighbourhood level.

The non-profit, non-governmental organisations landscape is nascent in Turkey, particularly with regard to those that work on behalf of Syrian refugees. Government data show a 22% rise in the number of organisations registered (from 4824 in 2011 to 6203 in 2016), but the data do not indicate their roles and relationships with the state, on whether they received funding, or on their primary focus (Mackreath and Sagnic 2017). Some civil society organisations have added a Syrian relief component, but there is a smaller subset of organisations that focus exclusively on Syrian-related issues. In Turkey's Syrian non-profit arena, the majority of organisations engage in the collection and distribution of donated clothing and food. Syrians are in need of basic support as most have exhausted their savings in exiting perilous situations in Syria and in securing a rental space. During the course of our fieldwork, we identified three additional non-profit organisations that have been very active in the Basmane area: Halkların Köprüsü Derneği, İzmir Müzisyenler Derneği, and ReVi Family. These organisations have been instrumental in supporting Syrian refugees achieve some degree of social cohesion and have focussed their Syrian engagement around a cultural space. We outline each of these groups in turn.

First, Halkların Köprüsü Derneği (The Association of Solidarity/The Bridge of the People) aims to promote peace and equality among the different groups in Turkey, and its efforts have now been extended to Syrians. The rise of İzmir as a migration hub compelled the organisation to focus on bridging refugee inclusion (Halkların Köprüsü Derneği 2017). In İzmir, the group initially concentrated on basic relief, but more recently, its focus has switched to specialised programming. Arts, food, and cultural programming are common, and the organisation also helps bridge the gap between Turks and refugees with disabilities. An example of programming offered in 2017 is 'One Woman One

Story Nights', whereby Syrian food is prepared by men and served to groups of 11–30 women, and the speaker(s), with the assistance of a translator, talk about their pre-war lives in Syria and the difficulties of living as a refugee. The core idea is to empower refugees to speak for themselves in their own words and to create a listening forum where locals can also learn first-hand about the everyday lives of fellow urbanites (Halkların Köprüsü Derneği 2017).

Second, İzmir Müzisyenler Derneği (Association of İzmir Musicians, 2017) participates in cultural and artistic relief for refugees. The group is known for its community event called 'Yeryüzü Sofraları', which is a big dinner open to everybody prepared with donations and efforts of volunteers. This initiative paves the way toward integrating different groups and promotes positive feelings among Syrian families (İlkses Gazetesi 2015). The Association of İzmir Musicians and Halkların Köprüsü Derneği also organise solidarity concerts and collect and distribute basic necessities (e.g. supplies, books, toys, clothes, winter boots, coats, shoes, blankets, floor mattresses and quilts).

Third, the ReVi Family organisation is a group of international and local volunteers in İzmir aiming to help the refugees with sustainable work opportunities and solutions by identifying the family's interests and skills and by engaging them in appropriate employment. It started to work in İzmir in early 2016 and already has provided assistance to more than 400 Syrian families in Basmane in rebuilding their lives. In addition, ReVi operates two kindergartens that serve approximately 120 children. To better serve these students, the organisation hired five Arabic speaking Syrian-trained teachers from the community. The group also provides assistance to older children to pursue a formal education, runs empowerment programs and provides employment opportunities for adults (e.g. knitting schemes where different types of clothing are handmade and retailed in their store as well as online). On Sundays, ReVi also visits one family for a Syrian dinner, and on these occasions a sum of money is paid by the participants for the meal cooked by a ReVi family (ReVi Family Organisation 2017).

After 8 years of living with precarity, Syrians are developing their own civil society in Turkey, adding a new component to the identity of civil society in Turkey, which has possible implications for the future Syrian presence in the country (Mackreath and Sagnic 2017). Cultural exchange, learning from each other, contributing to the economy as productive labourers and making the most of an opportunity to reuse existing rundown historic edifices can all be seen as evidence of refugees as change agents. Although their full potential is not yet realised, we argue that the influx of Syrian refugees increases awareness of Basmane, not only for the media, international humanitarian relief organisations, and academia, but also for İzmirians who did not know the area prior to the influxes. Nowadays, its historic potential is acknowledged more so than in the recent past, and Basmane's reputation as a historic and important neighbourhood is being rekindled, reinterpreted, and reestablished.

Conclusion

This paper explains how Basmane's built and social environment accommodated the temporary and permanent needs of refugees. The analysis sheds some light on a set of fluid dynamics to illustrate the lived and experienced reality of Basmane from the perspectives of refugees who are caught in a web in which they lack permanent legal status, experience circumscribed livelihoods in their temporary place of refuge, and are unable to return home (Hyndman and Giles 2017).

As Chacko and Price (2021) argue, various spatial scales ranging from architectural to urban are influential on minimising the impact of precarity. In Basmane, not only spatial, but also social dimensions tactics helped to reduce the impact of precarity of refugees. Basok et al (2015) named these tactics as 'self-making' and 'techniques of the self'. Relying on civil society and their own networks, Syrians engage in urban adaptation processes at the neighbourhood level (Ilcan, Rygiel and Baban 2018). For some, attending musical events, hosting dinners and engaging with local members of civil society are important opportunities to build social ties in İzmir. Importantly, at a more macro level, their everyday practices and tactics to create a sense of belonging play a role in yet another physical and social transformation of Basmane. İzmir, a city of cosmopolitan character throughout the ages, has welcomed many migrants and refugees. The influx of Syrian refugees adds another layer of diversity. This group is, for the most part, a transitory group due to factors relating to local and central governments. Thus an understanding of precarity is especially relevant during the period of their extended refugee status.

With few opportunities in a war-ravaged Syria, many refugees started to settle in Basmane and the surrounding areas, participate in the informal economy, make efforts to learn Turkish, access social services, and engage with civic society organisations. İzmir's residents are now grappling with the notion that this precarious group with a distinct culture and language are making claims on space, state, and civil society. İzmirians were initially welcoming to the short-stay 'guests', but as the flows swelled and areas such as Basmane were engulfed by outsiders, locals felt more estranged from parts of their city, especially its public spaces. This Basmane perception, however, is beginning to change as 'Little Syria' begins to function as an immigrant enclave. There are many unanswered questions about Syrians' transition from precarity and about their longer-term settlement. Will the existing Syrian-dominated area in Basmane continue to be consolidated as 'Little Syria'? Will other clearly demarcated Syrian enclaves form, or will Syrians diffuse into more private space and mixed neighbourhoods? Will return migration to Syria commence once the war is over? Moving deeper into protracted refugee status and possibly to other forms of 'belonging' will lead to further changes of selfhood of Syrian refugees in Turkey.

In conclusion, our case study shows the importance of developing longer- and mid-term rights and frameworks, rather than short-term needs-based rights (generally the international norm). Understanding the precarity of the refugees and their needs and tactics to belong involve their participation in the remaking of places, the rediscovery of downgraded neighbourhoods, and claims on space and on services. Such outcomes are important not only to Syrians in Turkey but to refugees in similar situations in many other parts of the world, such as Zimbabweans in South Africa, Somalis in Kenya, Romani in Canada, Africans in China, Burmese in Thailand, and Venezuelans in Colombia.

Indeed, many other segments of Turkish society also experience precarity even though Syrian refugees presently represent a quintessential form of precarity; we acknowledge similarities in precarity (but to different degrees in terms of space and mobility, labour and general insecurity) might allow for new and more broad-based struggles against precarity to emerge and new forms of collective organisation. Recognising that opportunities for inclusion, cultural exchanges, and adaptation and often resistance, are located in city neighbourhoods, we call for more research on different types of urban environments and the variegated ways that Syrian refugees participate in adaptation, engage with locals, and transform cultural realms, neighbourhoods, work, and educational environments in the process.

Disclosure statement

No potential conflict of interest was reported by the author(s).

References

Akgündüz, Y., M. Berg, and W. Hassink. 2015. *The Impact of Refugee Crises on Host Labor Markets: The Case of the Syrian Refugee Crisis in Turkey. Discussion Paper Series.* Bonn: IZA. http://ftp.iza.org/dp8841.pdf.

Baban, F., S. Ilcan, and K. Rygiel. 2017. "Syrian Refugees in Turkey: Pathways to Precarity Differential Inclusion, and Negotiated Citizenship Rights." *Journal of Ethnic and Migration Studies* 43 (1): 41–57.

Banki, S. 2013. "The Paradoxical Power of Precarity: Refugees and Homeland Activism." *Refugee Review* 1 (1): 1–20.

Banki, S. 2014. "Precarity of Place: A Complement to the Growing Precariat Literature." *Global Discourse* 3 (3–4): 450–463.

Basok, T., D. Bélanger, M. L. R. Wiesner, and G. Candiz. 2015. "Techniques of the Self in the Face of Precarity." In *Rethinking Transit Migration: Precarity, Mobility, and Self-Making in Mexico*, 72–88. London: Palgrave Pivot.

Bauder, H. 2016. "Possibilities of Belonging." *Antipode* 48 (2): 252–271.

Belanger, D. and Saracoglu, C. 2018. "The governance of Syrian refugees in Turkey: The state-capital nexus and its discontents." *Mediterranean Politics.*

Beşikçi, O. 2016. "Basmane field trip notes" Site trip for the ARCH 564 İzmir and Urbanization Course for İzmir University of Economics, Department of Architecture.

Bourdieu, P. 1963. *Travail et Travailleurs en Algerie.* Paris, France: Mouton & Co.

Castillo, R. 2016. "'Homing'Guangzhou: Emplacement, Belonging and Precarity among Africans in China." *International Journal of Cultural Studies* 19 (3): 287–306.

Chacko, E., and M. Price. 2021. "(Un)Settled Sojourners in Cities: The Scalar and Temporal Dimensions of Migrant Precarity." *Journal of Ethnic and Migration Studies* 47 (20): 4597–4614. doi:10.1080/1369183X.2020.1731060.

Crisp, J. 2003. *No Solution in Sight: The Problem of Protracted Refugee Situations in Africa.* Geneva: UNHCR.

De Certeau, M. 1984. *The Practice of Everyday Life.* Berkeley: University of California Press.

Demir, O. 2015. *Migration Policies, Social Concerns, and Syrian Refugees in Turkey.* Global Policy Paper 1. Ankara: Center for Migration Studies. http://globalpse.org/en/migration-policies-social-concerns-and-syrian-refugees-in-turkey/.

Erdoğan, M. 2017. "Kopuş"tan "Uyum"a Kent Mültecileri. Suriyeli Mülteciler ve Belediyelerin Süreç Yönetimi: İstanbul Örneği. Marmara Belediyeler Birliği.

Gavanas, A., and I. Calzada. 2017. "Multiplex Migration and Aspects of Precarisation: Swedish Retirement Migrants to Spain and Their Service Providers." In *Politics of Precarity: Migrant Conditions, Struggles and Experiences*, edited by C. Schierup, and M. B. Jørgensen, 118–137. Brill.

Global Human Assistance Report. 2016. Development Initiatives. http://devinit.org/wp-content/uploads/2016/06/Global-Humanitarian-Assistance-Report-2016.pdf.

Google Maps. 2019. *Map of İzmir.* https://www.google.com/maps.

Grant, R., and D. Thompson. 2015. "City on Edge. Immigrant Businesses and the Right to Urban Space in Johannesburg, South Africa." *Urban Geography* 36 (2): 181–200.

Halkların Köprüsü Derneği (Association of Solidarity/ The Bridge of the People). 2017. http://www.halklarinkoprusu.org/en/.

Heck, G., and S. Hess. 2017. "Tracing the Effects of the EU-Turkey Deal: The Momentum of the Multi-Layered Turkish Border Regime." *Movements* 3 (2): 35–57.
Hodge, P. 2015. "A Grievable Life? The Criminalisation and Securing of Asylum Seeker Bodies in the 'Violent Frames' of Australia's Operation Sovereign Borders." *Geoforum; Journal of Physical, Human, and Regional Geosciences* 58: 122–131.
Hubbard, B. 2015. "Money Flows with Migrants and Life Jackets Fill the Shops." *New York Times*, September 27. Cover Page.
Hyndman, J., and W. Giles. 2017. *Refugees in Extended Exile: Living on the Edge*. New York: Routledge.
İçduygu, A., and D. Şimşek. 2016. "Syrian Refugees in Turkey: Towards Integration Policies." *Turkish Policy Quarterly* Fall: 59–69.
Ilcan, S., K. Rygiel, and F. Baban. 2018. "The Ambiguous Architecture of Precarity: Temporary Protection, Everyday Living and Migrant Journeys of Syrian Refugees." *International Journal of Migration and Border Studies* 4 (1/2): 51–70.
İlkses Gazetesi. 2015. "Yeryüzü Sofraları Devam Ediyor." *İlkses Gazetesi*, 24 September. http://www.ilksesgazetesi.com/haber/yeryuzu-sofralari-devam-ediyor-11185.html.
İlkses Gazetesi. 2019. "CHP'nin İzmir Büyükşehir Belediye Başkan Adayı Tunç Soyer'den Mülteci Açıklaması: Belediyelere de Görevler Düşüyor." *İlkses Gazetesi*, 28 February. http://ilksesgazetesi.com/haberler/guncel/chpnin-izmir-buyuksehir-belediye-baskan-adayi-tunc-soyerden-multeci-aciklamasi-belediyelere-de-gorevler-dusuyor-65829.
International Organisation for Migration (IOM). 2017. *Mediterranean Migrant Arrivals Top 363,348 in 2016; Deaths at Sea: 5,079*. https://www.iom.int/news/mediterranean-migrant-arrivals-top-363348-2016-deaths-sea-5079.
İzmir Büyükşehir Belediyesi Akdeniz Akademisi. 2018. Basmane Çevresel Tasarım Önerileri. https://www.izmeda.org/yayimlar/projeler/basmane_web_son.pdf.
İzmir Müzisyenler Derneği (Association of İzmir Musicians). 2017. https://www.facebook.com/pg/İzmirmuzisyenleri/about/?ref=page_internal.
Karadağ, A. 2015. "Refugees of a City: The Socio-Spatial Impacts of Those Syrian Refugees Who Arrive in İzmir." In *Turkish Migration Conference 2015 Selected Proceedings*, edited by G. Seker, I. Sirkeci, A. Tilbe, M. Okmen, P. Yazgan, and D. Erogine, 118–125. London: Transnational Press.
Karşıyakahaber. 2015. "Suriyeli Göçmenler Kültürpark'tan çıkarıldı." *Karşıyaka Haber*, 9 August. http://www.karsiyakahaber.com/haber/suriyeli-gocmenler-kulturparktan-cikarildi/6007/.
Kasmir, S. 2018. "Precarity." In *The Cambridge Encyclopedia of Anthropology*, edited by F. Stein, S. Lazar, M. Candea, H. Diemberger, J. Robbins, A. Sanchez, and R. Stasch. Recuperado. http://www.anthroencyclopedia.com/ printpdf/282.
Kayın, E. 2004. "Oteller Sokağı/Oteller Bölgesi/Kemeraltı Neden, Nasıl Korunsun?" *Ege Mimarlık* 2004/4-52: 31–36.
Kayın, E. 2010. "Tarihsel ve Yaşamsal Kesişmeler: Basmane Oteller Bölgesi." *İzmir Dergisi* 2: 7. http://www.İzmirdergisi.com/İzmir/İzmir07/HTML/files/assets/basic-html/index.html#1.
Kirişçi, K. 2014. *Syrian Refugees and Turkey's Challenges: Going Beyond Hospitality*. Washington, DC: Brookings.
Kuzmanovic, G. 2016. *Refractions of Civil Society in Turkey*. London: Palgrave/Macmillan.
Levine-Rasky, C. 2016. "They Didn't Treat Me as a Gypsy: Romani Refugees in Toronto." *Refuge* 27 (11): 50–57.
Lobo, Michele. 201X. "Living on the Edge: Precarity and Freedom in Darwin, Australia." *Journal of Ethnic and Migration Studies*.
Mackreath, H., and S. Sagnic. 2017. *Civil Society and Syrian Refugees in Turkey*. İstanbul: Citizens' Assembly-Turkey. http://www.hyd.org.tr/attachments/article/214/civil-society-and-syrian-refugees-in-turkey.pdf.
Manjikian, L. 2010. "Refugee 'In-Betweenness': A Proactive Existence." *Refuge* 27 (1): 50–58.
Mazurana, D., K. Jacobsen, and L. Gale. 2013. *Research Methods in Conflict Settings: A View From Below*. Cambridge: University of Cambridge Press.

Melara, J. E., R. Grant, M. Oteng-Ababio, and B. Ayele. 2013. "Downgrading - An Overlooked Reality in African Cities: Reflections From an Indigenous Neighbourhood of Accra, Ghana." *Applied Geography* 36: 23–30.

Multeciler. 2019. Türkiye'deki Suriyeli Sayısı Ekim 2019. https://multeciler.org.tr/turkiyedeki-suriyeli-sayisi/.

Ortadogu Stratejik Arastirmalar Metkezi (ORSAM). 2015. *Effects of Syrian Refugees on Turkey. Orsam Report No. 195.* Ankara: ORSAM. http://www.orsam.org.tr/files/Raporlar/rapor195/195eng.pdf.

Özerim, G., and H. Crawley. 2016. "How a Turkish Neighbourhood Adapted to Its Syrian Refugees." *Middle East Eye*, 24 June. http://www.middleeasteye.net/columns/how-turkish-neighbourhood-adapted-its-syrian-refugees-1090199123.

Purcell, M. 2002. "Excavating Lefebvre: The Right to the City and Its Urban Politics of the Inhabitant." *GeoJournal* 58: 99–108.

ReVi Family Organisation. 2017. https://www.revifamily.org.

Saracoglu, C., and D. Belanger. 2018. "Mekan, Yer ve Şehir: Türkiye'de Suriyeli Karşıtlıpının Kentteki Görünümleri." *Eğitim Bilim Toplum Dergisi* 16 (62): 46–73.

Schneider, F., and D. H. Enste. 2013. *The Shadow Economy: An International Survey*. Cambridge: Cambridge University Press.

Senses, N. 2016. "Rethinking Migration in the Context of Precarity: The Case of Turkey." *Critical Sociology* 42 (7–8): 975–987.

Standing, G. 2011. *The Precariat: The New Dangerous Class*. London: Bloomsbury.

Tan, D. 2016. "Contextualizing Refugee NGOs in İzmir." In *Turkish Migration 2016 Selected Papers*, edited by D. Eroğlu, J. H. Cohen, and I. Sirkeci, 80–86. London: TPL.

Thompson, D. 2016. "Risky Business and Geographies of Refugee Capitalism in the Somali Migrant Economy of Gauteng, South Africa." *Journal of Ethnic and Migration Studies* 42 (1): 120–135.

Thompson, D., and R. Grant. 2015. "Enclaves on Edge: Strategies and Tactics in Immigrant Business Spaces in Johannesburg." *Urban Forum* 26 (3): 243–262.

TripAdvisor. 2017. Specialty Lodging, İzmir. https://www.tripadvisor.com/Hotels-g298006-c3-İzmir_İzmir_Province_Turkish_Aegean_Coast-Hotels.html.

Turkish Statistical Institute (TUIK). 2017. "Adrese Dayalı Nufüs Kayıt Sistemi Sonuçları." http://www.tuik.gov.tr/PreHaberBultenleri.do?id=24638.

United Nations High Commission for Refugees (UNHCR). 2016. From a Refugee Perspective. https://www.unhcr.org/5909af4d4.pdf.

United Nations High Commission for Refugees (UNHCR). 2017. Syrian Refugees in Turkey Frequently Asked Questions. http://www.unhcr.org/turkey/uploads/root/eng(69).pdf.

United Nations High Commission for Refugees (UNHCR). 2019a. Operational Portal Refuge Situations. https://data2.unhcr.org/en/situations/syria.

United Nations High Commission for Refugees (UNHCR). 2019b. Internally Displaced People. https://www.unhcr.org/sy/internally-displaced-people.

United Nations High Commission for Refugees (UNHCR). 2019c. UNHCR Turkey: Provincial Breakdown All Refugees and Asylum-Seekers in Turkey - September 2019. https://data2.unhcr.org/en/documents/download/71505.

Waite, L. 2009. "A Place and Space for a Critical Geography of Precarity?" *Geography Compass* 3 (1): 412–433.

Weise, Z. 2016. "Refugees Arrive in Turkish Ports to Find No More Smugglers." *The Telegraph*, 9 April. http://www.telegraph.co.uk/news/2016/04/09/refugees-arrive-in-turkish-ports-to-find-no-more-smugglers/.

Wissink, M., F. Düvell, and A. van Eerdewijk. 2013. "Dynamic Migration Intentions and the Impact of Socio-Institutional Environments: A Transit Migration hub in Turkey." *Journal of Ethnic and Migration Studies* 39 (7): 1087–1105.

Yıldız, A., and E. Uzgören. 2016. "Limits to Temporary Protection: Non-Camp Syrian Refugees in İzmir, Turkey." *Southeast European and Black Sea Studies* 16 (2): 195–211. doi:10.1080/14683857.2016.1165492.

YouCaring. 2017. "Help Us Help Refugees in İzmir." https://www.youcaring.com/syrianrefugeesstuckinİzmirturkey-690355.

Soft violence: migrant domestic worker precarity and the management of unfree labour in Singapore

Rhacel Salazar Parreñas, Krittiya Kantachote and Rachel Silvey

ABSTRACT
In Singapore, the temporary legal status of migrant domestic workers binds them in servitude to their employer-sponsor as their residency is contingent on their continuous and sole live-in employment with a sponsor whose permission they must secure in order to transfer jobs. This legal status technically renders domestic workers unfree and precarious as it gives employers tremendous power over domestic workers. Based on 30 in-depth interviews with employers, this article examines how employers in Singapore negotiate their power over domestic workers. We identify 'soft violence' as a tool that employer's utilise in their management of domestic workers. By 'soft violence', we refer to the practice of cloaking the unequal relationship in domestic work via the cultivation of a relationship of 'personalism' while simultaneously amplifying one's control of domestic workers. Representing a strategy utilised by employers to maximise the labour of domestic workers, 'soft violence' emerges from the paradoxical relationship of simultaneously *relieving* and *amplifying* servitude.

In most destinations, migrants with a domestic worker visa are bound labourers as their legal residency is contingent on their continuous and sole employment by their sponsor as it constrains their ability to change sponsors. This is the case in Canada, Great Britain, Israel, Taiwan, Singapore, and among others the United Arab Emirates (UAE) (Anderson 2000; Bakan and Stasiulis 2005; Lan 2007; Liebelt 2011; Mahdavi 2011). Scholars have argued that domestic workers who are bound labourers are subject to the 'persistence of the master/mistress servant roles' (Anderson 2000, 193) and become likely victims of abuse and labour trafficking (for examples, see discussions on Britain by Anderson [2000]; Lebanon by Pande [2013]; and the UAE by Mahdavi [2011]). Bound labourers, as they cannot freely quit their job without the permission of their employer, are arguably in a situation of unfree labour, who geographer Sallie Yea, writing on construction workers in Singapore, defined as 'any situation where workers cannot extricate themselves from an exploitative working situation, despite their desire to do so' (Yea 2017, 180). Unfree labourers, are however, not always exploited though we acknowledge that they are easily exploitable as well as precarious (Yea 2018).

The rise of unfree labour is not exceptional but part and parcel of the rise of 'global cities' in late capitalism (Sassen 1996). As argued by Sassen (1996), the advancement of capitalism coincides with the 'opposite turns of nationalism' in which the 'denationalization of economies' goes hand in hand with the 'renationalization of politics' (Sassen 1996). Indeed, the resurgence of populism in Europe and the United States alongside heightened anti-immigrant sentiments attest to this trend (Anderson 2013; Hayes and Dudek 2019). The exclusionary conditions of membership for temporary labour migrants whose labour is highly demanded likewise illustrate this contradiction in nationalist sentiments (Hahamovitch 2011). Focusing on one of the largest groups of temporary labour migrants across the globe, this article examines how the exclusionary terms of membership for migrant domestic workers shape the conditions of their labour. For domestic workers, it is their status as bound labourers subject to the arbitrary power of employers that defines the terms of their migrant exclusion and precarity.

This article accordingly examines the unfree labour of domestic workers on temporary contracts from the perspective of employers, focusing on the destination of Singapore, which is a high receiving country of domestic workers. Many scholars have paid attention to the effects of being an unfree worker on the labour conditions of migrant domestic workers, arguing that it results in the case of England in a 'master-slave relationship' (Anderson 2000); in the UAE and Lebanon in 'structural violence' (Mahdavi 2011; Pande 2013); and in 'labor trafficking' and 'contract slavery' in Lebanon (Jureidini and Moukarbal, 2004). While these previous works establish the susceptibility of domestic workers to abuse, they do not address the dynamics that sustain this abuse and precarity. In this article, we address this question by examining how employers act on their power over domestic workers who are tied to them in servitude as bound labourers, meaning workers whose legal residency is contingent on their sponsorship. In managing the bound labour of domestic workers, we found that employers practice 'soft violence', which we define as acting on while simultaneously cloaking their unequal relationship.

This article begins with an overview of the conditions that render migrant domestic workers to be unfree labourers exposed to oscillations in precarity. We follow with a discussion of the literature on migrant domestic work, addressing how the literature has attended to the unfree status of domestic workers. Then we proceed to describe our methodology and characteristics of sample, making a case for the unique perspective provided by interviews with employers, in other words, those in a position to abuse the unfree status of domestic workers. We then describe the emergence of 'soft violence', illustrating how the majority of employers claim the recognition of domestic workers as 'human' while simultaneously sustaining their unequal relationship by amplifying servitude. Employers amplify servitude through the common practices of withholding salaries, maintaining a relationship of debt bondage and among others imposing a curfew which underscores the scalar and temporal dimensions of their precarity (Chacko and Price 2021).

Our article extends current understandings of employer-employee relations in domestic work at the household scale by addressing the dynamics that sustain the unequal relationship that others have argued lends itself to 'structural violence', 'slavery', or 'trafficking'. Drawing from interviews with employers, we found that they do not necessarily resort to extreme force but instead turn to 'soft violence' to sustain unequal relations in domestic work. Soft violence is distinct from what Nixon (2013) refers to as 'slow violence', meaning the often invisible and gradual violence wrought by environmental disasters, and likewise distinct from what Galtung (1969) has described as 'structural violence', meaning a system's denial of basic human rights. Soft violence instead refers to a paradoxical process of simultaneously relieving and aggravating the unequal dependency of unfree labour and is thus an important aspect of temporary migrant precarity. As a process, soft violence emerges from a perspective of what anthropologist Pierre Bourdieu would describe as unrecognised privilege (Bourdieu 1977). It represents an enactment of 'symbolic capital', meaning the legitimation of the employer's power over the domestic worker and ability to determine and define the nature of their job. Contrary to the assertion that employers would uniformly act on their power and impose 'structural violence' to maximise the labour of domestic workers (Mahdavi 2011), we found that they strategically deploy what Hondagneu-Sotelo (2001) calls 'instrumental personalism' and accordingly recognise the humanity of domestic workers. They do so not only to extract labour but to also maintain 'symbolic capital' and legitimise the unfree status of domestic workers as bound labourers.

The unfree labour of migrant domestic workers

Various states across the globe legally recognise the reliance of their residents and citizens on the household work of foreign workers, thereby permitting them to sponsor the labour migration of domestic workers, especially to cities. The largest groups of foreign domestic workers to utilise this labour opportunity are Filipinos, estimated to reach 1.4 million, and Indonesians, estimated at 2.1 million (Parreñas, 2015; Parreñas, Silvey, Hwang and Choi, 2019). While Indonesians are primarily located in Asia and the Middle East, Filipinos are employed as domestic workers across the globe. The largest visa granting destinations for Filipino domestic workers are in the Middle East, but they also include Canada, Italy, Hong Kong, Malaysia, Singapore, and Israel (Parreñas, 2015).

While numerous states sanction the relegation of housework (including childcare and eldercare) to the market via the allocation of domestic worker visas to households, they simultaneously suppress the ability of such workers to maximise their market value by limiting their ability to freely participate in the labour market. In almost all destinations, migrant domestic workers cannot freely change their sponsors, which in turn results in their unfree status as bound labourers. Only Italy allows domestic workers to quit their job and secure a new resident-sponsor without restrictions. In the UAE, Kuwait, Lebanon, and other countries in the Middle East, domestic workers must secure the permission of their sponsor to transfer jobs prior to the end of their contract (Fernandez 2013; Mahdavi 2011; Pande 2013); in Israel, they can only change employers during their first 63 months of residency (Liebelt 2011); in Hong Kong, their flexibility to change employers is limited by the 'Two Week Rule' which requires they secure a new sponsor within two weeks of the termination of their employment to avoid deportation (Constable 2007); and as a final example, in Denmark, au pairs can only change employers twice during their 24 month stay in the country (Stenum 2011).

Migrant domestic workers in Singapore are likewise bound to their employer. The Ministry of Manpower (MOM) does not allow foreign domestic workers to work for more than one employer at a time. To change sponsors, even after the completion of their labour contract, foreign domestic workers are also required to secure the permission of their employer-sponsor. This legal condition has prompted Jolovan Wham, a local activist in Singapore, to claim that Singapore has its own *kafala* system. Indeed, the terms of incorporation for migrant domestic workers in Singapore mirror those of the *kafala*, meaning sponsorship system, in the Middle East. Under the *kafala*, the legal residency of a migrant domestic worker is contingent on their continuous employment with their sponsor. Aggravating this relationship of unequal dependency, domestic workers must also secure the permission of their sponsor to transfer jobs.

Other migrant contract workers, for example, South Asian construction workers in the UAE (Kathiravelu 2015) or Korean migrant workers employed in factories (Choo 2016), are likewise bound workers who must solely work for their employer-sponsor. Yet, differentiating and arguably placing domestic workers in a more vulnerable situation is the live-in requirement of their employment (Anderson and O'Connell Davidson 2003). Of all destinations that grant a domestic worker visa, only Canada and Italy legally permit the live-out employment of domestic workers. In all other destinations, domestic workers are required to reside in the home of their employers, which is a condition that heightens their risk of overwork as it results in extended work hours (Romero 1992) and at the same time aggravates the relationship of unequal dependence in domestic work (Jureidini 2010; Pande 2013).

Further aggravating the unfree status of domestic workers is the financial cost of migration, which domestic workers cover in most destinations (Pande 2013). They include the cost of the government required technical training programme in which domestic workers are given basic training in cooking and cleaning including the use of electronic appliances and gadgets, the cost of travel including airfare, passport and medical clearance, and finally the agency fee. The agency fee varies across destinations with the amount increasing according to average salary with lesser paying destinations costing less and higher paying destinations costing more. Due to differences in agency fee by country, Filipino domestic workers in Israel can expect to pay a sum total of approximately US$7000 for a guaranteed starting monthly wage of US$1100, in Hong Kong, they earn at least US$500 and accordingly pay approximately US$3000 to secure a labour contract; in Singapore, where they earn at least US$365, they can expect to pay at least two to six times this amount.[1] The fees Indonesian domestic workers pay likewise vary according to their average salary. While they must give up at least six to seven months of their salary to secure employment in Singapore or Hong Kong, it costs them no more than two to four months of wages for a job in the Kingdom of Saudi Arabia (KSA).[2] Notably, they can expect to earn less in KSA than in destinations in Asia.

The cost of migration limits the ability of domestic workers to change employers. While a responsibility of domestic workers, the cost of migration is usually covered initially by employers who would then incrementally reclaim this expenditure from their domestic worker via a salary deduction system. This historically had been the case in Lebanon (Pande 2013) and still is the case in Taiwan and Singapore.[3] While paying for their debt, the domestic work is technically 'unfree' (Lan 2007) as they are paid not a salary but instead an allowance of US$10-30. In Taiwan, Filipino domestic workers are subject to a salary deduction schema of up to twelve months (Lan 2007), in Hong Kong, they can work without pay for up to eight months, and in Singapore for two to six months.

Finally, domestic workers are perpetually bound to the sponsorship of their employer as they remain ineligible for permanent residency in most destinations. Only Italy allows domestic workers to apply for permanent residency, which they can do after five years of continuous employment with at least one sponsor (Parreñas, 2015). While participants in Canada's Live-in Caregiver's Program historically gained eligibility for permanent residency after two years of continuous employment in one household, the government amended this programme in 2014 and imposed a quota that restricts the number of domestic workers accepted as permanent residents (Black 2014). In Canada, domestic workers must now leave the country after four years of employment. In other countries, migrant domestic workers remain ineligible for permanent residency with some countries imposing a residency cap including Israel which limits the years of residency for domestic workers to five and Taiwan to twelve. With the exception of Canada and Italy, countries that grant a domestic worker visa usually follow the citizenship principles of *jus sanguinis* which results in the exclusion of the children of domestic workers from permanent membership and renders them 'born out of place' (Constable 2014).

The unfree status of domestic workers speaks of the conflicting political culture of domestic work. While states designate the responsibility of care and reproduction to the market by allocating residents the power to hire foreign domestic workers, the state simultaneously suppresses the ability of foreign domestic workers to fully participate in the market by binding them to employers. How employers manage this designated relationship of unequal dependency remains insufficiently analysed in the literature. This is not to say that scholars have not acknowledged the unfree status of domestic workers. Pande (2013), writing on Lebanon, and Yeoh and Huang (1998), writing on Singapore, see unfreedom as an abdication of state responsibility for standards of employment in domestic work and the ultimate designation of this labour as a private household responsibility. Some have observed that unfreedom places domestic workers in a locked-in situation that leaves them vulnerable to abuse (Bakan and Stasiulis 2005; Mahdavi 2011). Pratt (2012), looking at Canada's requirement that domestic workers continuously work for one household within a four-year window to qualify for permanent residency, and Constable (2007), commenting on the temporal restriction imposed by the 'Two Week Rule' for domestic workers in Hong Kong, have both noted that such conditions pressure domestic workers to accept less than ideal working conditions. Overall, the literature on the unfree labour of migrant domestic workers is relatively thin with the primary focus of discussion being on the effects of this structural factor on labour conditions. Missing from current discussions is the perspective of employers, which this article considers in its assessment of the unfree labour of migrant domestic workers.

Methodology

This article is based primarily on semi-structured interviews with 30 employers conducted in Singapore in 2014, which is supplemented by 40 hours of observation of employer visits to an employment agency in 2016.[4] We chose Singapore as a research site because it is a major destination for migrant domestic workers. Each year, thousands of domestic workers from Indonesia, the Philippines, Myanmar, India and Sri Lanka seek legal employment in Singapore, utilising the high volume of visas granted by the Ministry of Manpower [MOM]. In 2015, MOM issued 231,500 work permits to foreign domestic workers (Ministry of Manpower 2016). Legal conditions of domestic work in Singapore likewise reflect those of other destinations as domestic workers are ineligible for permanent residency, restricted to live-in employment, not protected by labour laws, and are bound workers whose legal residency is conditional to their continuous employment by a sponsoring employer. Because their place of employment is within private homes, their critical labour contributions are less visible in urban life.

Domestic workers are, however, protected by criminal and human rights laws most of which employers learn about in the mandatory online class required by MOM for all new employers to complete. It would be an offense, for instance, to inflict corporal harm on domestic workers including the withholding of food or imposing of physical abuse. The course educates employers on their challenges and obligations; informs them of the human rights of domestic workers including their right to basic food and shelter; and warns them of penalties against proven cases of employer abuse of domestic workers. Since 2004, domestic workers in Singapore have also benefited from the visible advocacy work of two organisations, Humanitarian Organization for Migration Economics [HOME] and Transient Workers Count Too [TWC2]. Efforts to raise public consciousness on the conditions of domestic workers have been the focus of both groups with HOME also providing shelter and assistance to victims of abuse. Both groups regularly conduct surveys and release information to the press on the conditions of domestic work. A joint campaign by the two organisations to mandate a weekly day off for domestic workers resulted in successful legal reform beginning on 1 January 2013. Due to efforts of government and nongovernmental organisations, employers in Singapore have a relatively high level of consciousness regarding the basic labour rights of domestic workers (e.g. right to 8 hours of rest per day, a weekly day off, three meals per day).

The interviews followed an interview guide in which we sought to gather detailed information about each participant's history of domestic worker employment, the employment process, the work standards and expectations, and their understanding and perception toward the law in regard to domestic employment. We did not explicitly ask employers about their negotiation of servitude but instead asked them to elaborate on pertinent conditions including the day off and agency fee. Doing so allowed us to gather sufficient data on their conscious or unconscious management of their sponsorship of workers. The interviews ranged from half an hour to one and a half hours in length. We also conducted interviews with various community leaders (e.g. staff at non-governmental organisations and at the Philippines Embassy), employment agency owners, and local researchers who have studied domestic workers. Finally, we observed the hiring process including interviews conducted by prospective employers in one employment agency. We took note of their hiring criteria and job standards including rules concerning the day off, use of mobile phone, Internet access, and work load.

To obtain a diverse sample, we solicited research participants from various sites (e.g. plazas, parks, and events) in different neighbourhoods of Singapore, ranging from the shopping district of Orchard Road to the working-class neighbourhood of Geylang. We also distributed and posted flyers in housing communities and at local associations. Several women responded to the flyers. We also relied on our own networks to identify potential interviewees. The interviews usually took place in the workplace of the respondent, in restaurants, or in their homes. All but two interviews were tape-recorded and fully transcribed.[5] Extensive notes were taken during the non-taped interviews. The interviews were all conducted in English by a graduate research assistant whose identity as a Thai of Chinese descent helped build rapport with the majority of Asian respondents. Their shared racial, social, and class status also facilitated a level of comfort, particularly as respondents frequently discussed issues of cultural conflicts and the difficulties they faced in employing domestic workers.

Characteristics of sample

Contrary to the popular belief that employers are only those of higher socioeconomic status, our interview sample represents a wide range of socioeconomic groups. Our assessment of the socioeconomic status of employers is based on their occupation, level of education, types of residence and their own self-evaluation. Our respondents include business owners (17 per cent), retailers (20 per cent), academics (20 per cent), stay-at-home mothers (17 per cent) and professional office workers (27 per cent). Their job titles include but are not limited to director of a private company, manager, consultant, sales associate, researcher, and clerk. Their levels of education vary from those holding a polytechnic degree to those having completed post-tertiary training. Illustrating the diverse class backgrounds of research participants, the types of residence of employers include large houses with yards, upscale private condominiums, government subsidised condominiums (HDB), and apartments.

Most of our interviewees are women (83 per cent), yet this does not mean that men employ domestic workers less as most of our interviewees are married. However, it does imply that women feel more fit to provide the details of employing domestic workers, explaining why only women had responded to our flyers and women employees in businesses approached were those more likely to agree to an interview. Indeed, it was primarily women who inquired about hiring a domestic worker in the employment agency we observed. Men never came alone and if they were there, it was to accompany their partner. This then reaffirms the claim that reproductive sphere responsibilities still primarily remain the responsibility of women (Huang and Yeoh 1996).

In our solicitation of research participants, the response rate was 80 per cent. Most of the employers interviewed are Asian (83 per cent) and a minority were Caucasian (13 per cent) or of mixed-heritage (3 per cent). Most employers (70 per cent) classified themselves as Chinese, while 7 per cent are Indian. Seventy per cent of the employers are Singaporeans, the rest are expats from Australia, Great Britain, the United States and South Korea. Some expats have been in Singapore for less than two years whereas others have been in Singapore for more than a decade. The majority of expats have been in Singapore for roughly two to five years.

As to be expected in dual-income households which represent the majority of our participants, most employers interviewed are married with children (73 per cent). Other participants are married without children (13 per cent) or single, divorced or widowed (14 per cent). The vast majority (80 per cent) of research participants are with children at home. Not surprisingly, most prospective employers we observed in an employment agency had sought domestic workers to assist them with childcare, though most expect their workers to be what is called an 'all around', as they are required to not only care but also cook and clean for the family. Rarely did a household rely on more than one domestic worker, resulting in the reliance of families on the domestic worker for a wide range of housework.

Most studies on domestic work neglect the perspectives of employers, instead choosing to account for the labour process solely from the perspective of the worker. Notable exceptions include the study of Hondagneu-Sotelo (2001) on Latino domestic workers in Los

Angeles and Lan's (2006) examination of domestic work in Taiwan. While our sample has several notable advantages over data used in most existing studies on domestic work, one shortcoming should be acknowledged. As our sample only includes employers who voluntarily agreed to an interview, it could be said that our sample excludes those who abuse their workers. Thus, our sample may exclude the worst-case scenarios faced by domestic workers in Singapore. This may be a potential source of sample selection bias. In the next section, we draw from our interviews with 30 employers to describe their management of the unfree status of domestic workers, illustrating 'soft violence' in the simultaneous relief and amplification of unfreedom by the majority of employers we interviewed.

Precarity, soft violence and the management of unfree workers

Standards of employment for domestic workers vary across households resulting in various states of precarity. This is because domestic work remains an unregulated occupation, as the work occurs in the private space of a home and remains excluded from regulation. In Singapore, domestic workers remain exempt from the Employment Act, thereby denying them the right to overtime pay, sick leave and other such employment benefits. As expected, the weak regulation of domestic work results in the inconsistency of labour standards. This is reflected in the day off. In Singapore, not all migrant domestic workers receive a weekly day off despite the recent change in law, as some are still denied a day off during the first six months of employment, others are only permitted a day off every other week, while others are restricted to one day off in a month.[6] A 2013–2014 survey with 195 domestic workers conducted by TWC2 confirms that 59 per cent of the domestic workers still do not consistently receive a weekly day off.[7]

This variation in standard of employment challenge claims of a uniform effect of unfree labour. Contrary to the assertion that unfree labour would uniformly lead to 'structural violence', which would, for instance, be established in the withholding of the day off for the vast majority of domestic workers, we instead found the emergence of 'soft violence' in the management of unfree labourers. In this section, we establish the use of 'soft violence' by describing the paradoxical process by which employers simultaneously relieve and amplify the servitude of domestic workers. The practice of 'soft violence' allows employers to sustain their relationship of unequal dependency with domestic workers, cloak their limits of freedom, and extend their relationship of inequality.

Relieving servitude

Employers maintain a wide range of perceptions of domestic workers. Some think of them as simpleminded, including a wealthy Chinese Singaporean housewife in her 40s who expressed a preference for Indonesian over Filipino domestic workers for their lower salary as well as lower level of intellect.[8] Some think of them as downtrodden. This includes a wealthy widower who thinks giving domestic workers a windowless bedroom constitutes of cruelty. Yet, the majority insists on seeing domestic workers as 'human' with basic rights. This includes a 65-year old Indian Singaporean clerk at an employment agency:

> The maid is not a servant to you. OK? Because we depends [*sic*] on them a lot, when we go to work, we expect the maid to be a housekeeper, to bring our children up and to upkeep the

> house and do the cooking for us. That's what I believe in and *they are human [emphasis our own]*. So all my life I never have any complaints with MOM.

While MOM raises awareness of domestic worker rights among employers, these rights, however, do not eclipse the power of the employer. As the elderly Indian employer continues, '... when in 6 months if they are not happy with me, I will tell them you are not happy, you wanna go back? I will be send you back'. Though mindful of the basic rights of domestic workers as 'human', employers are likewise aware of their relegated power as an employer of an unfree worker who is legally bound to be under their employ. This power includes their ability to not only fire but also deport domestic workers at will.

In general, the recognition of domestic workers as 'human' shapes how employers manage unfree labour and mitigates – although not completely – their maximisation of the labour of domestic workers. A push and pull dynamic characterise the recognition of the humanity of domestic workers. The recognition of domestic workers as human encourages employers to *relieve servitude* – granting adequate foods, providing breaks, allocating decent accommodation and allowing access to communication. However, this recognition does not eclipse labour expectations of employers, resulting then in a constrained recognition of humanity. While employers may insist that they view domestic workers as 'human', the vast majority of employers perceive domestic workers as their subordinate and accordingly impose boundaries that do not just create distance but also hierarchy (Lan 2006).

We witness the constrained relief of servitude in the food provisions allotted by employers to domestic workers. Many employers claim to maintain an 'open kitchen' policy.[9] However, there is an unspoken limit to the access of domestic workers to food, one that is rarely stated explicitly by employers but one that domestic workers seem to be expected to intuitively know. Our observations in the employment agency, for instance, indicate that employers may fire domestic workers for eating too much as employers with an open kitchen policy usually have an unspoken standard of what is acceptable for domestic workers to consume and those who cross the line are considered undisciplined and fired at will. Examples we witnessed of food consumption that led to the firing of a domestic worker include the selection of a large as opposed to a small apple from the refrigerator, the consumption of too large a portion of tofu on the dining table, or the failure to ask for permission to eat a banana. In addition to the unequal access of domestic workers to food, also establishing their subordinate status is the insistence of employers for domestic workers to not just eat separately but also only after the rest of the family. As a 58-year old Chinese Singaporean business professional states matter of factly, 'Normally, the maid would eat after we eat. That's the norm actually'.

The subordinate position of domestic workers suggests that most employers perceive domestic workers as workers and not 'one of the family', despite the common reference of 'aunty' that is designated to domestic workers. This is not to say that the designation of 'aunty' renders one to be a family member but it does signal familiarity and ease as opposed to distance and rigidity. Another indication that domestic workers experience a constrained relief from servitude comes in the provision of accommodations. Domestic workers are usually given decent accommodations but one that is of a lesser type than the rest of the adults in the household. Some admit to denying their domestic worker their own bedroom as they have them sleep in the living room or with children. Others have domestic workers sleep in a utility room without windows. Some, however, insist on always granting domestic workers a bedroom with a window.

The recognition of domestic workers as 'human' is also illustrated in the provision of a break. While employers recognise the need of domestic workers for a break, most give their own needs greater priority than those of the domestic worker. As a result, employers prioritise the completion of the work over the physical well-being of the domestic worker. Thus, most employers expect domestic workers to work continuously except during their designated break time. As a Chinese Singaporean stay at home mother with young children shared with us, 'I told her before she work [*sic*] for me, I say you cannot take a nap in the afternoon. No sleeping in the afternoon I told her'.

Likewise, most employers recognise the need of domestic workers for outside communication and accordingly grant them access to a mobile phone. However, they limit their access to 'non-working hours'. A 58-year old Chinese Singaporean, a human resources director, explains:

> Our rules you know we say during working hours, you're not supposed to stick on to the mobile phone or in a way ear phone [*sic*]. But you wouldn't know what they do because we're not home. So the official time for her take a break is from 1 to 3 pm [*sic*]. And then at night, I guess is when she can call home or whatever … So you know it's like office working hour … The maid is not supposed to watch TV, neither is the maid supposed to be making phone calls during working hours. They're supposed to look after the employer, the kids, the employers, or the employers' parents.

Although insisting that domestic workers do no more than work during working hours, employers do not necessarily see their home as a workplace as they do not fully but only selectively transfer rules one would have in a regular workplace. One standard rule they do not transfer is the eight-hour workday recommended by MOM as most expect at least a 12-hour workday from domestic workers that can begin as early as 6 am and end as late as 10 pm.

Finally, most recognise the need of domestic workers for outside communication but not at the cost of their labour productivity. Thus, the majority admit to limiting the freedom of domestic workers. They do so by either imposing a curfew during their day off, denying a day off, barring the use of the phone during work hours,[10] or banning them from engaging in romantic relationships. Employers choose to limit the freedom of domestic workers in order to maximise their labour. As the wealthy Chinese Singaporean in her 40s explains:

> Well first of all she will be busy talking to her boyfriend if she has a boyfriend, right? Then she will neglect her job right? Then she will have some, with a boyfriend she will not be able to concentrate and she may have some quarrel and some issues with the boyfriend. Then you won't have the mood to work, you're not in the right mood and all these troubles la.

Questioning the claim that they view domestic workers as human is the common disregard for the personal needs of domestic workers, including their potential desire for privacy or intimacy, as some employers prioritise their own needs at the expense of the said worker's personal well-being. Still, employers regularly insert recognitions of domestic workers as 'human' and in the process engage in *relieving servitude* albeit not at the cost of the worker's lower status in the household.

Amplifying servitude

> [You don't need to follow the law] because if there is a mutual [*sic*] between you and your helper and your helper willing to help you, why not? I mean as long as you pay them well and they don't complain. I mean rules are made but we don't need to strictly follow. As long as she think it's fair [*sic*]. (40-year old Chinese Singaporean sales clerk)

Employers might claim to perceive and treat domestic workers as 'human', but most do not question but instead aggravate the legal status of domestic workers as unfree workers. In Singapore, employers amplify the unfree status of domestic workers when they subject them to a relationship of temporary debt bondage, withhold their salary, or act on their power to deport them at will. This amplification enforces the subordinate status of domestic workers while easing the ability of employers to maximise the extraction of labour from workers who are not in a position to quit.

Employers are not necessarily malicious when they fortify their power over domestic workers. Some amplify unfreedom for the best of intentions. For instance, those who admit to withholding the salary of their domestic worker claim to do so for the good of the worker. This includes a 35-year old Chinese Singaporean sales executive, who thought it a reasonable arrangement for her to control the ATM card of her domestic worker:

> I don't want her to spend all then starts to have problems. So if she wants the money, we go together. We withdraw. Or if I don't have time to pick her up for withdraw, I will withdraw for her, show her all the receipt. Then every month the bank will send her the statement. She will see the statement.

More than a handful of our interviewees admit to withholding a portion of their domestic worker's monthly salary, informing us that their intention is 'good' as they wish to ensure that their domestic worker accumulates savings during the course of their employment. The same employers are also likely to withhold the passports of their domestic workers, though they claim that they do for their mutual protection. As the same sales executive explains, 'I feel that it's safer that I keep for her. She runs away, if anything happens she had quarrels with friends or her boyfriend she run away, the government wants to fine me la'. The practice of withholding salaries – akin to withholding passports – places domestic workers at risk of forced labour while increasing the power of employers over the worker and heightening employee precarity. For this reason, MOM strongly advises employers against doing both.[11]

Employers withhold the passport of domestic workers not necessarily to exert control over domestic workers but instead for their own legal protection. MOM holds employers responsible for domestic workers to remain in good legal standing. In addition to being required to cover a monthly levy to the government, employers must also ensure that their domestic workers reside in their abode and solely and continuously work for them. If the domestic worker is to run away, for instance, an employer could be held liable for a $5,000 bond (Ministry of Manpower 2018a). This suggests that migration regimes and legal infrastructures encourage the amplification of unfreedom by employers.

Employers also reinforce their relation of unequal dependency with domestic workers when they remind or act on their power to terminate or deport them. Threatening termination and deportation are disciplining mechanisms admittedly used by employers against domestic workers who miss their curfew, consume alcohol, pursue a romantic relationship or express dissatisfaction with their job. When they threaten termination or deportation, employers fortify their relation of unequal dependency and consequently diminish the ability of domestic workers to negotiate their labour conditions while intensifying their precarity. One employer, the earlier-cited wealthy Chinese Singaporean stay at home mother in her 40s, admitted to deporting her domestic worker without warning as she suspected her of stealing cash:

> I booked a ticket without letting her know until two hours before she left I asked her to pack and ask her to go off. I sent her straight to the airport and I cancel her permit, everything, the work permit ... Two hours I asked her to pack and send her off.

In Singapore, as is the case in various destinations in the Middle East, employers have the power to not only fire but deport domestic workers at will (Jureidini 2010). This is a disciplining strategy rarely used by employers we interviewed but it is one some feel rightfully entitled to.

Finally, the vast majority of employers we interviewed (22 of 30) subject domestic workers to a temporary relationship of debt bondage as they abide by the employment agency recommendation for domestic workers to cover the entire cost of labour migration. It is common practice in Singapore for employers to initially pay for the fee charged by the employment agency to place a domestic worker in their home. This amount varies across ethnicities as it is based on the monthly salary of domestic workers. The placement of a domestic worker from the Philippines, for instance, can initially cost an employer SG $3,000. Employers eventually retrieve these funds by deducting this cost from the monthly salary of the domestic worker. The Filipino domestic worker can expect to have their salaries withheld for as long as six months upon their initial placement in a Singaporean household. Indonesians, as they are paid a lower salary rate, are subjected to salary deductions for slightly longer at eight months. During this time, they can expect to receive no more than $40 a month for their payment.

In Singapore, domestic workers are expected to pay for the entire cost of their labour migration. This market standard is not one that employers tend to question but is one that they willingly embrace as an unquestioned norm.

> Upfront is the maid they borrow from the agent when they come to Singapore. So upfront will be 3K to 4K and the maid will not get any salary for like up to 8 months. For every month we just pay her some allowance like $20. Until the upfront is being cleared then we pay her full salary. Probably 6 months or 8 months onwards. (28-year old Chinese Singaporean)

> Umm we pay about ... I think I pay about $3000 plus, $3000 plus. That is because advance salary of the maid and then when they claim that they have to pay other site agent in advance. So actually the maid work for a few months la, like minimum 6 months without salary. It's not without salary, employers pay in advance, but because the Indonesian agent charge the maid I think at a very high price for the fee. And they end up with no salary for six months. So six months to eight months. (65-year old Chinese Singaporean manager of tourist company)

As is the case in Singapore, domestic workers in Taiwan likewise pay for the entire cost of their labour migration. The higher cost of migration to Taiwan results in a longer period of a 12- month salary deduction for domestic workers, a practice that subjects them to what Lan (2007) calls 'legal servitude'. According to Lan (2007), the forces of supply and demand work in favour of employers and allow them to pass all financial responsibilities for the placement of a foreign domestic worker in their home to the worker. Agreeing with Lan is a 35-year old Chinese Singaporean sales executive, who matter of factly states, 'Why the maid owe the agency fee? Because they want to come here … the maid pay [*sic*] the agency'.

Potentially curbing the forces of supply and demand is the moral consciousness of employers, who may find discomfort in their blatant aggravation of the servitude of domestic workers. Thus, some – particularly expat employers from the United States and Europe – choose to only hire transfer domestic workers, as the much lesser fee of a month's wage penalty charged domestic workers who are already in Singapore limits the length of debt bondage to no more than two months for Indonesians as opposed to six to eight months for those hired from their country of origin and one month for Filipinos. Notably, this set of employers do still subject their domestic workers to debt bondage, although for a much shorter period.

Other employers negotiate their moral discomfort by passing blame to the employment agency, who they describe as 'evil and unreasonable'. Expressing her outrage over the tendency of employment agencies to 'overcharge' is a 58-year old Chinese Singaporean jewellery store owner,

> They get no money for 6 months. The agency takes all the money. I feel bad for the maid but what can I do? It's 3000 plus, they have to give back to agency. I don't want to give to agency. Agencies are evil and unreasonable.

Yet, in her outrage, this employer disregards the actual costs incurred by the agency for the training and travel of the domestic worker. Moreover, it does not cross her mind to share this cost burden with her domestic work.

Indeed, only a minority (8) chose to bear some of the cost of the placement fee charged by employment agencies.[12] They include the earlier cited 40-year old Chinese Singaporean sales clerk, who expressed a moral responsibility to help ease the cost of migration of her domestic worker: 'I think as an employer we should bare half of the cost. Rather than the maid take everything because their salary are not much especially in Singapore'. It is perhaps not surprising then that her domestic worker has worked for her for more than 10 years. The minority who choose to incur some if not all of the cost of migration for their domestic worker are those more likely to have worker-friendly conditions in their home.

An elderly couple who has employed their Filipina domestic worker for nearly 28 years and are owners of a foot reflexology business are not the wealthiest of Singaporeans. Still, they insisted to cover the entire placement fee charged by the employment agency and opted to relieve her of any salary deduction. As they shared, 'We pay everything. Initially, before she comes, we have to pay for everything. It's about 2000 Sing dollars … She got no loan, nothing. First month, she can get her pay'. Reflecting their mindfulness, they do not micromanage the work or time of their domestic worker, who they know spends hours watching Korean television drama programmes every week. They insist on eating with her and are not one to discipline her as they leave her to manage their household. When asked if they ever had problems with their domestic worker, they mention her tendency to burn their clothes when ironing. When asked if they scold her for this, they insisted, 'no, never, never, never. Everybody makes mistakes'. This elderly couple proactively counters their structural position of unequal dependency with their domestic worker and mitigates her servitude by downplaying their authority and easing her bound status, which they, for instance, did by covering the entire cost of her migration including placement fees.

Yet most employers are unlike this elderly Chinese Singaporean couple. Most including locals, permanent residents and expats do not prioritise worker-friendly policies. Instead, they prioritise their concerns over those of their domestic worker including their need to extract the greatest amount of labour from the worker, their need to exclude her from precious family time and space, their need to minimise costs, and finally their need to reduce their vulnerability by increasing their authority over her.[13] They practice 'soft violence'. When doing so, employers become willfully blind to the unfree and precarious status of temporary domestic workers.

Conclusion

This article foregrounds the unfree status of migrant domestic workers in Singapore. It offers a window to the incorporation of low-wage migrant workers in cities across the globe and focuses on the household scale where soft violence and precarity varies among employers. With rare exception, this unfree status is one they share with migrant domestic workers in key migrant destinations in globalisation. This article asks, how do employers manage the power they hold over domestic workers who are bound to them in servitude? In Singapore, migrant domestic workers are beholden to their employer for their legal residency; their legal status is contingent on their continuous employment for the said employer and their ability to seek new employment likewise requires the approval of their employer who has the power to fire and deport them at will.

We identify the emergence of 'soft violence' as a common practice among employers in their management of servitude and precarity. 'Soft violence' is a process that fortifies their 'symbolic capital' (Bourdieu 1977), specifically their power to determine the conditions of employment of domestic workers. 'Soft violence', and the semi-good treatment of domestic workers, is the process by which the unfree status of domestic workers becomes morally and socially acceptable. Employers claim to recognise domestic workers as 'human', in the process relieving servitude and precarity, but at the same time, they act on their relationship of unequal dependency, thus simultaneously amplifying servitude. They relieve servitude in a variety of ways: maintaining an 'open kitchen' policy, allocating breaks during the day, granting a day off, and giving domestic workers access to a mobile phone including Internet. However, most simultaneously amplify servitude. Employers do this when they maintain a curfew, impose temporal limits on mobile phone access, or impose a 'partially open kitchen' policy. More significantly, the majority of employers amplify the unfree status of domestic workers when they withhold their salaries or subject them to a relationship of debt bondage.

Notes

1. Information gathered from interviews with outgoing migrants at offices of the Overseas Workers Welfare Administration in Manila on July 2016 as well as interviews with staff at employment agencies in Manila on August 2014.

2. Information gathered from interviews with domestic workers in Dubai in July, November, and December 2014.
3. In contrast, domestic workers in other destinations, for instance Israel, take out a private loan.
4. Employers visit agencies to make inquiries, interviews as well as to return domestic workers they wish to terminate.
5. The two interviewees were not accustomed to being recorded and expressed concern about their anonymity. To appease their worries, we agreed to not record our interview.
6. We make this assessment based on interviews and observations in an employment agency.
7. See Transient Workers Count Too (TWC2). 2015. The Right to Rest: The Effectiveness of the 'Day Off' Legislation for Foreign Domestic Workers. Transient Workers Count Too (TWC2).
8. Explaining why she prefers Indonesians over Filipinos, a Chinese Singaporean employer emphatically states, 'Salary is lower is one and other thing is communication, they are dumber. If you compare to Filipino, Filipino are smarter. So we prefer to have a dumber maid'.
9. In general, 'open kitchen' policy means that domestic workers are allowed to eat any food that is located in the kitchen without needing to ask for a permission from employers.
10. Employers observed in the employment agency include those who confiscate the mobile phone of the domestic worker from Monday to Friday or from 8 am to 8 pm from Monday to Saturday.
11. States the MOM employer handbook: 'You should not withhold the salaries of your FDW on the pretext of safekeeping her salary or delaying payment for extended periods' (Ministry of Manpower 2018b, 12).
12. The eight employers who opted to cover the cost of the placement fee include locals and expats as well as those from a variety of class backgrounds.
13. Explaining the vulnerability of employers is a 37-year old Chinese Singaporean journalist: 'The whole burden is thrown to us. If the maid comes in and said nope I want to go home, I don't want to work anymore, we got to provide her the air ticket to go back. All the money we paid, down the drain'.

Disclosure statement

No potential conflict of interest was reported by the author(s).

References

Anderson, B. 2000. *Doing the Dirty Work? The Global Politics of Domestic Labour*. London: Zed Books.

Anderson, B. 2013. *Us & Them? The Dangerous Politics of Immigration Control*. Oxford: Oxford University Press.

Anderson, B., and J. O'Connell Davidson. 2003. *Is Trafficking in Human Beings Demand Driven? A Multi-Country Pilot Study*. Geneva: International Organization for Migration.

Bakan, A., and D. Stasiulis. 2005. *Negotiating Citizenship: Migrant Women in Canada and the Global System*. Toronto, ON: University of Toronto Press.

Black, D. 2014. "New Rules for Federal Live-in Caregivers Program." *Toronto Star*. https://www.thestar.com/news/canada/2014/11/28/new_rules_for_federal_livein_caregivers_program.html.

Bourdieu, P. 1977. *Outline of a Theory of Practice*. Cambridge: Cambridge University Press.

Chacko, E., and M. Price. 2021. "(Un)Settled Sojourners in Cities: The Scalar and Temporal Dimensions of Migrant Precarity." *Journal of Ethnic and Migration Studies* 47 (20): 4597–4614. doi:10.1080/1369183X.2020.1731060.

Choo, H. Y. 2016. *Decentering Citizenship: Gender, Labor and Migrant Rights in South Korea*. Stanford, CA: Stanford University Press.

Constable, N. 2007. *Maid to Order in Hong Kong*. Ithaca, NY: Cornell University Press.

Constable, N. 2014. *Born Out of Place: Migrant Mothers and the Politics of International Labor*. Berkeley, CA: University of California Press.

Fernandez, B. 2013. "Traffickers, Brokers, Employment Agents, and Social Networks: The Regulation of Intermediaries in the Migration of Ethiopian Domestic Workers to the Middle East." *International Migration Review* 47 (4): 814–843.

Galtung, J. 1969. "Violence, Peace and Peace Research." *Journal of Peace Research* 6 (3): 167–191.

Hahamovitch, C. 2011. *No Man's Land: Jamaican Guestworkers and the Global History of Deportable Labor*. Princeton, NJ: Princeton University Press.

Hayes, A. R., and C. M. Dudek. 2019. "How Radical Right-Wing Populism Has Shaped Recent Migration Policy in Austria and Germany." *Journal of Immigrant and Refugee Studies. Online First May* 19: 2019. doi:10.1080/15562948.2019.1587130.

Hondagneu-Sotelo, P. 2001. *Domestica: Immigrant Workers Cleaning and Caring in the Shadows of Affluence*. Berkeley, CA: University of California Press.

Huang, S., and B. Yeoh. 1996. "Ties That Bind: State Policy and Migrant Female Domestic Helpers in Singapore." *Geoforum; Journal of Physical, Human, and Regional Geosciences* 27 (4): 479–493.

Jureidini, R. 2010. "Trafficking and Contract Migrant Workers in the Middle East." *International Migration* 48 (4): 142–163.

Jureidini, Ray, and Nayla Moukarbel. 2004. "Female Sri Lankan Domestic Workers: A Case of Contract Slavery?" *Journal of Ethnic and Migration Studies* 30 (4): 581–607.

Kathiravelu, L. 2015. *Migrant Dubai: Low Wage Workers and the Construction of a Global City*. Basingstoke: Palgrave Macmillan.

Lan, P. 2006. *Global Cinderellas: Migrant Domestics and Newly Rich Employers in Taiwan*. Durham, NC: Duke University Press.

Lan, P. 2007. "Legal Servitude and Free Illegality: Migrant 'Guest' Workers in Taiwan." In *Asian Diasporas: New Formations, new Conceptions*, edited by R. Parreñas and L. C. D. Siu, 253–278. Stanford, CA: Stanford University Press.

Liebelt, C. 2011. *Caring for the Holy Land: Filipina Domestic Workers in Israel*. New York: Berghahn Books.

Mahdavi, P. 2011. *Gridlock: Labor, Migration and Trafficking in Dubai*. Stanford, CA: Stanford University Press.

Ministry of Manpower. 2016. *Documents and Publications: Foreign Workforce Numbers*. Ministry of Manpower. http://www.mom.gov.sg/documents-and-publications/foreign-workforce-numbers.

Ministry of Manpower. 2018a. *Security Bond Requirements for Foreign Domestic Worker*. Ministry of Manpower. https://www.mom.gov.sg/passes-and-permits/work-permit-for-foreign-domestic-worker/eligibility-and-requirements/security-bond.

Ministry of Manpower. 2018b. *Your Guide to Employing a Foreign Domestic Worker*. https://epace.sp.edu.sg/EdulearnNETUpload/PACE/learningobject/File/0e963daa-0654-69eb-98c7-0e90df31 1224/FDW%20Material.pdf.

Nixon, R. 2013. *Slow Violence and the Environmentalism of the Poor*. Cambridge, MA: Harvard University Press.

Pande, A. 2013. "The Paper That You Have in Your Hand is My Freedom: Migrant Domestic Work and the Sponsorship (Kafala) System in Lebanon." *International Migration Review* 47 (2): 414–441.

Parreñas, Rhacel. 2015. *Servants of Globalization: Migration and Domestic Work*. Stanford, CA: Stanford University Press.

Parreñas, Rhacel, Rachel Silvey, Maria Cecilia Hwang, and Carolyn Choi. 2019. "Serial Labor Migration: Precarity and Itinerancy among Filipino and Indonesian Domestic Workers." *International Migration Review* 53 (4): 1230–1258.

Pratt, G. 2012. *Families Apart: Migrant Mothers and the Conflicts of Labor and Love*. Minneapolis, MN: University of Minnesota Press.

Romero, M. 1992. *Maid in the U.S.A.* New York: Routledge.

Sassen, S. 1996. *Losing Control? Sovereignty in an Age of Globalization*. New York: Columbia University Press.

Stenum, H. 2011. *Abused Domestic Workers in Europe: The Case of Au Pairs*. Brussels: European Commission.

Yea, S. 2017. "The Art of Not Being Caught: Temporal Strategies for Disciplining Unfree Labour in Singapore's Contract Migration." *Geoforum; Journal of Physical, Human, and Regional Geosciences* 78: 179–188.
Yea, S. 2018. "Unfreedom Unbound: Developing a Cumulative Approach to Understanding Unfree Labour in Singapore." *Work, Employment and Society* 32 (5): 925–941.
Yeoh, B., and S. Huang. 1998. "Negotiating Public Space: Strategies and Styles of Migrant Female Domestic Workers in Singapore." *Urban Studies* 35 (3): 583–602.

Temporary migrants and public space: a case study of Dongguan, China

Yining Tan

ABSTRACT

The development of the labour-intensive manufacturing sector in Dongguan, China, stimulated significant inflows of temporary migrants. However, their temporary status limits migrants' mobility and restrains their access to public resources available in the city. The community square in proximity to factories provides space for temporary migrant workers and their families to congregate, socialise and exercise during after-work hours. Grounded in theoretical discussions of the precarity of temporary migration and the intersection of migrants and urban space, this study uses participant observations and semi-structured interviews to examine the following questions: (1) What are the spatial and temporal patterns of temporary migrants' use of the community square? (2) How do temporary migrants' use of the community square indicate social inclusion or exclusion from the destination society? (3) How do temporary migrants experience precarity in spatial and temporal dimensions? The research findings suggest that the temporary status of migrants and fast-paced work schedules of manufacturing factories limit migrants' options for after-work leisure activities both spatially and temporally. The research has broad implications for the integration of temporary migrants in Chinese cities and the development of public space to enhance social belonging among underserved migrant populations.

Introduction

At a few minutes past 6:00 pm on a Wednesday, Meng, originally from Hubei Province but now an assembly line worker at a shoe manufacturing factory in Dongguan, China, walked to a community square about five minutes away from the factory to relax and exercise. The city of Dongguan is often referred to as the 'World's Factory' or 'Migrant City'. In 2017, Dongguan hosted around 4.39 million temporary migrants, more than twice the population of registered local residents (Dongguan Statistical Yearbook 2018a). Like many other migrant workers in Dongguan, Meng lived in the dormitory built on the factory premise, a common spatial arrangement employed by factory managers to increase production efficiency and oversee factory workers (Pun and Chan 2013). The community square was one of the very few places that Meng visited to escape briefly from crowded working and living conditions that were the norm for migrant workers. Like Meng, the temporary status of many migrants heightens their precarity (Chacko and Price 2021) and limits their spatial mobility and access to public resources in destination societies.

The new mobilities paradigm (Sheller and Urry 2006) argued that scholars should bring together the study of human mobility at the global scale with everyday concerns at the local scale. Migration processes are mediated not only by regulations and policies at the state level but also by everyday encounters in cities and neighbourhoods where these regulations and policies must be negotiated. Many scholars have examined the intersection of migrants and cities from both spatial and temporal dimensions. Spatially, human geographers view the city not as a bounded container but, rather, as a relational configuration for migrant populations. Scholars argued for everyone to have the right to the city (Harvey 2008; Lefebvre 1996; Mitchell 2003). Singer (2004) and Price and Benton-Short (2008) discussed the concept of 'immigrant gateway cities' and emphasised cities as critical entry points, nodes, and urban settlements. While existing scholarship has examined the role of cities in the migration process and the different modes of incorporation for migrants, less attention has been devoted to the everyday constitution of urban space and the role of temporary migrants as urban actors. A second strand of literature focuses on the temporal dimension. Bailey et al. (2002) coined the term 'permanent temporariness' to explain the transnational experiences of temporary migrant workers from El Salvador. Collins (2012) further expanded this term into conceptualizations of urban spatiality by discussing how the presence of significant numbers of temporary migrants produces 'both passing and more long-term transformations of the urban built environment' (322). The concept of 'permanent temporariness' offers an analytical starting point to consider the urban implications of such temporary mobility.

This research aims to advance the literature on the spatial and temporal dimensions of precarity and (im)mobility experienced by temporary migrants in non-Western context. Based on semi-structured interviews with temporary migrants and participant observations at a community square in Dongguan, China, this article focuses on the spatial and temporal dimensions of migrant precarity in relation to public space. Specifically, this study aims to understand the following: (1) What are the spatial and temporal patterns by which temporary migrants use the community square? (2) How do temporary migrants' uses of the community square indicate social inclusion in or exclusion from the destination society? (3) How do temporary migrants experience precarity in spatial and temporal dimensions?

In the following sections, the article will provide an overview of the relevant literature that examines the precarity of temporary migration and its relations to urban public space. Following a contextualisation of temporary migrants in China and an explanation of the research methods employed, the article will analyse the research findings according to uses of space, social inclusions and exclusions in the locality of the community square, and the destination society.

Literature review

The precarity of temporary migrants

Traditional migration studies were anchored in the analysis of permanent migration, ignoring, until recently, non-permanent migration and its effects on economic and socio-cultural landscapes (Baláz, Williams, and Kollar 2004; Parreñas 2010; Robertson 2014). While some scholars believed temporary migration might transform into permanent settlement, initiating chain migration and the establishment of ethnic communities (Castles 2006; Hugo 2003), others argued that the restrictive policies and regulations in destination societies prevent temporary migrants from moving into permanent settlement (Waldinger and Fitzgerald 2004). Meanwhile, the dichotomy between temporary and permanent mobility was challenged. King (2002) argued for a deconstruction of the binary of migration and pointed out that there are 'different degrees of temporariness' (King 2002, 93) rather than clear-cut distinctions between temporary and permanent migration. Moreover, the idea of 'permanent temporariness' suggests the ways in which the temporary status of migrants has both a passing and long-lasting effect on 'bodies, families, and social fields' (Bailey et al. 2002, 139), as well as urban space and the built environment (Collins 2012).

Embedded in the temporality of migration are the restrictions imposed on temporary migrants by the receiving societies. Migration status is associated significantly with the rights and identities of residents (Joppke 2007). The precarity of temporary migrants is reflected in various spatial scales, including international, national, city and neighbourhood levels (Chacko and Price 2021). Immigration law structures 'the vulnerability of those who enter by assigning them to various categories of precariousness, ranging from illegality though permanent temporariness, transitional temporariness, and permanent residence to citizenship' (Macklin 2010, 332). Castles and Davidson (2000) described the 'differential exclusion' of migrants in some host countries, which encourages migrant workers to be temporary sojourners rather than long-term residents. Their temporary status turns migrant labourers into precarious workers over whom employers and managers have particular and wide-ranging mechanisms of control (Anderson 2010; Lewis et al. 2015).

On the scale of urban life, the temporal restrictions also influence temporary migrants' everyday migration experiences. Temporary migrants are usually not entitled to local citizenship (Smart and Smart 2001) and are restricted from obtaining more affordable public housing, medical services, public education, and pensions, which are available only to permanent residents (Fan 2002; Solinger 1999). While some scholars believed that integration could be achieved over time (Alba and Nee 2003; Perlmann and Waldinger 1997), other researchers argued that barriers such as language differences, discrimination, and lack of educational qualifications would prevent the full integration of temporary migrants (Gans 2007; Portes and Zhou 1993). In short, the temporary status of migrants is likely to put them in precarious and uncertain conditions and limits their social and spatial mobility in destination cities.

The intersection of temporary migrants and public space

Acknowledging the precarity of temporary migrants is not to suggest that migrants do not have any influence over the ongoing constitution of destination societies. The migration-development paradigm perceives migrants as agents, rather than instruments of development (Muniandy and Bonatti 2014). While the challenges and hardships experienced by temporary migrants have been examined quite thoroughly (Anderson 2010; Lewis et al. 2015), less attention has been paid to temporary migrants' roles in reproducing and contesting urban space (Bork-Hüffer 2016). Temporary migrants, as a group of urban dwellers, are constantly restructuring space–time relations (Bailey et al. 2002). Glick Schiller and Çağlar (2009) examined various pathways for migrant incorporation and the interrelations between migration and urban transformation. Similarly, Tardiveau and Mallo (2014) maintained that temporary migrants actively shape the urban space in both temporary and permanent ways.

Among all urban space, public space is viewed as a 'third place', in addition to work space and living space (Oldenburg 1989). Yet, the functions and meanings of public space are different across cultural traditions and may be experienced very differently by various groups (Németh and Schmidt 2011). As an essential component of cities, public space could be inclusive of all residents ideally. While there is abundant research on the structural exclusions experienced by temporary migrants as a result of their temporary status, only recently have scholars begun to explore the social inclusions that temporary migrants experience in relation to public space. Social interactions between strangers in public space can be meaningful and conducive to social cohesion in a multicultural society (Peters 2010).

Meanwhile, public space not only provides opportunities for people to congregate, socialise and recreate, but it is also reshaped by the everyday involvement of its users. In their study of female domestic migrant workers in Singapore, Yeoh and Huang (1998) investigated the spatial segregation of marginalised groups as well as the strategies migrant workers employed to use public space and negotiate their own identities in the process. The public space in the Central District of Hong Kong is contested through its use by both Filipino migrant workers and cosmopolitan professionals in the post-colonial cultural landscape (Law 2002). Thus, temporary migrants are making and remaking transient urban spaces through their presence in, visits to, and uses of public space. My research brings conversations about the precariousness and influence of temporary migrants to bear on the scale of neighbourhood and public space.

As stated by Bell and Ward (2000), population movement involves both temporal and spatial dimensions. This paper aims to examine the intersections of temporary migrants and public space from the perspective of space–time and people-place relations. Grounded in the literature on the precarity of temporary migrants and the intersection of temporary migrants and urban space, this study enhances our understanding of how the uncertainty associated with the temporary status of migrants is mitigated or strengthened through visiting and using public space, as well as how migrants' uses of public space affect their senses of belonging and the locality of the destination city.

Temporary migrants in China

In China, the temporary status of internal migrants is not determined by the length of their stay, but rather by the country's household registration system (*hukou*). Under this system, temporary migration is defined as 'migration that involves no change in migrants' official household registration' (Yang and Guo 1999, 935). The system serves as a tool to regulate migration within China, especially rural to urban relocations. These temporary moves are likely to be self-initiated and involve migrants of low skill levels and social-economic statuses (Li 2006; Sun and Fan 2011). Despite living and working in urban areas, most rural-urban labour migrants retain their official permanent residence in places of rural origins. On the one hand, the receiving cities are highly selective regarding migrants' skill levels, human capital, and socio-economic statuses, making it difficult for temporary migrants to officially obtain urban *hukou* (Zhu and Chen 2010). The change of residency status also has implications at the local and state levels, as it involves a 'transfer of welfare entitlement' (Li and Siu 1997, 65) and the associated government obligations. On the other hand, the risks related to migration and the uncertainties of employment prospects may also influence temporary migrants' intentions to permanently settle in the destination (Yang and Guo 1999). Zhu's (2007) survey findings indicated that job stability, income levels and availability of social insurance are the three major underlying factors that affect migrants' intentions and capability for permanent settlement.

Temporary residency status not only has far-reaching influences on migration experiences, but also on settlement patterns and urban forms in the destination cities. According to Lawrence (1995), housing availability, affordability and residential environment are the major characteristics that define housing quality for migrants. To increase work efficiency, many manufacturing factories build on-site dormitories to manage the production and reproduction processes of their workers (Pun and Chan 2013). Self-help housing in Chengzhongcun (*urban village*) (Zhang, Zhao, and Tian 2003) also enables temporary migrants to settle temporarily in rapidly urbanising city centres. In migrant cities such as Dongguan, factory dormitories and rented apartments have become the housing choices for temporary migrants due to limited access to other housing options (Wu 2002, 2004). Scholars have shown the relationship between the working poor's unfavourable housing conditions and an increasing desire for public and open space in the city (Shaw 2004; Wolch, Byrne, and Newell 2014).

In addition, the temporary mode of migration affects the spatial arrangement of family members. The ineligibility for public education and the high expenses of child-care put more pressure on temporary migrants, leading to changes in household strategies that result in either split households (Chang, Dong, and MacPhail 2011; Ye and Lu 2011) or the chain migration of relatives (Yang and Guo 1999). Consequently, the transient population and their lack of access to social welfare indirectly leads to changing demographic profiles in destination cities.

Earlier studies on the everyday migration experiences of rural-to-urban migrants in China focused largely on their working environment and housing conditions (Jiang 2006; Shen and Huang 2003). Recently, scholars started to pay attention to aspects of their after-work leisure life. Chen (2007) observed migrant workers' participation in square dancing in Beijing and found that the improvised uses of urban spaces in streets and community parks helped enliven urban space and engage temporary migrants. Due to the lack of high-quality public facilities in urban villages, residents' nightlife activities were constrained to low-end commercial and recreational activities in public space that had access to lighting and required few expenses (Song, Pan, and Chen 2016).

The community square analysed in this paper is located in Tangxia Town of Dongguan (Figure 1), which hosted 368,983 temporary migrants in 2017, more than six times that of the locally registered population (Dongguan Statistical Yearbook 2018b). Located in the Pearl River Delta region and the Guangzhou-Shenzhen economic corridor, Dongguan benefitted from policy incentives during the country's economic reform in 1978 and has become a major recipient of foreign investment in the labour-intensive manufacturing sector. The increasing demand for cheap labour stimulated waves of migrant workers from

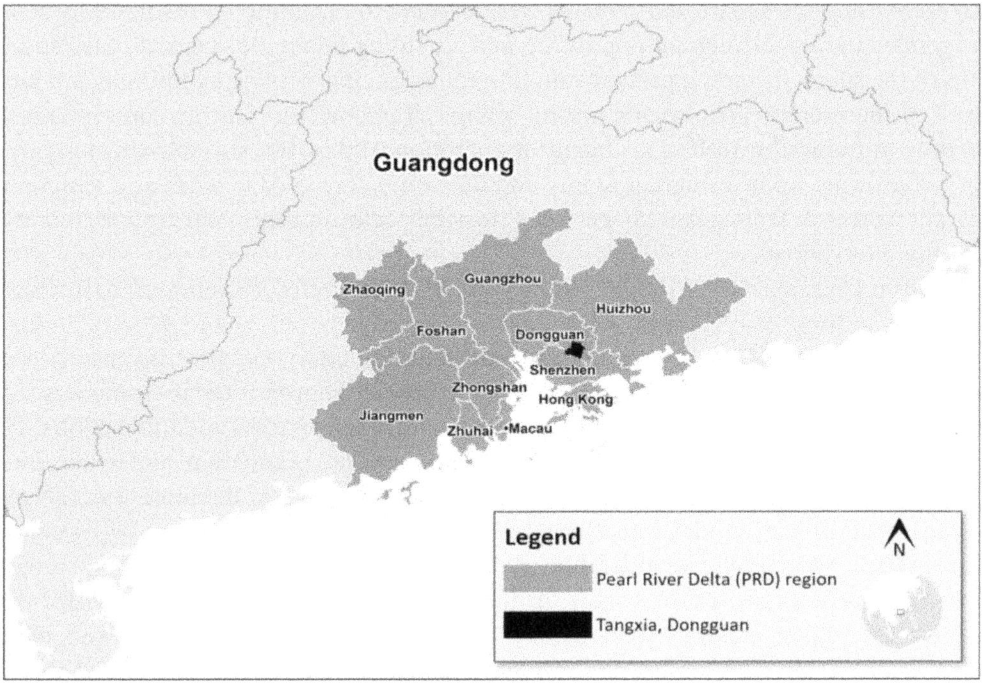

Figure 1. Location map of Tangxia Town in Dongguan, China.

other parts of China, and large numbers of temporary migrants facilitated the development of labour-intensive manufacturing industries in the city. In 2017, around 79% of the employed persons in Dongguan worked in manufacturing industries (Dongguan Statistical Yearbook 2018c). Therefore, the demographic and economic structures of the city are highly intertwined and may have significant implications for its urban and social landscapes.

Methods

This study employed participant observation and semi-structured interviews to gather primary data. I visited the community square at different times of the day (8 am, 12 pm, and 5 pm to 9 pm) to observe the uses of the space. When visitors started to congregate in the square at night, I spent time observing and taking notes regarding approximate numbers of visitors, the physical appearances of the visitors, their uses of space and their interactions. In total, I spent 85 h in the community square to collect data from participant observations. There were times when I was having conversations with interviewees and they were greeted by acquaintances and started conversations among themselves in Mandarin Chinese. The conversations may or may not have had direct relevance to my research questions, but observing their tone and body language when they were interacting with each other provided valuable information about their perceptions of the spatial and social dynamics of the public space and the destination society.

Interviewees were identified using the purposive sampling method to ensure that a diversity of temporary migrants was represented. I approached these migrants while they were using the square. Participants were selected to maximise representations in age and gender among the migrant population and also to represent the diversity of usage patterns of the space, including participation in group dancing, playing badminton and table tennis, using exercise instruments, sitting, using cell phones, etc. During conversations, I not only introduced myself as a student of migration studies, but also told them my own story of growing up in a migrant family and how my father used to work as a temporary migrant worker in Dongguan. My personal story helped me quickly gain rapport and trust with the interviewees.

Between December of 2016 and January of 2017, I collected 16 valid semi-structured interviews in Mandarin Chinese. Each interview lasted between 20 and 40 min. Some of the interviewees said that they could not stay long for interviews because they needed to go back to the factory for the night shift. The relatively shorter interview time was supplemented by the time I spent in the square observing usage patterns and interactions. The interviewees' demographic profiles varied in age, gender, occupation and educational attainment. Ranging in age from 20 to 63 years old at the time of the interview, the participants included seven males and nine females. None of the interviewees had a college degree. Their occupations included housewife, worker in a factory assembly line, owner of a small business and other worker in the labour-intensive manufacturing sector. For dual-wage families, children were mostly taken care of by grandparents, who either stayed in the hometown or became migrants themselves and sometimes found jobs at local factories or started their own businesses.

All of the interviewees either lived in dormitories built on the premises of factories or rented apartments that were close to their workplaces. Among the 16 participants, nine lived in dormitories and seven in rented apartments, a common arrangement for migrants who lived with their family members. None of the interviewees had private cars, and their movement in the city was highly dependent on public transportation, walking and biking. Fourteen participants reported walking five to twenty minutes to the community square, while the other two said they used bikes to commute between the square and their primary residence.

The interviewees were asked about the frequencies and lengths of their visits, the distances from their living/work places to the square, their activities and usage patterns in the space, their social interactions with other users, the influences of visiting the square on their migration experiences and future settlement plans, the effects of their visits to the square, the neighbourhood and the city. I recorded the interviews and then transcribed and translated them into English for further coding and content analysis. A hybrid of deductive and inductive approaches was employed to create coding schemes (Charmaz 2000). First, I manually developed the coding structure based on research questions and theories. For example, codes such as 'social inclusion' and 'social exclusion' were created to capture the experiences of migrants in the community square and the city. Then, I used an inductive and data-driven coding strategy that allows for themes and patterns to emerge from the fieldwork. For instance, I created 'children-related networks' as a new theme that emerged from conversations with participants and my observations in the square.

Spatial and temporal uses of the community square

Spatially, the community square was divided into different uses, such as exercise equipment and sports courts, open space, a sunken plaza and berms next to the green space.

Each of the areas catered to the diverse needs of different user groups, serving visitors with a variety of demographic profiles and leisure behaviours. The basketball and badminton courts on the east side of the community square engaged both active and passive uses, with some participants playing while others watched. The designated uses of the space were simultaneously accompanied by improvised uses, reflecting the initiatives of urban residents and 'a revival of civic spirit' (Talen 2015, 145).

There was an immense contrast between the uses of the community square during the day and at night (Figure 2). The community square was almost empty during the day and started to receive more visitors after 6:00 pm, which was the typical time for factory workers to be released from work. In a manufacturing town like Tangxia, the temporal rhythms of work, life and leisure for temporary migrant workers are closely related to factory schedules. After work, the migrant workers came to the community square either alone or in small groups, each navigating their own way of using the space. Hua and Ling both came from the same province, and they worked at assembly lines in a factory that manufactures suitcases and travel bags for export. They each earned 2,000 RMB a month, in addition to the free meals and lodging provided by the canteen and dormitories built on the factory premise. Although the living costs were minimised for Hua and Ling, the conflation of work and living space limited the spatial boundaries of their daily movement. 'What are your after-work activities?' I asked. Ling said,

> Mostly I would just spend my after-work time with my phone in my room (in the dormitory) to watch shows and movies and listen to pop music. The work itself is tiring. Sometimes we have nightshifts when the factory gets a big order and needs it done quickly. I don't have much free time, and even when I do, there is not much to do. Well, there are some shopping streets and supermarkets 20 minutes' bus ride away. I would sometimes go there. But I come to this square more often. It's just a few minutes' walk away from my factory, and it has open space and trees, which are good for health.

Hua nodded and added, 'factory life is boring. The square gives us a little break'. Within walking distance from several factories, the community square provided migrant workers with an opportunity to escape temporarily from the segregated and stressful life of the factory during short periods of time away from work.

The temporality of square visits was reinforced by the families of migrant workers, who also tended to visit the community square much more often in the evenings even though

Figure 2. The community square during the day (left) and at night (right). By author.

they were not restricted by factory schedules. When I met Huifang a few minutes past 7:00 pm, she was sitting and watching her child play with other children in the square. Huifang was a housewife in her early thirties. She met her husband in Dongguan and quit her factory job after getting married. Her husband was a manager at an electrical firm and could contribute 6,000 RMB a month to the household income. After paying for rent, food, and other expenses, they also needed to send remittances to assist with the education of Huifang's brother-in-law. Although not confined to work space during the day, Huifang was still more likely to visit the square in the evenings. She said that the presence of other visitors enhanced her experience,

> I go to the market to buy groceries in the morning and then prepare food for my family. Then I do some laundry and play with her [signalling to her daughter who was playing with a girl of her age while I conducted the interview] for a while before she takes a nap. My life is mostly trapped in the small one-bedroom apartment that we rent, and I sometimes feel I am disconnected from the outside world. Visiting the square becomes a good way for me to see other mothers and talk or simply watch the kids play.

Huifang intentionally waited until after 6:00 pm to bring her child to the square to get together with other children and their parents. Visiting the square was a temporary escape from her unfavourable residential space. Although Huifang no longer worked in a manufacturing factory, she was still part of the temporary labour migration. Her living situation was affected by that of other migrants, particularly her husband, and even non-migrants such as her brother-in-law.

During the interviews, the migrants sometimes brought up that they 'chose to' visit the square at night. However, the time that migrants chose to visit the square was largely constrained by external factors, such as the work schedules of factories, institution regulations and urban development in the host society. The work schedule of the factory town impacted not only the timetables of the temporary migrant workers but also the daily schedules of their family members. The temporary residency status of migrants and their relatively disadvantaged socio-economic positions limited their options for housing and after-work leisure activities and their use of space in the city.

Illusive inclusion

Social integration is a process rather than an outcome (Penninx et al. 2004). The interviewees indicated that they knew very few local residents and their social interactions in the community square were mostly with other temporary migrants. For example, Huifang said she mostly talked with other mothers who shared similar migration background. Likewise, Meng told me that he had not interacted with any locals in the square. The lack of social interactions between temporary migrants and locals partly resulted from the temporary migrants being the dominant population in the city. Jin, who worked at an electrical factory and had lived in Dongguan for three years, mentioned that she faced a language barrier when socialising with locals because she could not understand Cantonese, a local dialect in Guangdong Province. She said,

> I know some of the seniors in the square are locals, but I never talk to them. I can't speak Cantonese, and they don't speak Mandarin. My friend is from another part of Guangdong province, and she can understand it, so I guess it is easier for her to adapt to life here in general.

Yet, the language barrier did not seem to be a hurdle for all. Mr. Zong said,

> Dongguan has such a high number of migrants from all over the country. We all have various dialects and accents, but most of the time we have no difficulty understanding each other speaking Mandarin Chinese.

In a city where temporary migrants far outnumber local residents, the language difference is less likely to be a barrier to migrants visiting the community square. Instead, the users of the community square were connected by other linkages, such as children and common interests in group activities.

During my observations and interviews, I was impressed by the children-related social networks and economic entrepreneurship. Parents or grandparents who brought children to the community square found it easier to get to know and socialise with other parents. Sometimes my interviews were interrupted by greetings between my participants and other parents who visited the square at the same time. The local government also encouraged children's visits and uses of the community square by only issuing business permits for children-related activities, such as toy cars, air-filled castles and mini fishponds. At 5:00 pm every day, Mr. Zong, the owner of a business that rents toy cars, set up the cars in the square, waiting for children to come to play. Mr. Zong was in his sixties and had lived in Dongguan for about twenty years. His two daughters migrated to Dongguan for jobs in the late 1990s, and he followed them two years later. At first, he helped take care of his grandchildren. As the grandchildren grew up and moved to other cities for school, he bought toy cars and rented them out for children to play with in the square. Over his two decades' stays in Dongguan, Mr. Zong transitioned from raising his own grandchildren to enriching the lives of other temporary migrants' children. Mr. Zong came to Dongguan as a part of chain migration, and his involvement in the toy-car renting business also affected the lives of other migrants. Owners of the children-related businesses were temporary migrants themselves, and their entrepreneurship illustrated further economic integration into local society. However, their social connections and economic activities were strongly space-based and could not be easily transferred out of the context of the community square once temporary migrants left the space.

In addition to children-related networks, the temporary migrants who visited the community square were also connected by group activities such as square dancing and ball games. For example, the open space in the centre of the square provided venues for square dancing from around 7 pm to 9 pm every night, serving as the hub of social networks. Square dancing, a form of group exercise in urban China, not only attracted visitors, especially women and seniors, to participate in the activity, but also appealed to audiences who simply enjoyed watching others dance. The local government hired two dance instructors to lead the square dancing every night, suggesting that they were motivated to encourage more females and seniors to visit the square, as well as more flexible and diversified uses of the public space. After retiring in her hometown, Fang, in her fifties, moved to Dongguan to help take care of her grandchildren. For Fang, participating in square dancing every night was not only a form of exercise, but also an opportunity to socialise and get involved in urban life, 'I used to feel I didn't belong to the city when I first came here. All I had were my children and grandchildren. Now I feel I have met more people and know more things'. However, the social connections established among temporary migrants were closely tied to their presence in the community square and were likely to vanish as soon as they left the space. Except for one interviewee who said that she sometimes visited the square with her neighbours, all other informants stated that they would meet and greet other visitors in the space but barely kept in contact with them after they left the square, indicating the temporary nature of integration into Dongguan's urban life. Nanhua, a housewife who had lived in Dongguan since 2010, said,

> Yeah, I have met a few people here, but we didn't really keep much contact afterward. If we bump into each other in the square, we would say hi, but that's it. You know, with the high turnover of people here, it is difficult to maintain contact when we move with our jobs frequently.

Ling, who had just arrived in Dongguan, expressed similar feelings,

> I usually come to the square with Hua. We are laoxiang [meaning: people who share the same hometown], and we now work in the same factory. There are some faces that I frequently see in the square, but I never really know them. Well, if I see them again in supermarkets, we may greet each other. But you know, I never make plans with them to go to supermarkets together. Not even once.

For temporary migrants like Nanhua and Ling, the community square served as a social hub for them to congregate, socialise and participate in group activities. Visiting the community square created a sense of belonging that enabled temporary migrants to escape from work and household chores and to be integrated into urban life temporarily. Nevertheless, the social inclusion experienced by temporary migrants in the community square was rather illusive. Spatially, the social connection established among temporary migrants in the community square was not likely to be transferred to other social occasions in other parts of the city. Temporally, the social connection was formed when migrants visited the square, but it quickly disappeared after they left the space. The illusive nature of the social inclusion experienced by temporary migrants further highlights the scaler and temporal dimensions of precarity.

Structural exclusion and the permanent temporariness in migration

Although all the interviewees agreed that visiting the community square enriched their after-work migration experience and improved their health conditions, it did not necessarily lead to full socio-spatial inclusion into the destination society (Antonsich 2010). Instead, the study confirms the spatial immobility experienced by temporary migrants (Joppke 2007). Their decisions on where and when to go for after-work leisure activities were structured largely by external factors such as factory regulations and the urban environment. Economic conditions and long working hours limited the temporary migrants' options to travel further and enjoy more diversified urban lives in the destination societies (see also Parreñas, Kantachote, and Silvey 2021). As a result, the community square in close proximity to their primary residence and workplace became the 'third space' (Oldenburg 1989) for them to have a temporary escape from their highly stressful and segregated lives.

Their spatial immobility was also coupled with social immobility that further constrained them. None of the interviewees had a college degree, and their temporary migration status was reinforced by their low levels of skills and educational attainment. The labour-intensive manufacturing factories in Dongguan provided job opportunities for the low-skilled migrant workers. However, although the temporary migrants benefited from factories' hiring demands and policy relaxations during the first stage of their migration, they did not enjoy many opportunities for upward mobility in their post-migration experiences.

The possibility to transition from temporary migration to permanent settlement was largely dependent on migrants' economic opportunities and the institutional regulations on the *hukou* system. Yanping, a 33-year-old migrant worker, had a sorrowful look in her eyes when she brought up the separation between her and her family. Due to the restrictions of the *hukou* system, her children were not eligible to attend public school in Dongguan, and the private school was too expensive for her family to afford. She said,

> Well, my children are still back in the hometown, a 20 hour train ride away. My parents-in-law take care of them. They visited here during their summer breaks, but I couldn't afford for them to go to school here. You know, I don't have a Dongguan hukou, so my children are not able to go to public school. They are really frustrated.

The left-behind children in the hometown and separation from family members have prevented some migrant workers from settling permanently in Dongguan. Chunhua expressed her feeling of hopelessness in becoming a permanent resident of the city,

> The city wants more educated and skilled migrants. I barely finished middle school and now end up working in assembly lines. There's no way I can be qualified for applying for the hukou here. For now, I just save as much money as I can before I eventually return to my hometown.

Both Yanping and Chunhua had lived in Dongguan for about two years, and both worked as assembly line workers in the same garment manufacturing factory. Although the community square provided them with space to relax and integrate into the city's urban life temporarily, they were still structurally excluded from gaining access to Dongguan's educational resources and higher wage job opportunities.

The permanence of temporary migration was demonstrated at both individual and national levels. For migrant individuals, although the availability of manufacturing jobs that enabled temporary migrants to work and reside in cities seemed to strengthen their mobilities, their potential for upward mobility was hardly realised. The provision of accessible public space in close proximity to migrants was influential in shaping their everyday movement patterns and improving their migration experiences; however, their ability to settle down depends more on institutional factors, such as restructuring the household registration system, improving public welfare and public education, and providing adequate training for temporary migrants to improve their competitive strength in the job market. Otherwise, it is difficult for temporary migrants to end their temporary status and move into permanent settlement.

At the national level, the existence of the *hukou* system and the regional differences in social and economic development also fuel the sustaining flows of temporary migration across regions. In recent years, as the manufacturing sector in Dongguan has undergone restructuring, the traditional labour-intensive industries have been phased out in the city's economic structure. Many manufacturing operations were relocated to inland provinces where both land and labour are relatively less expensive. Mr. Zong had lived in Dongguan for twenty years, although he was still registered as a temporary migrant. He observed that the number of temporary migrants has decreased sharply in the past decade, and the number of visitors to the community square has also declined accordingly. Similarly, Feng said that compared to a few years ago, an increasing number of labour workers from his village were willing to seek job opportunities in cities closer to their hometown instead of moving a long distance to Dongguan because the income gap between the two places had gradually narrowed. The slower growth in Dongguan's temporary migrant population did not suggest the ending of the temporary migration flow in the country. In contrast, the rising number of destinations for temporary migrants in other parts of China illustrates both the permanent temporariness and precarity of low-skilled labour migration at the national level.

Conclusion

In China, the movement of people, including temporary migrants, is closely regulated by the government and the household registration system. Some of the restrictions imposed on the temporary migrants directly result from institutional regulations, while others are the outcomes of economic immobility, low educational attainment and skill levels. When examining the everyday immobility and uncertainties experienced by temporary migrants, restrictions are evident in both spatial and temporal dimensions.

Through an examination of the intersections between temporary migrants and public space, this paper focuses on the everyday uses of the community square by temporary migrants and examines the people-space relations exhibited in the process. Spatially, the low socio-economic status of temporary migrants limits their travel options and circumscribes the boundaries of urban space they may reach in the destination city. Temporally, the fast-paced work schedules of manufacturing factories limit the availability of time to enjoy leisure activities after work. Despite constraints emanating from income level, after-work time and commuting options, many of the temporary migrants chose to visit the community space, as it was unlikely to incur extra costs. The community square in this study was in close proximity to factories and, thus, served as a critical venue for temporary migrant workers to spend their free time after work.

The visiting schedules of temporary migrants created a contrast between the landscapes of the community square during the day and at night. The presence of temporary migrants and their engagement in activities in the community square during after-work hours enlivened the space and enhanced their own wellbeing. Since these leisure and social activities were place-specific, the transformations of the space were closely tied to the visit times of the temporary migrants. Nevertheless, as the flow of temporary migrants into Dongguan is relatively continuous, the impacts on the urban environment tend to be long-lasting. Yet, the temporary migrants only experienced a temporary integration into urban life during the time they visited the community square and were more likely to return to their segregated urban life afterward. Finally, although visiting the community square was likely to enhance the positive migration experience of the temporary migrants, they were essentially excluded from full integration into local society by structural forces. As a result, the temporary status of migrants was likely to become permanent.

These research findings contribute to the literature on cities and migrants by examining the spatial movements of temporary migrants and their uses of public space. The study also expands the literature on 'permanent temporariness' from transnational immigration studies to migration studies, and confirms the immobility and uncertainty experienced by temporary migrants that results from their temporary residency status and its associated social disadvantages. The research findings also highlight the active roles that temporary migrants play in reconstructing the public space in the receiving societies.

In addition, the study was conducted in the context of Dongguan, a migrant-receiving city in China. The definitions of temporary and permanent migrants in China are highly associated with the country's particular household registration system. As public space is experienced differently across cultures, the intention of the study is not to build a new model for Asian cities, but rather to illustrate the diversity of experiences in different geographical locations. Unlike in similar studies of public space and migrants in cosmopolitan cities such as Singapore or Hong Kong, the city of Dongguan is undergoing rapid urbanisation as a result of globalisation. The economic and social dynamics exhibited in the case of Dongguan may be applied to understanding the everyday interactions between migrants and cities in emerging economies.

The findings of the study will help local policy makers and planning institutions to design and maintain public spaces in a manner that better accommodates all residents, regardless of their residence status, class, age and gender. The study also informs local governments regarding the need to balance the economic and social development of temporary migrants and engage transient urban residents with more opportunities to experience urban life. There is no homogenous way of using public space among temporary migrants. Age and gender are two critical variables that may influence the visiting experiences; women and seniors are oftentimes even less privileged within the temporary migrant populations. Different usage patterns of the community square existed between families with children and migrants who were single. In future work, more studies could focus on particular groups of temporary migrants and examine how temporality is highlighted in their interactions with others in public space.

Acknowledgement

The author would like to thank all the participants in the research. She is thankful to Dr. Wei Li, and Dr. Emir Estrada for providing important feedback. The author is also very grateful to the anonymous referees and the organizers of the special issue, Dr. Elizabeth Chacko and Dr. Marie Price, for their critical comments and suggestions.

Disclosure statement

No potential conflict of interest was reported by the author(s).

References

Alba, Richard D., and Victor Nee. 2003. *Remaking the American Mainstream: Assimilation and Contemporary Immigration*. Cambridge: Harvard University Press.

Anderson, Bridget. 2010. "Migration, Immigration Controls and the Fashioning of Precarious Workers." *Work, Employment and Society* 24 (2): 300–317.

Antonsich, Marco. 2010. "Searching for Belonging–an Analytical Framework." *Geography Compass* 4 (6): 644–659.

Bailey, Adrian J., Richard A. Wright, Alison Mountz, and Ines M. Miyares. 2002. "(Re)Producing Salvadoran Transnational Geographies." *Annals of the Association of American Geographers* 92 (1): 125–144.
Baláz, Vladimír, Allan M. Williams, and Daniel Kollar. 2004. "Temporary Versus Permanent Youth Brain Drain: Economic Implications." *International Migration* 42 (4): 3–34.
Bell, Martin, and Gary Ward. 2000. "Comparing Temporary Mobility with Permanent Migration." *Tourism Geographies* 2 (1): 97–107.
Bork-Hüffer, Tabea. 2016. "Migrants' Agency and the Making of Transient Urban Spaces." *Population, Space and Place* 22 (2): 124–127.
Castles, Stephen. 2006. "Guestworkers in Europe: A Resurrection?" *International Migration Review* 40: 741–766.
Castles, Stephen, and Alastair Davidson. 2000. *Citizenship and Migration: Globalization and the Politics of Belonging*. New York: Routledge.
Chacko, Elizabeth, and Marie Price. 2021. "(Un)Settled Sojourners in Cities: The Scalar and Temporal Dimensions of Migrant Precarity." *Journal of Ethnic and Migration Studies* 47 (20): 4597–4614. doi:10.1080/1369183X.2020.1731060.
Chang, Hongqin, Xiao-yuan Dong, and Fiona MacPhail. 2011. "Labor Migration and Time Use Patterns of the Left-Behind Children and Elderly in Rural China." *World Development* 39 (12): 2199–2210.
Charmaz, Kathy. 2000. "Grounded Theory: Objectivist and Constructivist Methods." In *The Handbook of Qualitative Research*, edited by N. K. Denzin, and Y. S. Lincoln, 2nd ed., 509–535. Thousand Oaks, CA: Sage.
Chen, Caroline. 2007. "*Dancing in the Street in Contemporary Beijing: Improvised Uses and Long-Life Practices Within the Urban System.*" Proceedings of the 6th Conference of the Pacific Rim community design Network, Quanzhou, Fujian, China.
Collins, Francis L. 2012. "Transnational Mobilities and Urban Spatialities: Notes From the Asia-Pacific." *Progress in Human Geography* 36 (3): 316–335.
Dongguan Statistical Yearbook. 2018a. "2-5 Temporary Residents and Labor Over Years." Accessed 29 September 2019. http://tjj.dg.gov.cn/website/flaArticle/tjnj/2018/directory/content.html?02-05-0.
Dongguan Statistical Yearbook. 2018b. "14-8 Migrant Population by Town." Accessed 29 September 2019. http://tjj.dg.gov.cn/website/flaArticle/tjnj/2018/directory/content.html?14-08.
Dongguan Statistical Yearbook. 2018c. "2-13 Employed Persons in Urban Areas by Registration Status and Sector (2017)." Accessed 29 September 2019. http://tjj.dg.gov.cn/website/flaArticle/tjnj/2018/directory/content.html?02-13.
Fan, C. Cindy. 2002. "The Elite, the Natives, and the Outsiders: Migration and Labor Market Segmentation in Urban China." *Annals of the Association of American Geographers* 92 (1): 103–124.
Gans, Herbert J. 2007. "Acculturation, Assimilation and Mobility." *Ethnic and Racial Studies* 30 (1): 152–164.
Glick Schiller, Nina, and Ayse Çağlar. 2009. "Towards a Comparative Theory of Locality in Migration Studies: Migrant Incorporation and City Scale." *Journal of Ethnic and Migration Studies* 35 (2): 177–202.
Harvey, David. 2008. "The Right to the City." *New Left Review* 53 (1): 23–40.
Hugo, Graeme. 2003. "Circular Migration: Keeping Development Rolling?" *Migration Policy Institute*, June 1. Accessed 29 September 2019. https://www.migrationpolicy.org/print/4844#.XZFzIDbsbIW.
Jiang, Leiwen. 2006. "Living Conditions of the Floating Population in Urban China." *Housing Studies* 21 (5): 719–744.
Joppke, Christian. 2007. "Transformation of Citizenship: Status, Rights, Identity." *Citizenship Studies* 11 (1): 37–48.
King, Russell. 2002. "Towards a New Map of European Migration." *International Journal of Population Geography* 8: 89–106.

Law, Lisa. 2002. "Defying Disappearance: Cosmopolitan Public Spaces in Hong Kong." *Urban Studies* 39 (9): 1625–1645.

Lawrence, Roderick J. 1995. "Housing Quality: An Agenda for Research." *Urban Studies* 32 (10): 1655–1664.

Lefebvre, Henri. 1996. "The Right to the City." In *Writings on Cities: Henri Lefebvre*, edited by E. Kofman and E. Lebas, 76–115. Oxford: Blackwell.

Lewis, Hannah, Peter Dwyer, Stuart Hodkinson, and Louise Waite. 2015. "Hyper-precarious Lives: Migrants, Work and Forced Labour in the Global North." *Progress in Human Geography* 39 (5): 580–600.

Li, Bingqin. 2006. "Floating Population or Urban Citizens? Status, Social Provision and Circumstances of Rural–Urban Migrants in China." *Social Policy and Administration* 40 (2): 174–195.

Li, Si-Ming, and Yat-Ming Siu. 1997. "A Comparative Study of Permanent and Temporary Migration in China: the Case of Dongguan and Meizhou, Guangdong Province." *International Journal of Population Geography* 3: 63–82.

Macklin, Audrey. 2010. "Freeing Migration from The State: Michael Trebilcock On Migration Policy." *The University of Toronto Law Journal* 60 (2): 315–348.

Mitchell, Don. 2003. *The Right to the City: Social Justice and the Fight for Public Space*. New York: Guilford Press.

Muniandy, Parthiban, and Valeria Bonatti. 2014. "Are Migrants Agents or Instruments of Development? The Case of 'Temporary' Migration in Malaysia." *Journal of Ethnic and Migration Studies* 40 (11): 1836–1853.

Németh, Jeremy, and Stephen Schmidt. 2011. "The Privatization of Public Space: Modeling and Measuring Publicness." *Environment and Planning B: Urban Analytics and City Science* 38 (1): 5–23.

Oldenburg, Ray. 1989. *The Great Good Place: Café, Coffee Shops, Community Centers, Beauty Parlors, General Stores, Bars, Hangouts, and how They Get You Through the Day*. Saint Paul: Paragon House Publishers.

Parreñas, Rhacel Salazar. 2010. "Homeward Bound: The Circular Migration of Entertainers Between Japan and the Philippines." *Global Networks* 10 (3): 301–323.

Parreñas, Rhacel Salazar, Krittiya Kantachote, and Rachel Silvey. 2021. "Soft Violence: Migrant Domestic Worker Precarity and the Management of Unfree Labour in Singapore." *Journal of Ethnic and Migration Studies* 47 (20): 4671–4687. doi:10.1080/1369183X.2020.1732614.

Penninx, Rinus, Karen Kraal, Marco Martiniello, and Steven Vertovec. 2004. *Citizenship in European Cities: Immigrants, Local Politics and Integration Policies*. Aldershot: Ashgate.

Perlmann, Joel, and Roger Waldinger. 1997. "Second Generation Decline? The Children of Immigrants, Past and Present: A Reconsideration." *International Migration Review* 31 (4): 891–920.

Peters, Karin. 2010. "Being Together in Urban Parks: Connecting Public Space, Leisure, and Diversity." *Leisure Sciences* 32 (5): 418–433.

Portes, Alejandro, and Min Zhou. 1993. "The New Second Generation: Segmented Assimilation and Its Variants Among Post-1965 Immigrant Youth." *Annals of the American Academy of Political and Social Science* 530 (November): 74–96.

Price, Marie, and Lisa Benton-Short, eds. 2008. *Migrants to the Metropolis: The Rise of Immigrant Gateway Cities*. Syracuse, NY: Syracuse University Press.

Pun, Ngai, and Jenny Chan. 2013. "The Spatial Politics of Labor in China: Life, Labor, and a New Generation of Migrant Workers." *South Atlantic Quarterly* 112 (1): 179–190.

Robertson, Shanthi. 2014. "Time and Temporary Migration: The Case of Temporary Graduate Workers and Working Holiday Makers in Australia." *Journal of Ethnic and Migration Studies* 40 (12): 1915–1933.

Shaw, Mary. 2004. "Housing and Public Health." *Annual Review of Public Health* 25: 397–418.

Sheller, Mimi, and John Urry. 2006. "The new Mobilities Paradigm." *Environment and Planning A: Economy and Space* 38 (2): 207–226.

Shen, Jianfa, and Yefang Huang. 2003. "The Working and Living Space of the 'Floating Population' in China." *Asia Pacific Viewpoint* 44 (1): 51–62.
Singer, Audrey. 2004. *The Rise of New Immigrant Gateways*. Washington, DC: The Brookings Institution.
Smart, Alan, and Josephine Smart. 2001. "Local Citizenship: Welfare Reform Urban/Rural Status, and Exclusion in China." *Environment and Planning A: Economy and Space* 33 (10): 1853–1869.
Solinger, Dorothy J. 1999. *Contesting Citizenship in Urban China: Peasant Migrants, the State, and the Logic of the Market*. Berkeley: University of California Press.
Song, Hongyang, Mingmin Pan, and Yiyong Chen. 2016. "Nightlife and Public Spaces in Urban Villages: A Case Study of the Pearl River Delta in China." *Habitat International* 57: 187–204.
Sun, Mingjie, and C. Cindy Fan. 2011. "China's Permanent and Temporary Migrants: Differentials and Changes, 1990–2000." *The Professional Geographer* 63 (1): 92–112.
Talen, Emily. 2015. "Do-it-Yourself Urbanism: A History." *Journal of Planning History* 14 (2): 135–148.
Tardiveau, Armelle, and Daniel Mallo. 2014. "Unpacking and Challenging Habitus: An Approach to Temporary Urbanism as a Socially Engaged Practice." *Journal of Urban Design* 19 (4): 456–472.
Waldinger, Roger, and David Fitzgerald. 2004. "Transnationalism in Question." *American Journal of Sociology* 109 (5): 1177–1195.
Wolch, Jennifer R., Jason Byrne, and Joshua P. Newell. 2014. "Urban Green Space, Public Health, and Environmental Justice: The Challenge of Making Cities 'Just Green Enough'." *Landscape and Urban Planning* 125: 234–244.
Wu, Weiping. 2002. "Migrant Housing in Urban China: Choices and Constraints." *Urban Affairs Review* 38 (1): 90–119.
Wu, Weiping. 2004. "Sources of Migrant Housing Disadvantage in Urban China." *Environment and Planning* 36: 1285–1304.
Yang, Xiushi, and Fei Guo. 1999. "Gender Differences in Determinants of Temporary Labor Migration in China: A Multilevel Analysis." *International Migration Review* 33 (4): 929–953.
Ye, Jingzhong, and Pan Lu. 2011. "Differentiated Childhoods: Impacts of Rural Labor Migration on Left-Behind Children in China." *The Journal of Peasant Studies* 38 (2): 355–377.
Yeoh, Brenda SA, and Shirlena Huang. 1998. "Negotiating Public Space: Strategies and Styles of Migrant Female Domestic Workers in Singapore." *Urban Studies* 35 (3): 583–602.
Zhang, L., Simon X.B. Zhao, and J. P. Tian. 2003. "Self-help in Housing and Chengzhongcun in China's Urbanization." *International Journal of Urban and Regional Research* 27 (4): 912–937.
Zhu, Yu. 2007. "China's Floating Population and Their Settlement Intention in the Cities: Beyond the Hukou Reform." *Habitat International* 31: 65–76.
Zhu, Yu, and Wenzhe Chen. 2010. "The Settlement Intention of China's Floating Population in the Cities: Recent Changes and Multifaceted Individual-Level Determinants." *Population, Space, and Place* 16: 253–267.

Consuming the neighbourhood? Temporary highly skilled migrants in Montreal's Mile End

Gabrielle Désilets

ABSTRACT
The neighbourhood of Mile End, in Montreal, Canada, is known to be a transient, multicultural hub, home to successive waves of migrants. It is internationally acclaimed in popular travel blogs and world lists of 'hip' neighbourhoods on the basis of indicators such as number of artists per square kilometre, café culture, and established independent shops. Yet a core of socially involved and rooted residents nurture the village-like vibe of the area. In the past decades, the eastern industrial zone of Mile End has seen a concentration of IT, gaming and film industries rise considerably, especially with the arrival of a large multinational company that brought a significant demographic of mostly affluent professional 20- and 30-something males. Local companies are recruiting temporary high-skilled migrants to respond to a growing demand for various types of designers and programmers. This paper documents the localised everyday life experience of temporary professional migrants' in the neighbourhood. It considers migrants' influence on the revitalisation of the area, and their the impact on the urban culture. Ethnographic data on how temporary migrants' struggle for integration into forms of civic engagement are juxtaposed against their transnational urban lifestyles mostly defined by modes of consumption.

Global economic forces, like environmental disasters and war move people across the globe at an accelerated pace and these features in our newsfeeds everyday. One dimension of international migration we seldom read about is the movements of skilled professionals from one city to another for temporary or longer terms. At a local level, these people, and the industries that employ them, impact urban economies and the lives of the migrants and non-migrants alike. Several authors have examined the consequences of creative cities' policies and the new economy on urban social and spatial fabric (Catungal, Leslie, and Hii 2009; Centner 2008; Rantisi and Leslie 2010; Sprague and Rantisi 2018). These economic forces and the human cost to this mobility are closely tied to the organisation of global labour and 'a "just-in-time" delivery of workers' (Dauvergne and Marsden 2014, 233). In this context, temporary migration, both skilled and unskilled has gained notable importance.

The development of temporary worker programmes has accelerated in post-industrialised nations in the past decades (Dauvergne and Marsden 2014; Chacko and Price 2021).

From 2006 onward, Canada's numbers of immigrants entering on a temporary sojourn outnumbered those entering with a permanent status (Pellerin 2011). High skilled temporary workers are privileged over lower-skilled temporary workers in that their work permits are much less regulated. They are less likely to be separated from their families (having access to work visas for their spouses and access to schools for their children), have more renewal options, and better access to permanent residence (Dauvergne and Marsden 2014). Accordingly, immigration regimes arise that select for an individual's ability to rapidly integrate into the labour market and to create minimal burden on state-sponsored social services. Points systems, which are used in Australia, New Zealand, Canada and the UK, effectively rank prospective migrants according to characteristics that quantify their desirability as workers (Robertson and Runganaikaloo 2014, 2).

Following a neoliberal framework, states and cities must compete internationally to attract highly skilled migrants, encouraging their settlement, while lower skilled migrants are subject to unequal regulatory regimes that insure their return to their home country when labour needs are reduced (Parreñas, Kantachote, and Silvey 2021). Highly skilled migrants are nonetheless affected by migration policies where 'states increasingly using periods of temporariness as a "testing ground" (Rajkumar et al. 2012) during which migrants must perform or accumulate desirable attributes that can grant them extended, repeat or permanent stays' (Robertson 2015, 51–52). On the other hand, being defined by their skills in high demand in multiple locations, these skilled workers are depicted as individualistic 'creative subjects [and] as hedonistic free agents' (Peck 2007, 36 in Catungal, Leslie, and Hii 2009, 1096). In this article, I draw attention to the underlying contradiction between policy discourse on the attraction and retention of talent, and the long-term integration and civic participation of these skilled migrants in Quebec.

Contemporary migration studies have given little attention to the mobility of professionals, to voluntary and privileged migrants and even less so to highly skilled temporary workers. We often take for granted their social 'integration' because they are not considered 'vulnerable' or 'problematic' migrants and are instead considered 'desirable' because they are arguably good for the economy. Immigration policies in countries like Canada, Australia, U.S. and New Zealand have facilitated rather than limited these privileged migrants' rights, such as the right to apply for permanent residency (Rajkumar et al. 2012). In this research, through an examination of highly skilled temporary migrants' place-making practices and representations of place at the scale of the neighbourhood, I seek to shed new light on these migrants' local participation and social integration in the neighbourhood.

This paper seeks to offer a more nuanced picture of the highly skilled migrant experience. The example of working-holiday makers, international students and other 'middling migrants' convey the complexities of categories based on visa statuses, departing country, transition periods, bridge permits and motives for sojourning to a foreign country (Chacko 2021). Based on a case study of highly skilled temporary workers in Mile End, I argue that circular and multi-destination patterns of movement are far more common for an increasing number of people *on the move.*

In line with the papers presented in this special issue, this article seeks to uncover the intricate relationship between the migrants who live with a temporary permit, who act as *temporary* neighbours, and the cities, the neighbourhoods and the communities that compose the everyday urban social fabric (Chacko and Price, 2021). This paper aims to contribute to the discussion on the underlying contradictions of a migration system that favours temporary migration to fill labour market fluctuating cycles of supply and demand, and the need for territorial democracies to welcome temporary migrants as equal citizens (Bauböck 2011).

By looking at the everyday experience of highly skilled temporary migrants working in creative industries in Montreal, this research uncovers these migrants' experience of privilege and of temporality. This experience is accentuated by the transnational, ideological, and material ties that these migrants maintain with other places. Being temporarily *in place*, their posture can be compared to that of tourists, consuming place and transforming it. They are drawn to experiential destinations in which place branding and place marketing are important. In a globalised labour market, professional status and transnational ties influence participants' everyday lives, the way they interact with colleagues, family and friends, near and far, and these relations are marked by temporariness and transience (Robertson 2015). In this context, the city is merely a background for the main focus, which is on work. More specifically, in this article, I explore the relationship between temporariness and the commodification of neighbourhood life. As described by many commentators (Catungal, Leslie, and Hii 2009; Peck 2005) the creative ecosystem of Mile End may have become more about marketing, consumption and real estate development, than about genuine creativity (Peck 2005).

The highly skilled temporary migrants encountered in this research sought out an international and comfortable sense of place in Mile End. Here, cosmopolitanism understood as a means to 'consume' the other (Hannerz 1996) is apparent in the way some of the Mile End's commercial streets have been transformed in the past fifteen years in response to economic development and to the tastes of these new demographics, one that is similar in some ways to the dot-comers described by Centner (2008) in San Francisco. It is time to question the impact of the temporalities of migration regimes on the individuals' experience and on the receiving communities' social dynamics of cohabitation. State policies on migrant selection as well as on the construction of cultural districts (Sprague and Rantisi 2018) 'have inclusionary and exclusionary impacts on different actors' (Catungal, Leslie, and Hii 2009, 1097), and in this case study, have transformed the neighbourhood of Mile End in Montreal from a bohemian multicultural hub to an international global village.

Skilled and privileged temporary migrants: towards a more nuanced approach to 'Middling Migration'

Middling migration is a term that was initially coined by Conradson and Latham (2005) in a special issue of JEMS entitled *Ordinary and Middling Transnationalism* (Conradson and Latham 2005), to identify the mobility of people belonging to the transnational 'middle class', either in the country of departure or of arrival, or both (Smith 2005). What distinguishes these migrants is that they have voluntarily and personally chosen to migrate, often for the purpose of working (and/or studying) abroad, and sometimes in precarious – or temporary – jobs that do not necessarily correspond to the level of qualification or to the social status and class they benefited from in the country of departure. Elaine Ho describes these migrants of the middle as 'self-initiated mobile professionals' (Ho 2011a, 730) or 'self-initiated work migrants' (Ho 2011b). The question of visas categories, residence status or citizenship is decisive in the lived experience of these migrants (Rajkumar et al. 2012). Although most of them originally migrate to work abroad, many of them begin their migration journey with a study visa, hence the importance of considering student mobility in the study of 'middling migration' (Robertson 2011; Robertson and Runganaikaloo 2014; Chacko 2021). Many contemporary authors have written about current trends in the internationalisation of education and about access of a greater number of people to higher education especially in emerging economies (Heiman, Freeman, and Liechty 2012). Unsurprisingly, there is a renewed interest in the social sciences on the emergence of a 'new' global middle class (Donner 2017).

Several studies report the importance of international mobility for people from the 'new' global middle classes, considering new class dynamics in emerging economies (Marsh and Li 2015; Rutten and Verstappen 2014; Rutz and Balkan 2009). In many cases, such as migrants from Eastern Europe studied by Parutis (2014), young Indians studied by Rutten and Verstappen (2014), Singaporeans studied by Ho (2011b), or graduate students from countries of the European Union studied by Kennedy (2010), these migrants' personal trajectories are marked by constraints and opportunities. As Kennedy points out (2010), mobility becomes the preferred way of constructing personal trajectories and the individualisation of pathways, for these young migrants. Thus, job opportunities and career paths are just as important as the desire to travel, to see the world and/or to flee from a life considered too restrictive or lacking in professional advancement opportunities. The terms referring to this class of migrant are varied but include: 'professional migrants', 'nomadic workers' and 'ordinary' middle-class migrants (Conradson and Latham 2005; Kennedy 2004; Scott 2006); 'young global professionals' (Fechter 2007), and 'transnational knowledge workers' (TKWs) (Colic-Peisker 2010).

According to Lasch (1995), professional migrants form a 'new' class because their livelihood does not necessarily rest on property ownership, but on their ability to manipulate information, knowledge and professional expertise.[1] In a Bourdieusian analysis, their status depends on distinction and symbolic capital (Bourdieu 1979). Their investment in education and information as opposed to property, which distinguishes them from the rich bourgeoisie, the ascendency of which characterises an earlier stage of capitalism, and from the old proprietary class that made up the bulk of the population (Lasch 1995, 34). As such, and in contrast to the mostly White Ivy-league educated 'dot-comers' of the internet-based new economy described by Centner (2008), the new class we are referring to here is more varied in terms of its social, ethnic and national origins.

This 'new' class ethos also rests on a willingness and ability to be globally mobile. In this context, mobility has immersed the psyche of people, and in many professional domains, it is now presented as *a passage obligé*: one must move to make it professionally. Yet, as I will demonstrate in this article, there is a human and personal cost to mobility. The mobility of highly skilled temporary migrants is seldom associated as being part of the issues surrounding temporary migration since privileged and voluntarily moving professionals are considered free agents, moving with relative ease and freedom when compared to the trajectories and everyday experience of labour migrants, asylum seekers or undocumented migrants. Following in the footsteps of Robertson (2015) who addresses the importance of the temporal and processual dimension of migration, this article seeks to depart from a binary opposition between disenfranchised low skill workers and highly skilled mobile elite and to draw attention to the wide spectrum of temporary labour migrants. Heterogeneous and multidirectional flows mean people move in increasingly diverse ways, migration is no longer conceived as a one-way linear flow leading to settlement and integration. Categories of 'visitors' and 'sojourners' are more flexible, and transition from one status to another has repercussions – in time – on the perception of 'integration' as much as they have repercussions on forms of identification. As Robertson rightly argues, talking from McHugh: 'individuals who ostensibly have similar trajectories or physical mobility can have differing "place-attachment" and temporal identities – such as being rooted, being suspended or being footloose' (Robertson 2015, 51). Furthermore, these emotions and relations will inevitably change with the passage of time and the scale of analysis.

An ethnography of Mile End

The neighbourhood of Mile End, in Montreal, Canada, has historically seen various waves of immigration since the first settlements in the Saint-Louis du Mile End Parish. The area became the home of a succession of groups from the French-Canadian, British and Irish lower middle classes, and to European migrants that seized the opportunity given by the arrival of the tramway connecting a new residential area to the city centre. In the 1970s, after the exodus of European migrants in response to upward social and spatial mobility to the outer suburbs, the temporary decline of the neighbourhood was again inverted by a first wave of gentrification. This new wave brought students, artists and bohemian middle-class professionals – the 'creative class' described by Florida (2002) – attracted by the revival of the housing market lead by Portuguese migrant entrepreneurs. This means that a blend of Francophones, Anglophones and allophones, Jews, Protestants and Catholics have cohabited with other ethnic and religious minorities in the area since the early twentieth Century (Richard, Rose, and Germain 2015). In the Saint-Viateur East (SVE) district of Mile End, the railway and the textile industry, central to the local economy for decades, also contributed to the movement of workers and people in and out of the area. Today, the central location of Mile End, just a ten-minute bus ride from Montreal's business district, and major universities, is the main hub for students, professionals, visitors and tourists who flock the streets of Mile End all year long.

Cities and neighbourhoods with an industrial past were the theatre of the 'back to the city' (Polèse 2014) movements by creative industries that occurred in the 1980s and 1990s in North America and Europe (Catungal, Leslie, and Hii 2009; Sprague and Rantisi 2018; Centner 2008). The Saint-Viateur East district (SVE) then saw a plethora of artists, architects and designers who seized the opportunity provided by affordable large open space structures left behind by the deindustrialisation of the area. Yet, the revival of the SVE, which has seen the most change in recent years, really began with the arrival of a major player, a multinational video game company. As such, in the past decades, the SVE has seen a concentration of IT, gaming and film industries rise considerably, bringing a significant demographic of mostly affluent professionals, single 20- and 30-something males, also known as Richard Florida's *Creative Class* (2002). The number of jobs exploded twofold in four years, from 7,500 jobs in 2012 to 13,000 jobs in 2016 (Field notes, interview, Ville de Montréal, Arrondissement Plateau-Mont-Royal). The Mile End is now also a hotbed for the Montreal Start-up scene, and most recently an emerging global hub for

AI. The diminishing numbers of traditional artists – who can no longer afford the exploded real estate prices – now sit side by side with well-established internationally acclaimed multinationals in the gaming, entertainment and VFX industries. More so, the young people who move from across the province, from the rest of Canada and from other countries to study at the four established universities, animate the neighbourhood nightlife and underground music scene. This influx of people in an otherwise largely residential area is striking at lunchtime when workers swarm St-Viateur Street in groups of six or seven men eager to find a take-out lunch or restaurant to share a meal while talking business.

Canada's immigration policy now geared towards temporary skilled migrants, local companies are recruiting internationally to respond to a growing demand for various types of designers and programmers which cannot be filled by local talent. I choose to anchor this project in the Mile End because of its reputation as a 'creative ecosystem' in the Montreal Landscape, and because of the strategic position of Montreal in attracting mobile labour in the video game, VFX, and AI industries. The established reputation of Mile End as a creative and artistic hub is further supported by census data that presented the borough of Plateau Mont-Royal, in which the Mile End is located, as the largest concentration of artists per capita in 2006, representing 8 percent of its population (Hill Stratégies Recherche 2006 in Pilati and Tremblay 2007).

The neighbourhood 'branding' and the digitisation of tourism with peer review structures, such as *Airbnb* and similar web platforms, have put Mile End on the world's Top Lists of 'Cool neighbourhoods' to live in (Wisenthal 2016). The flourishing economic activity has also fostered the arrival of successions of art galleries, specialised shops, cafes, restaurants, underground bars and music venues. More recently, traces of mass tourism such as double-decker buses, foodie establishments, craft beer and specially tailored guided walking tours are attracting foreign tourists and workers from across Canada. This influx of people is arguably leading to a new migration wave influencing the transformation of the neighbourhood with raising rent prices pushing small independent shops and low-income residents out of the area.

I sought to better understand the specific experience of migrating to Montreal for work by observing the everyday life of highly skilled migrants in the Mile End. I have integrated into the area to become part of its scenery. I have spent considerable amounts of time observing and recording the comings and goings of people through: naturalistic observations (in cafés, street corners, restaurants, businesses, cafeterias, shops, etc.); conversations with shop owners, municipal representatives and other community groups. I have participated in many networking events for the community, and within the businesses with which I have established collaboration for my project (social events and drinks, public forums, etc.) And I have reviewed traditional and social media focusing on the Mile End. I recorded data on highly skilled temporary migrants' particular lifestyles, and on their modes of mobility and settlement. This fieldwork was juxtaposed and put in perspective of my own personal experience growing up and as a young adult, during the 1990s and 2000s, on the streets, in the parks, and the cafes of Mile End.

The key method and empirical material of this research consists of 20 semi-structured interviews (of an average of 1.5 h each) with skilled temporary migrants working and or living in the neighbourhood and its surroundings. The 20 participants interviewed are highly skilled temporary migrants who work and/or live in the Mile End. They are aged between 26 and 37 (average = 31.5) and come from various countries: seven participants are from France, four from Romania, two from Brazil, and one from each of Sweden, Hungary, Belgium, Italy, Mexico, Colombia and the United States. The sample has a balanced number of men and women (9/7), despite of the overrepresentation of men in the employment sectors covered by this study. Three of the female respondents are the spouses of men who work in the sector and who have accompanied them in their migratory project. Only four participants are single, several have arrived as a couple (12) and there are three families with young children. I asked detailed information about their perceptions and uses of the neighbourhood spaces and about their habits in and around Mile End.

The professionals I met through this research highlighted their preference to live close to their workplace and enjoy an urban lifestyle: the vast majority of participants (18/20) live in the neighbourhood or in the neighbouring areas of the SVE Sector. All participants possessed undergraduate (45%) or graduate (55%) university degrees in their country of departure. Most participants (12/20) did not have French as their mother tongue but spoke English well, and many spoke more than three or four languages. Although French is the official language in the province of Quebec, and is a determinant factor in the selection of immigrants to the province, most of my interlocutors who did not speak French considered it was a lacuna in their experience of Montreal, yet the strong majority asserted that it is not essential to live in the Mile End.

The question of visa categories, status of residence or citizenship is crucial in the everyday experience of migrants. At the time of our interview, 10 participants had temporary status; a closed visa[2] of between one and three years according to the employer's contract, only one person had a working-holiday permit, and one participant had a post-graduate three-year work permit. One participant had a one-year a closed work permit from the French government VIE program. Finally, five participants had recently obtained their permanent residence after sojourning in Canada with a closed work permit and could thus reflect about their recent immigration experiences as temporary workers in the SVE district.

The city as a mere background: temporality and a focus on work

Decades of theorisation on transnationalism, translocal social ties and their impacts on everyday experience now point towards the effects of temporary visa categories on migrant's experience of place and on their position of being and feeling 'in-between', in transition (Oner, Durmaz-Drinkwater, and Grant 2021). For many of the people encountered in this research, the temporariness of their visa status gave them an opportunity 'to try' a life in Canada without having to leave everything behind more permanently. For many, it was an opportunity to try something different and new. The temporary status of their stay also meant they had the opportunity to return to a comfortable middle-class position in the home country if they judged it was a better option for them. For some, this 'fast track' migration facilitated by a temporary employment permit allowed them to initiate their immigration process to Canada.

Roselyn and Edouard, a Romanian couple in their 30s who had recently acquired permanent residence after four years of temporary permits, told me they had started thinking about migrating outside of Romania despite their comfortable professional lifestyle there.

In Romania, they owned an apartment, a car and had jobs that kept them busy until late most nights. Their original plan was to move to another European country, to remain close to their families. They wanted to have 'an international experience' and had also considered Canada. One of their friends had been to Canada on vacations and returned with a tourist magazine and some stories that really sparked their interest. After *Googling* 'immigrating to Canada' they attended a seminar on immigration offered at the Canadian embassy in Bucharest. They realised the procedures were long and complicated and they considered the move to be too risky if they did not have jobs upon arrival. They said they were not willing to compromise their careers and start again from zero.

As an employee of a large multinational video game company, Edouard was working with teams scattered in different countries. When his supervisor suggested a move to Montreal, Edouard and Roselyn saw this opportunity as a sign, one that precipitated their plan to move abroad.

> My manager who was living in France back then told me that there's a new team that was going to be built here. We worked really good together he said if I'm interested … We analysed it for a few weeks, specially the cold I would say. We decided [to move to Canada] in probably three weeks. (Edouard, Romania, Business intelligence, 36 years-old)

The couple said the decision was easy to make. Edouard would be working with the same people, and as an inter-company transferee, he thought he would not have to go through the same arduous process of acculturating to a new company as a newly arrived permanent resident. He said he would be 'living in a bubble because if you work in an international company you get to have like a very good salary and then you get to have medical insurance, so compared to other people I mean we were ok' (Edouard, Romania, Business intelligence, 36 years-old).

Lucas, a 37 years-old Brazilian, also left a comfortable situation in his home country. Lucas was self-employed in Brazil, specialised in advertising with clients all over the world. His wife, a federal lawyer who was still in Brazil at the time of our interview, was about to join him in Montreal. Lucas' immigration project started when he found out about a Montreal based company during a conference in Brazil. He started dreaming of working for them. Since there is no equivalent industry in Brazil, Lucas trained on his own, and worked on his demo reel for a couple of years before sending it to Montreal to see whether the company had an interest in his work. He was hired six months before I met him, as a 3D generalist for that entertainment Media Company located in the Mile End. He had never been to Canada before, and he confessed he would have moved anywhere in the world to work for that company:

> If the company was not here, if it was I don't know, in another country, I would be there, anywhere, China, Hong Kong you know! It is my main motivation for being here. (Brazil, 3D generalist, 37 years-old)

Lucas told me that many of his friends in Brazil were thinking of immigrating to Canada for a better quality of life in terms of personal safety. As a middle class Brazilian, wearing a watch outside is very risky and everyone wears their backpack in the front. The security issue is such that people walk quickly into their homes to avoid an attacker from entering with them. For him, business was good in Brazil and there was no shortage of clients, but he said he was working all the time under stressful conditions. He felt that Canada could offer him a more balanced professional life;

> We had a very good life over there. And for sure, money was not the motivation to come to work here at [the company]
>
> *Q: Because you would get paid more in Brazil?*
>
> Yes, yes, because for example, I earned more money, but on the other hand I had to work a lot, and when you freelance, you have to keep searching, you have to be the businessman, etc. So I was a little bit tired of this. (Lucas, Brazil, 3D generalist, 37 years-old)

Again, like Edouard, Lucas might not have moved to Canada without a job offer. Yet, his move to Montreal was driven by career advancement in specialised projects and by gaining a lighter workload and more personal safety, it was not motivated by a higher salary. This example shows that for many temporary highly skilled migrants, their migration project is not tied to a desire to become part of a new society but instead to develop their professional and international career.

Brett, a 28-year-old American who had been working in Montreal for over two years as a 3D lighting artist had a similar account. He also did not know anything about Montreal prior to moving there for work. He was hired when he was still in school in Florida. He received his NAFTA visa, flew to Montreal on Saturday, and started work on Monday. His first employer paid for his flight and two weeks of furnished accommodation and between his first job and the one he had when we met, he went from one temporary contract to another, having to exit the country to renew his visa each time. He says that in the VFX industry, it is not uncommon to have six months contracts, and there is a very high turnover of employees, especially in entry-level positions. Brett was offered a job in Florida in between contracts but he decided to remain in Montreal for the better quality of life – which for him was shorter commute time by foot or public transport, and no extra payment for health insurance. He chose to stay because Montreal is one of the centres of the VFX industry in North America and has many career prospects. At the time of our interview, and because the NAFTA visa is unrestricted in Canada, he sees no incentives to apply for permanent residency. Although he says he does not go out much, he loves the proximity to work and to shops in Mile End. Brett's professional life, working extensive hours on consistently tight schedules, and his passion for what he does influences his experience in Montreal much more than the setting and neighbourhood life. Again, his motivation is not to become a long term Montrealer, but rather to take advantage of the opportunities offered by the city's booming VFX ecosystem.

In these previous accounts, these migrants benefited from the temporary migration scheme to experience something new without having to commit and spend time and energy in permanent immigration procedures. What gives them this unique opportunity is their in-demand skills and professional experience. In this context, provinces and cities wanting their share of the benefits of immigration tend to have strategies that do not promote migrant welfare or integration (see Dobrowolsky 2011) instead, in the case of Mile End, it is the creation of a predominantly English-speaking 'international' village that is the draw. This is a striking contradiction in the context of Quebec where the command of the French language has dominated the selection criteria for immigration for decades. Furthermore, by being temporary migrants, they spend several years living in-between places, evaluating their different opportunities, and in the meantime, not being fully recognised as political agents neither in the country of departure or of arrival.

Another example of how temporality plays into the trajectories of skilled migrants is Carl, a 26-year-old Belgian who is a Marketing Director for a successful start-up in the Mile End. After three years in Montreal, he is professionally drawn to the Silicon Valley for career advancement, but the coveted H1B visa for highly skilled workers in the United States is difficult to obtain as a European. Carl arrived in Montreal on a working-holiday visa, and then shifted through different visa categories including several closed work permits. He confessed to not really knowing what would be his next move. His family and friends are in Belgium and some in other countries, and at that point, he did not wish to apply for permanent residency in Canada. He lives in the present moment, and he does not know how the three major dimensions of his life will pan out: work, international family life, and financial or real estate investments. He recently committed to something bordering engagement, a one-year gym membership. Carl has always been actively involved in his community at home in Belgium. His father is the mayor of his hometown. His temporary status is a big part of his lack of commitment in Montreal, he gives the impression of still being 'travelling through' Montreal, enjoying his young professional lifestyle of going out to underground bars, barbeques in the parks, weekend brunches and cultural events.

For Edouard, Lucas and Carl, professional and transnational networks take precedence in their everyday life and migration experience to Montreal to the detriment of local ties in local affairs or with longer term or native residents, especially in the earlier days of migration. This distance is negotiated voluntarily or not, and for some people encountered during fieldwork, they still lived and worked as temporary sojourners even after 11 years in Montreal. Carl's example illustrates the importance of transnational and professional ties in his everyday life. Almost each night after work, Carl goes out to professional networking events, to meet people or to entertain clients. During daytime, Carl's routine is punctuated with stories and events of his family members and friends spread across the world with the use of social digital media.

> We have a WhatsApp family group. My little sister is doing an exchange in Chile, my other sister is travelling around the world during a year. My dad takes photos of my mom, of their meals, of drinks with friends. Sometimes my parents Skype with my sister and I, I just connect while I'm at work, I put on my headphones and I chat with them while I work. ([*My translation from French*] Carl, Belgium, Marketing director, 26 years-old)

A characteristic shared by many participants is their consideration of professional life as an integral part of their lifestyle, and this is a common trait among middle-class professionals living in global urban centres. They are career driven; they choose the job or the industry, not the city. They are passionate about their work and their work overlaps with their personal life. In the following section, I analyse how patterns of mobility among highly skilled temporary migrants play out in the type of neighbourhood and the related urban lifestyles they favour, acting as a feedback loop for change at the neighbourhood and street level, towards the construction of an international village such as the Mile End.

Mobility in an international village

With many companies selecting Mile End as a place to grow their businesses, the neighbourhood draws a young hip crowd supporting its reputation as the Hipster capital of Canada (Anonymous 2016). It is burgeoning with restaurants and bars to suit the tastes of the bearded young male professionals and the flocks of incoming tourists. The Mile End is renowned as a foodie hub acclaimed in popular travel blogs because of features such as: number of artists per square kilometre, café culture, and established independent shops. Yet, one element that captures the attention of newcomers and longer residents alike is the fact that a rooted core of residents nurtures the village-like vibe of the area.

Ariane is a 27-year-old French-Portuguese, born and raised in France, who works as a Content Project Manager for a large video game company in the Mile End. She had been in Montreal for over a year when we met and tells me she was hired as part of a France-Quebec government alliance for the mobility of young professionals on a temporary work permit for two years. She came to Montreal with her boyfriend, a French-Italian who has been very active online, finding everything and anything about life and lifestyle around her future workplace. She said that her boyfriend was very attracted to the Mile End after reading so many reviews about it online. Ariane talked to me about the village feel of Mile End:

> The houses are really cute, with the stairs and all, I find it has something of Old Montreal [...] you see, it's like a village, a village in the city, and I find that really nice. ([*My translation from French*] French, VIE France-Quebec internship program, 27 years-old)

One feature of this atmosphere is the fact that many residents tend to remain in the neighbourhood to live, work, shop and seek entertainment. Others have lived in the area for several decades. As such, it is very common to see the same people on the streets, walking their dog or sipping their morning coffee at the same corner, every day. Not only is it often described as a village-like area, it is a place where most participants feel at home. Participants describe the neighbourhood as a place where it is easy to fit-in as a foreigner, it is very 'international'.

Lucas, described above, was also pleased by the welcoming attitude of his next door neighbours in Mile End who came over to introduce themselves and offered to help when he moved in. They invited him to a few house parties where most guests also came from somewhere else, spoke English and little or no French just like him, helping him settle in. For Brett who came from the United States and could stay on a temporary and unrestricted NAFTA visa, it was even a strategic choice to work for a British based company where all communications are in English, avoiding having to learn French for work, for a visa or to live and shop around the Mile End.

Roselyn and Edouard, the Romanian couple introduced earlier reported similar experiences socialising in the Mile End. They never felt like strangers and they mostly hang out with people who have also migrated to Montreal from other countries. Talking more specifically about the array of shops in the area, Roselyn and Edouard said:

> I mean what's a foreigner in Mile-End? I think that there's no country that is not represented in Mile-End. There's a Polish patisserie and the sales woman is Romanian, there the *charcuterie Hongroise* where you have people speaking Romanian and they have Romanian products. I have never felt as an outsider in Canada in general. But especially in Mile-End and Plateau ... (Roselyn)

Not only are people generally very welcoming, the fact that they are immigrants is a valued feature. The presence of many tourists and visitors, the high numbers of domestic and foreign students from the nearby universities, and the migration history of the neighbourhood further make Mile End a place where it is easy to function in the English *lingua franca*, in an otherwise vastly francophone but also bilingual and allophone city. The international tone of the area further relates to the consumer lifestyles and tastes, the everyday habits of the new demographic of the area; the mobile and transient 'middling migrants'. In the Mile End, being 'different' and being from somewhere else is something many people have in common; as such it becomes something to be valued. As Edouard says:

> I never had the feeling of being an outsider that's the cool thing and especially by people who ask you where you're from and you say Romania «oh! I have a lot of Romanian friends. You guys are awesome» and whatever. So, this kind of feedback is really nice. (Edouard, Romania, Business intelligence, 36 years-old)

Anaïs, a French woman of mixed background working in the area on a post-diploma work visa talked about the multiple 'minorities' present in the neighbourhood, rendering it a place to make friends easily as a foreigner. She said it is a place where there are many immigrants and many Anglo-Canadians – a minority group in francophone Quebec – who come from provinces outside Quebec making it a welcoming community:

> You see, I think there is a solidarity of minorities between the immigrants and the Anglos. Between Anglos and non-Quebecers. Put simply, they're like immigrants from the inside. I remember, for many people who migrate like me, maybe I'm wrong but it seems easier to create stable links with non-Quebecer Canadians than with Quebecers. True, true … […] it's easier in the early days to make links with another minority. […] Myself, I have lots of friends from Vancouver and Toronto who are in the same situation of wanting to create bridges. ([*My translation from French*] Anaïs, Post-diploma bridge visa, France, 27 years-old)

Participants talked a lot about the diverse backgrounds of their friends, their openness to new experiences and to diversity (sexual orientation, ethnicity) and their middle-class lifestyle with habits such as eating out in restaurants for dinner, brunch, etc. Roselyn and Edouard further assert their inclination towards cultural diversity by distancing themselves from the Montreal Romanian community they considered too inward looking for their tastes.

> They eat Romanian, they're very religious I mean they go to the church they dress, they speak Romanian. We like to mix it. I think the beauty of being here is the opposite of hanging out with Romanians. (Roselyn)

Carl also mentioned the familiarity and the conviviality of the relationships he has formed with colleagues he met in the Mile End, people who also came from different backgrounds. Yet, very few mentioned friendship ties with locally born Quebecois, further supporting the perception of Mile End as an international village.

> I started to go out a lot and to party with people from (the Company), and startups are very family-like, so … they're all nice people, lots of immigrants too, we get along well, so naturally we become friends. ([*My translation from French*] Carl, Belgium, Marketing director, 26 years-old)

Distinction and consumer lifestyle

As a neighbourhood of transit, where intellectuals, students, middle-class professionals, children of working-class migrants, and now tourists and temporary skilled migrants, distancing themselves from the white, francophone, catholic, Quebecois 'majority' is a practice that defines long term as well as newcomer residents of the Mile End.

As argued in the previous section, the Mile End is described as an international neighbourhood. This qualification is always a red flag in the ears of an anthropologist, relaying ethnicity as less important, and emphasising class and other forms of capital as more defining features in the social fabric. Analysing this data thus led me towards changes in consumption patterns on the main commercial streets in the neighbourhood, reflecting the tastes and habits of the urban dwellers of the area (see Centner 2008). This can be observed through the rapidly growing numbers of design boutiques and franchised stores that are slowly replacing the more traditional ethnic shops, further emphasising the rapid increase in niche tourism that is slowly transforming the Mile End into a 'destination'.

A means to distinguish oneself is through lifestyle and tastes (Bourdieu 1979; Giddens 1991). Many participants share a 'middle class professional' consumer lifestyle, based on similar characteristics to the participants of Germain's (2009) study of individual households in two of Montreal's neighbourhoods. These households were composed of individuals who possessed tertiary qualifications; a certain level of income or socio-economic status; had everyday practices that gave material form to their identity narratives.

Most participants talked to me about their relation to the neighbourhood in some form of consumption, mainly in terms of outings in shops, cafes, restaurants and bars. Jean and Carl, two Frenchmen in their 20s, describe what they do outside of work in the area. Brunch, pub grubs and other lunchtime meals are evoked and they appreciate the variety and diversity of cuisines in the area. In their scarce free time, people talked about going out to top-rated restaurants and bars, speciality shops, visiting the city and its surroundings:

> In our free time, which is mostly weekends [...] we go to the cinema, to the restaurant, to bars... we try to find a good brunch and we go to places our friends recommend [...] we visit, discover the neighbourhood, parks nearby. ([*My translation from French*] Jean, France-Germany, Community developer, 33 years-old)

In Germain's article (2009) there is a clear relation between consumer lifestyles, habits and behaviours as tied to certain professions or types of industries located in specific neighbourhoods. I argue here that there is a link between the Mile End's creative industries, and the 'global work' structure in which they are embedded. Further, global middle-class ethos relate to the temporality and the international mobility that characterise the lifestyles of the temporary migrants encountered in this research. In such a context, little attention is given to local politics and civic participation.

Anaïs, whose trajectory was introduced above, talked at length about political participation and contemporary circular migrations criticising the French 'expatriates'[3] in Montreal, a group she has originally been a part of until she realised her desire and need to break into local French Quebecois circles. She said she was eager to find more permanent, anchored relationships and to have a better grasp of the city in which she had been living for some years. She explains her frustrations of not knowing about the political system, about the inner workings of institutions, and the meaningful micro-social details that take time to learn, especially when one remains within newcomers' networks. She thinks that this lack of local knowledge of the immigrant contributes to the 'distance' one can feel towards long-term residents. Talking about the reasons why she decided to stay away from her former French friends and to try making long term local friends, she says:

> It's better. Yeah! You're always on that second level of society, always on a parallel to reality. Oh, Ok! Interesting. Or you're also at a level of consumption, let's say [...] I have friends like that, it's ... a French friend ... I find that her relation to the territory and to society is a rapport of consumption. ([*My translation from French*] Anaïs, France-Guadeloupe, project coordinator, 27 years-old)

Returning to the notion of temporality, Anaïs describes how her approach to being in Montreal has changed over time. As she suggested in an earlier quote, while she found it easier in the beginning to socialise with other migrants or 'minorities' like Anglo Canadians and French newcomers in Mile End, she has grown more and more critical of what she calls the 'expat culture',

> I had already lived this migratory reality ... I call it 'expat' in France. In Europe we call it the Erasmus culture, that was established with the Erasmus Network, European Union in Schengen in the 90's, I think ... 80's-90's ... a student system to allow exchanges [...] but what you consume, it's very experiential. ([*My translation from French*] Anaïs, France-Guadeloupe, project coordinator, 27 years-old)

Temporality and the position in-between has consequences for the migrants who risk being positioned as visitors, remaining like transient tourists for years – never fully recognised as legitimate social agents. It further has profound effects on the local communities, especially in the neighbourhood of Mile End, a former socially diverse immigrant suburb that has been transformed into what some commentators called a *Hipster Disneyland*, a growing trend in several post-industrialised urban centres across the world (Maly and Varis 2016; Michael 2015; Schiermer 2014). Carl's experience of Mile End reflects this reality as he describes the hipster culture as something he likes and something he was aware of because of online data he could gather prior to coming to Montreal.

> Mile-End is a bit between two vacant lots. I feel kind of drawn to that, I like street art, so ... [...] [In my memories] the Mile-End was the Hipster place where I wouldn't have wanted to live right away ... In my head, I felt more Plateau. Mile-End was nice, but just for brunch! [...] but I started going out on Saint-Viateur and started to understand the cultural side. How the traditional culture got *hipsterized* into a fashion about everything, bagels, Olympico Café that hasn't changed, that still has Italian football player posters on the walls. Why is it hot? [...] The whole VICE thing started here and then, the fact that there are Jews, it reminds me of Brooklyn which is still the cool neighbourhood in New York. Here, it's the same thing. It's cool to navigate between the ancient and the new and to get different visions of things. ([*My translation from French*] Carl, Belgium, Marketing director, 26 years-old)

As Carl's account shows, there is a feedback mechanism between, global trends and lifestyles, global labour and globally mobile professionals. The high numbers of transient people in Mile End shape the type of sojourn they experience, and in turn, transform the place.

Conclusion

This article aimed at providing an empirical dimension to the global economic forces and industries that favour temporary and mobile labour in a neoliberal context. While much work has been done on the fate of lower skilled temporary workers, looking at highly skilled temporary workers and similar 'Middling migrants' sheds new light on the implication of this kind of mobility on the everyday lives of migrants themselves, who remain afloat, distanced from the communities in which they live temporarily, sometimes for decades. But also importantly, this case study highlights the need for researchers to pay closer attention to the impact of the temporality of sojourners, for this 'just in time' labour, on cities and on the specific neighbourhoods in which temporary 'talents' settle.

Developed under three themes: *temporality*, *mobility* and *consumer lifestyles*, the data presented in this article shows how transnational ties and professional status influence the everyday experience of the participants encountered in this research. Personal relationships are marked by temporariness and transience, and the city and neighbourhood are merely a background for the main focus on work, sometimes to the detriment of other spheres of their lives like personal and family time. Highly skilled migrants' experience in the Mile End is thus influenced by the multiplicity of individual migrant trajectories present on site.

Heterogeneous, multidirectional and circular migration flows mean people move in increasingly diverse ways, and migration can no longer be conceived as a one-way linear flow leading to settlement and integration. Categories of 'visitors' and 'sojourners' are more flexible, and transition from one status to another has repercussions – in time – on perception of 'integration' as much as they have repercussions on migrants' forms of identification. Juxtaposed against the migration history of Mile End, complex flows have created an internationally flavoured and comfortable place where my participants find many like-minded people and, experiencing relatively minimal precarity despite their temporary status. Yet, the analysis cannot forgo the consumerist dimension of cosmopolitanism expressed by the participants' lifestyles and taste for diversity. Their presence, along with that of global tourists, has modified the commercial streets and residential market, leading to exclusionary dynamics affecting the very diversity on which the reputation of the neighbourhood was formed.

Migration literature has focused on issues of settlement and integration. Temporary migration literature has, in turn stressed the importance of including temporary migrants as equal citizens. In the context of the attraction and retention of desirable highly skilled migrants, it is timely to question the impact of the temporalities of migration regimes on the individual's experience and on the receiving communities' social dynamics of cohabitation. On one hand, highly skilled and highly mobile temporary migrants risk suffering from social disconnection and isolation, from a lack of place-based belonging. But more so, a more important mass of temporary disconnected sojourners may increase the already important social and political disengagement at the heart of some of the social tensions and fears of immigration to urban settings.

Memories, routines and habits are formed over time. It takes many encounters and contacts with local shop owners, neighbours, community centres receptionists and library clerks to create bridges and community. How can temporary migrants negotiate community and engagement, participation and social inclusion in the city, and should they? Considering the data presented here, should highly skilled temporary migrants be given equal citizen rights despite what could be interpreted as a lack of involvement in public affairs and citizenship? Shouldn't economic development policies geared towards the attraction of highly skilled workers also consider the high mobility of this demographic and their lack of long term investment in the society? While these questions exceed the scope of this paper, researchers and urban policy makers as well as community activist should pay closer attention to the way consumer lifestyle and consumption-driven experience of place, combine with the notion of temporality, constrict the type of experience people have in one locale, rendering the city and its longer-term inhabitants as a mere background.

Notes

1. Again, referring to Richard Florida's Creative Class (2002).
2. A closed visa means that the visa holder is tied to a fixed-term contract with a specific employer and has to exit the country to renew the visa if there is any change to the employment contract.
3. For a discussion of the 'expatriate' as a migrant category see (Cranston 2017; Désilets 2015).

Disclosure statement

No potential conflict of interest was reported by the author(s).

References

Anonymous. 2016. "The 15 Coolest Neighbourhoods in the World in 2017." In 2016. How I Travel. Meet the World's Most Interesting Travelers.

Bauböck, R. 2011. "Temporary Migrants, Partial Citizenship and Hypermigration." *Critical Review of International Social and Political Philosophy* 14 (5): 665–693. doi:10.1080/13698230.2011.617127.

Bourdieu, P. 1979. *La Distinction: Critique sociale du jugement.* Paris: Les éditions de minuit.

Catungal, J. P., D. Leslie, and Y. Hii. 2009. "Geographies of Displacement in the Creative City: The Case of Liberty Village, Toronto." *Urban Studies* 46 (5-6): 1095–1114. doi:10.1177/0042098009103856.

Centner, R. 2008. "Places of Privileged Consumption Practices: Spatial Capital, the Dot-Com Habitus, and San Francisco's Internet Boom." *City and Community* 7 (3): 193–223. doi:10.1111/j.1540-6040.2008.00258.x.

Chacko, Elizabeth. 2021. "Emerging Precarity Among International Students in Singapore: Experiences, Understandings and Responses." *Journal of Ethnic and Migration Studies* 47 (20): 4741–4757. doi:10.1080/1369183X.2020.1732618.

Chacko, Elizabeth, and Marie Price. 2021. "(Un)Settled Sojourners in Cities: The Scalar and Temporal Dimensions of Migrant Precarity." *Journal of Ethnic and Migration Studies* 47 (20): 4597–4614. doi:10.1080/1369183X.2020.1731060.

Colic-Peisker, V. A. L. 2010. "Free Floating in the Cosmopolis? Exploring the Identity-Belonging of Transnational Knowledge Workers." *Global Networks* 10 (4): 467–488.

Conradson, D., and A. Latham. 2005. "Transnational Urbanism: Attending to Everyday Practices and Mobilities." *Journal of Ethnic and Migration Studies* 31 (2): 227–233.

Cranston, S. 2017. "Expatriate as a 'Good' Migrant: Thinking Through Skilled International Migrant Categories." *Population, Space and Place, n/a-n/a*, doi:10.1002/psp.2058.

Dauvergne, C., and S. Marsden. 2014. "The Ideology of Temporary Labour Migration in the Post-Global era." *Citizenship Studies* 18 (2): 224–242. doi:10.1080/13621025.2014.886441.

Désilets, Gabrielle. 2015. "'Third Culture Kids' as Serial Migrants' Children: Understanding Some of the Impacts of a Highly Mobile Transnational Upbringing." In *Migration, Diversity and Education: Beyond "Third Culture Kids"*, edited by Saija Benjamin and Fred Dervin, 143–162. London: Palgrave Macmillan.
Dobrowolsky, A. 2011. "The Intended and Unintended Effects of a New Immigration Strategy: Insights From Nova Scotia's Provincial Nominee Program." *Studies in Political Economy* 87 (1): 109–141. doi:10.1080/19187033.2011.11675022.
Donner, H. 2017. "The Anthropology of the Middle Class Across the Globe." *Anthropology of This Century* 18). http://aotcpress.com/.
Fechter, Anne-Meike. 2007. *Transnational Lives: Expatriates in Indonesia*. Aldershot: Ashgate.
Florida, R. 2002. *The Rise of the Creative Class: and how It's Transforming Work, Leisure, Community and Everyday Life*. New York: Basic Books.
Germain, A. 2009. "Le Quartier au Coeur du Mode de vie des Ménages Solos Dnas la Ville Centrale." In *Habiter Seul, un Nouveau Mode de vie?*, edited by A. G. Johanne Charbonneau and Marc Molgat, 199–217. Québec: Presses de l'Université Laval.
Giddens, A. 1991. *Modernity and Self-Identity: Self and Society in the Late Modern Age*. Redwood City: Stanford University Press.
Hannerz, U. 1996. *Transnational Connections: Culture, People, Places*. London: Routledge.
Heiman, R., C. Freeman, and M. Liechty. 2012. *The Global Middle Classes: Theorizing Through Ethnography*. Santa Fe: SAR Press.
Ho, E. L.-E. 2011a. "Identity Politics and Cultural Asymmetries: Singaporean Transmigrants 'Fashioning' Cosmopolitanism." *Journal of Ethnic and Migration Studies* 37 (5): 729–746.
Ho, E. L.-E. 2011b. "Migration Trajectories of 'Highly Skilled' Middling Transnationals: Singaporean Transmigrants in London." *Population, Space and Place* 17 (1): 116–129. doi:10.1002/psp.569.
Kennedy, Paul. 2004. "Making Global Society: Friendship Networks among Transnational Professionals in the Building Design Industry." *Global Networks* 4 (2): 157–179.
Kennedy, P. 2010. "Mobility, Flexible Lifestyles and Cosmopolitanism: EU Postgraduates in Manchester." *Journal of Ethnic and Migration Studies* 36 (3): 465–482.
Lasch, C. 1995. *The Revolt of the Elites and the Betrayal of Democracy*. New York: Norton.
Maly, I., and P. Varis. 2016. "The 21st-Century Hipster: On Micro-Populations in Times of Superdiversity." *European Journal of Cultural Studies* 19 (6): 637–653. doi:10.1177/1367549415597920.
Marsh, L. L., and H. Li. 2015. *The Middle Class in Emerging Societies: Consumers, Lifestyles and Markets*. New York: Taylor and Francis.
Michael, J. 2015. "It's Really not hip to be a Hipster: Negotiating Trends and Authenticity in the Cultural Field." *Journal of Consumer Culture* 15 (2): 163–182. doi:10.1177/1469540513493206.
Oner, Asli Ceylan, Bahar Durmaz-Drinkwater, and Richard J. Grant. 2021. "Precarity of Refugees: The Case of Basmane-İzmir, Turkey." *Journal of Ethnic and Migration Studies* 47 (20): 4651–4670. doi:10.1080/1369183X.2020.1732591.
Parreñas, Rhacel Salazar, Krittiya Kantachote, and Rachel Silvey. 2021. "Soft Violence: Migrant Domestic Worker Percarity and the Management of Unfree Labour in Singapore." *Journal of Ethnic and Migration Studies* 47 (20): 4671–4687. doi:10.1080/1369183X.2020.1732614.
Parutis, Violetta. 2014. "'Economic Migrants' or 'Middling Transnationals'? East European Migrants' Experiences of Work in the UK." *International Migration* 52 (1): 36–55.
Peck, J. 2005. "Struggling with the Creative Class." *International Journal of Urban and Regional Research* 29 (4): 740–770. doi:10.1111/j.1468-2427.2005.00620.x.
Pellerin, Hélène. 2011. "De la migration à la mobilité : changement de paradigme dans la gestion migratoire. Le cas du Canada." *Revue Européenne des Migrations Internationales* 27 (2): 57–75.
Pilati, T., and D.-G. Tremblay. 2007. "Le Développement Socio-économique de Montréal: La Cité Créative et la Carrière Artistique Comme Facteurs D'attraction?" *Canadian Journal of Regional Science/Revue Canadienne des Sciences Régionales* XXX (3): 475–496.
Polèse, M. 2014. "Why (Some) Downtowns Are Back: Lessons From the Urban Resurgence." *City Journal* (Winter). http://www.city-journal.org/2014/24_1_downtowns.html.

Rajkumar, D., L. Berkowitz, L. F. Vosko, V. Preston, and R. Latham. 2012. "At the Temporary–Permanent Divide: how Canada Produces Temporariness and Makes Citizens Through its Security, Work, and Settlement Policies." *Citizenship Studies* 16 (3-4): 483–510. doi:10.1080/13621025.2012.683262.

Rantisi, N. M., and D. Leslie. 2010. "Materiality and Creative Production: The Case of the Mile End Neighborhood in Montréal." *Environment and Planning A: Economy and Space* 42 (12): 2824–2841. doi:10.1068/a4310.

Richard, M., D. Rose, and A. Germain. 2015. "Les trajectoires contrastées des banlieues de l'immigration de la région montréalaise." In *Travailler et cohabiter: l'immigration au-delà de l'intégration*, edited by S. Arcand and A. Germain, 145–169. Québec: Presses de l'Université Laval.

Robertson, S. 2011. "Cash Cows, Backdoor Migrants, or Activist Citizens? International Students, Citizenship, and Rights in Australia." *Ethnic and Racial Studies* 34 (12): 2192–2211. doi:10.1080/01419870.2011.558590.

Robertson, Shanthi. 2015. "The Temporalities of International Migration: Implications for Ethnographic Research." In *Social Transformation and Migration: National and Local Experiences in South Korea, Turkey, Mexico and Australia*, edited by Stephen Castles, Derya Ozkul, and Magdalena Arias Cubas, 45–60. London: Palgrave Macmillan UK.

Robertson, S., and A. Runganaikaloo. 2014. "Lives in Limbo: Migration Experiences in Australia's Education–Migration Nexus." *Ethnicities* 14 (2): 208–226. doi:10.1177/1468796813504552.

Rutten, M., and S. Verstappen. 2014. "Middling Migration: Contradictory Mobility Experiences of Indian Youth in London." *Journal of Ethnic and Migration Studies* 40 (8): 1217–1235.

Rutz, Henry, and Erol M. Balkan. 2009. *Reproducing Class: Education, Neoliberalism, and the Rise of the New Middle Class in Istanbul.* New York: Berghahn Books.

Schiermer, B. 2014. "Late-modern Hipsters." *Acta Sociologica* 57 (2): 167–181. doi:10.1177/0001699313498263.

Scott, Sam. 2006. "The Social Morphology of Skilled Migration: The Case of the British Middle Class in Paris." *Journal of Ethnic and Migration Studies* 32 (7): 1105–1129.

Smith, M. P. 2005. "Transnational Urbanism Revisited." *Journal of Ethnic and Migration Studies* 31 (2): 235–244. doi:10.1080/1369183042000339909.

Sprague, M., and N. M. Rantisi. 2018. "Productive Gentrification in the Mile-Ex Neighbourhood of Montreal, Canada: Exploring the Role of the State in Remaking Urban Industrial Clusters." *Urban Research and Practice*, 1–21. doi:10.1080/17535069.2018.1448109.

Wisenthal, M. 2016. "Montreal's Mile End may just be the coolest 'hood' in Canada: Maybe even cooler than Portland." *Life Travel.* http://www.theloop.ca/8-reasons-why-mile-end-may-be-the-coolest-hood-in-canada/.

Promising precarity: the lives of Dublin's international students

Mary Gilmartin, Pablo Rojas Coppari and Dean Phelan

ABSTRACT
There has been a considerable growth in the number of international students in Dublin, Ireland. In this paper, we first explore the broader context for this growth, showing the ways in which international student migration to Dublin has been facilitated, and the consequences in terms of the creation of different categories of international student migrants. We then discuss the experiences of international student migrants in Dublin by focusing on precarity and promise. We use Lorey's tripartite understanding of precarity (2015. *States of Insecurity: Government of the Precarious*. London: Verso) to show how international student migrants in Dublin experience legal precarisation, economic precarity and personal precariousness. This is, we argue, mitigated by promise (Ahmed 2010. *The Promise of Happiness*. Durham: Duke University Press), as international student migrants seek to navigate their way through precarity in place. The paper offers important insights into the complexity of international student migration, based on the lived experiences of migrants themselves.

Introduction

The number of international students, defined as 'those who have crossed borders for the purposes of study' (OECD 2013, 1), is significant. In 2011, the OECD estimated that there were around 4.3 million students enrolled in tertiary education outside their country of citizenship, with around 40 per cent studying in European countries (OECD 2013, 1–2; European Migration Network 2012, 10–11). These numbers have increased considerably since 2000 (King and Raghuram 2013, 128), driven by the complex interplay between structural forces such as neoliberal reform and globalisation (Beech 2017) and individual migrant aspirations (Carling and Collins 2018).

There is a growing awareness of, and attention to, the recent increase in international student numbers and its broader implications. One broad body of research focuses on the internationalisation of higher education, with institutions of higher education increasingly encouraged to act on a global scale through the recruitment of international students (see Gürüz 2011; Beech 2018; Kehm and Techler 2007). Another body of research emphasises mobility capital, specifically how international students hope to, or actually, benefit from time spent studying abroad, whether this benefit is academic, economic, social and/or cultural (Brooks and Waters 2013; Findlay et al. 2012; King and Raghuram 2013; Madge, Raghuram, and Noxolo 2015; Murphy-Lejeune 2002; Park 2011; Prazeres 2013; Van Mol and Timmerman 2014). Despite this growing attention, there are also recognised gaps in our knowledge of international student migration. There is uneven spatial coverage of the phenomenon, with the situation in some countries (e.g. the UK, the US, Australia and Canada) well documented and analysed, while less attention is paid to other countries. There is no standard global definition of 'international' or 'foreign' student and, consequently, no reliable source for 'statistical data on international flows of foreign students' (Prazeres 2013, 809). Equally, there is no standard definition of 'student', and so the focus of research tends to be on degree or credit mobility (King and Raghuram 2013, 129). This misses out on a range of other types of international student migration, of which migration related to less formalised language education is particularly important. Across all categories of international student migrants, there are gaps in our understanding of people's lived experiences. As Raghuram points out, student migrants are 'not easily categorisable as students alone' (2013, 140–141): they are also workers, family members, activists, locals. The emphasis on study thus serves to minimise other aspects of the lives of international students. It obscures key ways in which international students are embedded in, affected by, and influence, the places where they study and live.

In this paper, our focus is on international students in Dublin, Ireland. From our experiences of living and working in Dublin, we recognised that international student migration to Ireland and Dublin has clearly increased in recent years. This was in part a response to broader governmental and place-based initiatives (Department of Education and Skills 2010, 2016; Gebhardt 2011). The visible effects of international student migration included a growth in the number and size of language schools, an increased international student presence in universities and colleges, and international students working in public-facing sectors such as retail and restaurants. However, while the issue of international student migration has been addressed in policy-related research (see, for example, Finn and O'Connell 2012) and mentioned in more general accounts of migration to Ireland (see, for example, Gilmartin 2015), specific studies of the experiences of international students are limited and tend to focus on university students (Dunne 2009; O'Connor 2017; O'Reilly, Ryan, and Hickey 2010; Sheridan 2011). Our work with Migrant Rights Centre Ireland (MRCI), a migrant-focused non-governmental organisation, indicated that international students in Ireland were facing considerable challenges, many of which were not captured in policy or academic research. In particular, MRCI records clearly showed that many international students in Ireland were experiencing difficulties in relation to work and to their migrant status. While the presence of international students was visible in Dublin, their embodied experiences of living and working in the city were mostly hidden.

The main aim of this paper is to make the experiences of international students in Dublin visible, paying particular attention to how international students experience and respond to the difficulties they face. In the first section, we investigate the specific context of Ireland. We analyse the conditions under which international student migration to Ireland increased in recent years, paying particular attention to the different types of migrants and the legal frameworks that enabled and restricted their migration and their lives. In the second section, we provide a detailed discussion of the lived experiences of international student migrants in Dublin, Ireland. In doing so, we draw from in-depth interviews with international student migrants and associated professionals to discuss their embodied experiences in Dublin, particularly as they negotiated a rapidly changing legal and policy framework. We frame our discussion of embodied experiences through the lens of precarity (Lorey 2015) and promise (Ahmed 2010; Park 2011). Precarity is a defining characteristic of the lives of international student migrants. For international students, precarity extends beyond employment to take three key forms – legal, economic, and personal – that intersect in place in specific ways. In this section, we show how precarity is grounded for international students in Dublin. However, the lives of international students are not just marked by precarity, but also embody promise. We therefore also discuss how promise offers a way of navigating through precarity in place. We conclude with an assessment of the relevance of the embodied experiences of international students in Dublin, Ireland – what we call promising precarity – for our understanding of contemporary migration.

International student migration to Ireland

In 2017, the Irish Minister for Education and Skills, Richard Bruton, launched Ireland's second *International Education Strategy*. This strategy covers the period from 2016 to 2020; the first covered the period from 2010 to 2015. The first strategy had, as its key objective, that Ireland would become a world leader 'in the delivery of high-quality international education' (Department of Education and Skills 2010, 29). By the time the second strategy was published, the objective had become a vision for international education, namely 'to support Ireland to become internationally recognised for the development of global citizens through our internationalised education system and a market leader in attracting international student talent'. In both strategies, increasing the number of international students in Ireland is seen as crucial, in part because of their considerable value to the Irish economy (Department of Education and Skills 2016, 20).

The definition of international student in Ireland requires some consideration. In general, students from other European Economic Area (EEA) countries are not defined as international. Instead, international students are understood as from outside the EEA, studying in Ireland for a period of at least three months. This includes both those who are required to get a student visa in advance of arriving in Ireland (e.g. from China and India) and those who have a visa waiver (e.g. from the US, Malaysia, Canada and Brazil). The Irish Naturalisation and Immigration Service (INIS) provides data on annual student visa applications, and these are shown in Table 1. Between 2011

Table 1. Irish Study Visa Applications.

Year	Number of applications	Number granted	Grant rate (%)
2011	5412	4741	87.6
2012	7790	6939	89.1
2013	10,850	9099	83.9
2014	12,348	10,462	84.7
2015	11,882	10,343	87.0
2016	11,984	10,072	84.0

Source: INIS 2013; Personal communication with INIS 2017.

and 2016, there was a 112 per cent increase in the annual number of study visas granted. In 2016, the first year for which this data is available, around 65 per cent of the visas issued were for 'Long Stay D visas', which cover stays of over three months.

The definition of student in Ireland also requires some attention. International students in Ireland generally study in three sectors: higher (tertiary) education; further (post-secondary) education; and (English) language education. The last publicly available audit of international student migrant stock in Ireland dates to March 2009, when it was estimated that there were 34,557 people registered: 38.82 per cent in higher education; 26.01 per cent in further education; and 30.02 per cent in the English language sector (Department of Justice and Equality 2009). An answer to a parliamentary question in 2014 suggested that there were around 36,000 non-EEA students in Ireland: 40 per cent of whom were degree students, and 38 per cent of whom were language students. However, these figures were described as a 'snapshot' and 'not reliable' by the Minister, Frances Fitzgerald (Fitzgerald 2014). The uncertainty over numbers is also visible in the Department of Education and Skills' recent report (2016, 50–57), which relied on a survey to capture data on English language students, and does not distinguish between EEA and non-EEA students. Comprehensive statistics are also not available in relation to where international student migrants live. However, the Higher Education Authority (HEA) calculates that of the 16,169 full-time students enrolled in publicly funded third-level institutions in 2015–2016, 8,455 (52.3 per cent) were in the Dublin region (HEA 2016). Of the 130 institutions that are recognised for the purposes of granting student visas, 78 (60 per cent) are in Dublin (INIS 2017). This clearly shows the concentration of international students in the city of Dublin and its hinterland.

The international student regime in Ireland is managed through a system of legal requirements. At the most basic level, some international students are required to get a student visa in advance of arrival in Ireland, and all international students are required to register with the Garda National Immigration Bureau (GNIB) shortly after arrival. In order to get a visa, be allowed into Ireland, and to register with GNIB, a potential international student has to provide a letter of acceptance from a recognised education provider, proof of payment of the entire course fee, evidence of monetary support of between €3000 and €7000 for stays of over 6 months, and evidence of private medical insurance (Finn and O'Connell 2012, 30). At this point, international students are given a Stamp 2 in their passport, which entitles them to work for up to 20 h a week for 7 months of the year, and for up to 40 h a week for 5 months. Their time as Stamp 2 holders does not count for the purposes of citizenship. Additionally, they have no family reunification rights, and they do not have access to public funds.

This straightforward description of the current international student regime in Ireland masks its volatility in recent years. Moves to change the international student regime began in 2010, when an Interdepartmental Committee made suggestions for a 'new immigration regime for full-time non-EEA students' (Department of Justice and Equality 2010). The recommendations of the Interdepartmental Committee were underpinned by a belief that the existing regime was leading to wide-scale abuse by both students and education providers, described as 'disreputable colleges … [and] students who do not attend their classes' (Department of Justice and Equality 2010, 2). Following on from this report, a number of significant changes were introduced. Key changes are listed in Table 2.

Table 2. Key changes to the International Student regime in Ireland, 2011–2017.

Date	Change
1 January 2011	New time limits
1 April 2011	New funding requirements on first registration
19 November 2012	Doubled fees for an immigration certificate of registration
January 2015	Changes to Student Work Concession
1 October 2015	Changes to the holiday entitlements of language students
January 2016	New list of eligible programmes
	Reduction in permission for language students (from 1 year to 8 months)
June 2017	Changes to Third-Level Graduate Programme

While these are all significant changes, the January 2015 amendments to the Student Work Concession have created particular difficulties. The so-called Student Work Concession was first introduced in 2001 (Finn and O'Connell 2012, 36) as part of a broader strategy to make Ireland attractive to international students. Initially, students were permitted to work up to 20 h a week during term time, and 40 h a week outside term time. This changed in January 2015, and students are now only permitted to work 40 h a week during specific periods of the year: from May to August, and from 15 December until 15 January. The stated reason for the change was to 'align the work concession with the traditional academic year' (Department of Education and Skills and Department of Justice and Equality 2014, 12). Of course, few international students in Ireland study under these traditional academic structures, so this change has created further difficulties for students in terms of what is legally possible for them in Ireland.

Volatility in relation to international student migration policy has been a feature in many countries in recent years, such as the UK, Australia, Canada and the US (Mavroudi and Warren 2013; Sá and Sabzalieva 2018). In Ireland, language students – over a third of all international student migrants according to the Minister – have been the particular target of these recent changes, with new hierarchies of international students emerging, and favoured treatment for those studying for postgraduate and undergraduate degrees. However, even with these hierarchies, international students in Ireland occupy an uneasy position: encouraged to come to the country but marginalised on arrival. As a consequence, their experiences are often marked by precarity. In the next section, we turn to the issue of precarity in the lives of international students. We begin by developing our understanding of precarity, and then show how precarity offers insights into the lived experiences of international student migrants in Dublin, Ireland.

Precarity and international student migrants

The question of precarity has received considerable attention from social scientists in recent years. Guy Standing defines the 'precariat' as workers who lack access to a range of forms of labour security, such as employment, job and income security (2014, 17–18). Standing clearly states that migrants are a large share of the global precariat (2014, 153–159). Anderson (2010) develops the relationship between precarious work and modern migration, noting that immigration regimes are crucial for creating precarious workers, while Chacko and Price (2021) underscore the fluctuations in precarity experienced by temporary workers over time. Precarity has also been discussed in relation to the specific circumstances of international student migrants. Standing identifies student mobility as one of the key features of modern migration (2014, 153–159), though he does not address the forms of precarity experienced by international student migrants. In her discussion of international students in Australia, Robertson shows the complex identities of international students and highlights their 'extended precarity' as they seek more permanent forms of status, which in turn leaves them more vulnerable to labour exploitation (Robertson 2013; 2015). Precarity was highlighted by Susan Thomas (2017) in her ethnographic study of indebtedness among Indian students at a US university and by Chacko (2021) in her study of integration and precarity of international students in Singapore. While discussions of international student mobility often highlight experiences at work – particularly the transition from study to work – this can ignore the complexity of international students' subject positions (King and Raghuram 2013), and the multiple ways in which they might experience precarity.

From our perspective, the precarious – broadly defined – offers a productive way to consider the experiences of international students. Our starting point comes from Isabell Lorey, who defines precarity as 'a category of order that denotes social positionings of insecurity and hierarchization' (in Puar 2012, 165). In a later publication, Lorey expands on her understanding of precarity, distinguishing between its three forms: precariousness, precarity, and (governmental) precarisation (Lorey 2015). Precariousness, Lorey writes, is an existential state, the common form of human existence. Precarity creates differentiations and hierarchies in this existential state. As Lorey describes it, 'the precariousness shared with others is hierarchized and judged, and precarious lives are segmented' (Lorey 2015, 21). Precarisation is a form of governance that relies on the destabilisation of employment, and of the conduct of life (Lorey 2015, 13). This approach moves beyond precarity as outcome to focus on the process of precarisation, including its politicisation, thereby offering an alternative approach to considering the lives of international student migrants.

We chose to research the issue of precarisation in Dublin because of the significant concentration of international students in the city. We did so through in-depth qualitative interviews with current and former international students in Dublin and with people who worked in the international student industry. We focused on recruiting participants from four leading countries of origin – China, Brazil, United States and Venezuela – with a range of education experiences (language schools, further education and higher education). Participants were recruited through personal contacts and through gatekeepers, including MRCI. Information about interviewees is provided in Table 3. Additionally,

Table 3. Overview of interviewees.

Code	Name	Country of origin	Gender	Description
01HEChina	Li	China	Male	Student – Higher education
02HELSChina	Mei	China	Female	Student – Higher education and language programme
03LSBrazil	Joao	Brazil	Male	Student – Language programme
04LSBrazil	Adriana	Brazil	Female	Student – Language programme
05LSVenezuela	Sofia	Venezuela	Female	Student – Language programme
06LSBrazil	Paulo	Brazil	Male	Student – Language programme
07FEHEBrazil	Daniel	Brazil	Male	Student – Further education and higher education
08HEUS	Amy	United States	Female	Student – Higher education
01PROFIreland	Patrick	Ireland	Male	International student recruitment
02PROFLSIreland	Alan	Ireland	Male	Teacher – Language programme
03PROFLSIreland	Maria	Ireland	Female	Teacher – Language programme

we sought to interview professionals working in related services. We recruited professionals through personal contacts and through cold-calling companies. The interviews were semi-structured in order to allow interviewees to describe their social worlds, opinions and experiences in their own words, while providing room for them to raise issues and concerns that we might not have otherwise considered. We conducted the interviews in English, in sites chosen by the interviewees, which ranged from office spaces to public cafes. All interviews were audio-recorded and later transcribed and thematically analysed. In total, we interviewed eight current or former students and three professionals, with each interview lasting for a minimum of 90 min.

Through our analysis of the interviews, we identified three key ways in which the precarious is experienced. The first is legal precarisation, relating to immigration status. The second is economic precarity, relating to the cost of studying and living in Dublin, and the difficulties in finding decent work. The third is what we call personal precariousness: the ways in which precarity affects the 'intimate spheres' of people's lives (Robertson 2015, 942), such as relationships, health and wellbeing. We first show how insecurity and hierarchization permeate each of these interconnected aspects of the lives of international students in Dublin, and then offer an alternative reading that focuses on promise and hope.

Legal precarisation

The legal regime in Ireland, particularly its volatility, was a source of considerable anxiety for the students we interviewed. Drawing from Lorey, we describe this as legal precarisation, because it is a form of governance that destabilises the lives of international students in Dublin. The changes to time limits, introduced in January 2011 (Table 2), created considerable difficulties for existing students. These changes drew distinctions between students based on their programme of study. People studying for degrees were permitted to stay in Ireland for a maximum of seven years, while people studying at language schools or on non-degree programmes could stay in Ireland for a maximum of three years. The second changes, introduced in January 2016, reduced the time that language students could remain in Ireland from three years to two years. Joao, from Brazil, told us that laws were changing too quickly and too often. 'I think since I arrived here they must have changed like five times .... That's hard, because you can't plan your future like that', he said. Sofia, a language student from Venezuela, who said that legal changes had made her future uncertain, also raised the issue:

> If you renew before October, you can get one year, but after, not. And ... if I would renew it will be February, so after October, it's just for 8 months. That's what I'm not sure if I'm going to stay in Ireland. I'm not sure.

Adriana, from Brazil, also highlighted the legal changes, telling us:

> I'd say like there are lots of girls complaining that they don't know what they are going to do now with the new laws, because they really want to stay, but having only eight months and not being able to work for most of the time is going to be hard for them.

While Joao and Sofia emphasised the time limits on visa for non-degree and language students, Adriana raised another important legal change. When the Student Work

Concession was changed in January 2015, it created difficulties for people who were relying on employment income to fund their studies and living expenses. These significant structural changes to the international student regime have thus created conditions of legal precarity. To an extent, this was recognised in the Student Probationary Extension scheme, which was introduced by the Department of Justice and Equality after the new time limits came into force in January 2011. This scheme allowed students who were affected by the changes in time limits to register for an additional two-year probationary period. However, there were no such concessions in relation to changes to the work concession though, as Adriana pointed out, those changes were also creating significant problems for students living in Ireland.

Adriana, when we met her, was concerned that the recent legal changes would lead to an increase in the number of international students who become undocumented. Certainly, the experience of the Migrant Rights Centre Ireland (MRCI) suggests that this is a pressing issue. In the period between 2013 and 2016, MRCI assisted 956 people who had moved to Ireland as students and subsequently became undocumented. The main countries of origin were Mauritius, Brazil, China, Venezuela and Pakistan, and a considerable proportion were unemployed. While none of the people we interviewed were undocumented at that time, many spoke about their fear of losing their status in the future, or of periods in the past where their status was uncertain. In some instances, these fears were linked to the structural changes to the student regime. In other instances, people were not directly affected by the structural changes, but they expressed profound concerns about their future or recounted stories of previous insecure status. Mei, a Chinese woman, had moved to Dublin to study at a higher education institution. She failed her course, which meant she was no longer eligible for a student visa. Though not legal, she used personal contacts to obtain a student visa for a language course, and managed to get the visa renewed without meeting the attendance requirement. Others spoke about the ways in which they manipulated the attendance requirement for language schools so as to maintain their right to a visa. This included sharing information about schools and teachers who were lax in their approach to attendance, or immigration officials who bent rules, or how to pay for additional language courses in order to appear to meet the requirement (see also Pan 2011). While people told us these stories from the vantage point of a more secure legal status, the fear they experienced was still present, if less immediate. Daniel, for example, told us about his anxiety over the expiry of his GNIB registration before he was able to secure his status on a graduate scheme. His educational institution told him not to worry, that it 'would be fine', but he said he was 'really concerned':

> I was getting distracted, and I was getting sort of, I don't know, I just, I didn't, I barely, I didn't really feel any motivation to work or do anything, so it kind of took over most of my thoughts during those days.

For Daniel, anxiety over his legal status spilled over into all aspects of his everyday life, showing how legal precarisation and economic precarity are closely interconnected.

Economic precarity

There is an extensive literature that links migration and economic precarity. This literature pays particular attention to migrant experiences at work and as workers, through sectoral concentration, poor pay and conditions, and vulnerability to exploitation (see Anderson 2010; Lewis et al. 2015), often in global cities (Wills et al. 2010). However, despite a recognition of the importance of work in the lives of international students (Raghuram 2013), their experiences as workers are often relegated to their experiences as students. Instead, discussions of work tend to highlight post-study careers, whether these are in the country of study as part of the search for a more secure legal status, or in the country of origin (Collins et al. 2017; Findlay et al. 2012; Van Mol 2014; Waters 2009).

In Dublin, as elsewhere, research that deals specifically with the experiences of international students as workers is limited. The small body of research that focuses explicitly on international students in Ireland is effectively silent on the topic of work (Dunne 2009; O'Connor 2017; O'Reilly, Ryan, and Hickey 2010; Sheridan 2011). A small number of exceptions provide some insights into this aspect of the lives of international students. In her research on workers in low-skilled service industries in Dublin – catering, cleaning and security – McPhee found that many moved to Dublin using student visas (McPhee 2016). Smith's research with au pairs found that many had come to Ireland on student visas and became au pairs 'due to the lack of employment options and the need to finance their studies and stay' (Smith 2015, 173). Pan's ethnographic study with Chinese student migrants in Dublin showed they often worked in service industries with a reputation for exploitation of staff (Pan 2011, 278). Data from MRCI shows that, of the people they assisted in the period from 2013 to 2016 who had first entered Ireland as students, 22.5 per cent worked in the food and accommodation sector, 16.2 per cent in the retail sector, and 9.6 per cent in the care sector (25.8 per cent were unemployed at the time they approached MRCI). These sectors – such as hospitality, retail and care – are particularly open to worker exploitation (see MRCI 2012a, 2012b, 2015a, 2015b). This evidence suggests that 'student-workers' (Collins 2018) in Dublin, like their counterparts in Australia, New Zealand and Denmark, are vulnerable at work and may be taken advantage of (Campbell, Boese, and Tham 2016; Collins 2018; Wilken and Dahlberg 2017).

Difficulties at work in Dublin were a common story among the people we spoke to. Sofia's first job was in a bakery, and she told us:

> [I]t was a really really bad experience, because I didn't know and I didn't sign a contract. And after that, after one month and a half, the place just closed, and I didn't receive any money, any payment.

While she expressed positive sentiments about her next job, which was in the restaurant industry, it was clear from her description of the job that her conditions of employment were not ideal. For example, when asked if she knew her hours of work in advance, she said that her employers did a weekly roster, but 'if the place was busy, they ask you to work more'. She did not get any additional pay for these additional hours, but was just paid at the regular hourly rate. Adriana told us about her cleaning job with an agency. Having worked there for a year, she asked for holidays at Christmas. In response, her employer let her go 'with no further reasons or justifications or anything'. Some people worked illegally: for cash in hand payments, or for more hours than permitted, putting them at risk of contravening their work concession. Most of the people who worked had irregular hours which, if they were attending a language school, made it difficult for them to maintain the required attendance level and hold down their job. When

Joao, from Brazil, started working four hours a day, he had to miss two hours of his class. As he said, 'there was not a lot I could do because I had to work to live here. I had to earn money.' People found ways around not having the required level of attendance (Pan 2011, 269). Overall, though, it is difficult to balance attendance requirements with precarious work, which intensifies the experiences of economic precarity of international students in Dublin.

Economic precarity is related to the types of work available to international students in Dublin, but also to the cost of living in the city, which includes the cost of studying and of legal compliance. When Joao said that he needed to work to live in Ireland, he mentioned why:

> I had to save money to renew the visa, to buy the course, I have to buy insurance, well, insurance comes with the course in the school

At the language school Joao attended, his six-month course cost €800, and he also had to pay another €300 for a new GNIB registration. Adriana also mentioned how the cost of GNIB registration had increased, from €60 when she first arrived in Ireland, to €300 today. For Paulo, also, the cost of studying was a burden. He talked about a rapid increase in fees for a degree course that he started but did not finish: from €3200 in the first year to €3900 in the second year, an increase of almost 22 per cent. The cost of studying and GNIB registration created, in effect, an economic trap for international students in Ireland. Their ability to work depended on having a study visa; the cost of studying meant that they had to work and, in the process, jeopardised their status as students. The cost of living in Dublin, particularly housing, was also an issue for many of the people we met. Migrants are particularly vulnerable in the current housing crisis in Dublin, because they are concentrated in the mostly unregulated private rental sector (Kitchin, Hearne, and O'Callaghan 2015; Gilmartin 2015). This was evident in the stories people told us about their experiences of finding and retaining a place to stay. Living in overcrowded accommodation was common. Mei told us that she shared a two-bedroom apartment with four other people. Joao stayed in a studio apartment that he shared with five other people:

> It was a tiny, tiny place. I paid €180. But there was a condition. There was 1 bed like … a double bed, and I had to sleep two weeks in the double bed and two weeks on the mattress on the floor … . So that's what I did. Just to save some money.

While some students availed of on-campus accommodation, it too was considered expensive. Amy, from the United States, said that it cost over €8,000 a year to stay in a campus apartment, 'and it's only going up'.

While our initial interest was in the experiences of international students at work in Dublin, our research also uncovered another related form of economic precarity. This was experienced by people working in education industries, in particular those involved in English language teaching. It was difficult to find people in the English language industry to talk to us, which we initially thought was connected to the recent exposure of rogue language schools, described by Alan as 'dodgy schools and visa factories'. The small number of professionals who agreed to talk to us showed us that economic precarity was not restricted to international students, but was also experienced by many of those who taught them. Maria, an experienced English language teacher with postgraduate qualifications, said 'security of employment is an absolute joke'. Maria also drew attention to the different treatment of native and non-native English teachers, describing what she saw as 'definite exploitation' in terms of pay, regardless of skills or ability. While the issue of casualisation in Irish universities has come under critical scrutiny (Courtois and O'Keefe 2015), this has not been the case for the English language industry. Instead, when attention is focused on the English language industry, it tends to be framed as a source of potential reputational damage to broader internationalisation efforts. The extent to which both workers and students in the industry are open to exploitation is conveniently ignored.

Personal precariousness

While legal and economic precarity were clearly present in the embodied experiences of international students and teachers in Dublin, this was not sufficient to capture the range of ways in which people experienced, and articulated, their everyday lives. In our analysis of interview data, we also encountered a third, interlinked form of precarity that we describe as personal. This includes the types of 'intimate' issues identified by Robertson in her discussion of international students in Australia: romantic relationships, having children, and ease of general mobility (Robertson 2015, 942). However, our understanding of personal precariousness is broader, and also includes the 'messy complexity of emotions' experienced and expressed by international student migrants (Boccagni and Baldassar 2015, 76).

Many of the people we spoke to mentioned relationships. In some instances, people had been able to secure their status in Ireland because of a romantic relationship – including marriage and de facto relationships. This caused anxiety, particularly for some of the women we met. Adriana had got married to her Irish husband and, because of this, was granted a Stamp 4 visa. Yet she clearly struggled with the marriage and what this meant for her. She told us:

> It was mixed feelings. It was good for jobs but I remember kind of thinking about him and saying ok, this is strange, everybody will think I got married because of the passport and you know the advantage of working full time. This is bad.

For Adriana, marriage affected her sense of self in two key ways. The first was that it affected her sense of independence. Rather than being fully self-reliant, she was dependent on another person to secure her legal status and to improve her economic status. This is because, as a language student, she had no other clear options for making her immigration status more permanent. The second was that she was very concerned with how her marriage would be perceived by others. In particular, she felt that she would be perceived as dishonest, marrying only for legal status. While she insisted this was not the case, she repeated that she had 'mixed feelings' a number of times during the interview.

Others struggled with relationships, though often individualised this struggle. For example, Li spoke about linguistic and cultural differences that affected his everyday experiences in Ireland, mentioning the 'language barrier' and describing his English as 'too bad' to pick up jokes. Daniel told us that it was hard for him to even try to be in a relationship, for two reasons. The first is that he thought there was a general level of indifference or hostility to people of his nationality, saying 'they are tired of Brazilians and that's obvious'. In his direct experience, this had led to him being rejected because of his nationality, though this contrasts with the Brazilians and Latin Americans interviewed by Marrow (2013), who commented on favourable treatment in Ireland. The second was that he thought that people would doubt his sincerity and his motives, similar to Adriana's concerns. He said this affected his self-esteem, and how he approached people, making him much more cautious and reticent.

While relationships were an important part of the discussions we had with many international students, the question of the future surfaced in all the interviews, whether with students or professionals. Recent research on international migrants has emphasised the need to use temporal perspectives for the study of migration and mobility (Collins and Shubin 2015; Robertson 2016; Robertson and Ho 2016). Collins and Shubin, for example, caution against understanding migration through a conventional life-course approach, which 'overemphasizes individuals' capacity to manage time as an objective, external entity that leads to particular endpoints' (2015, 103). Certainly, research on international student migration is often concerned with those endpoints: qualifications, social and economic capital, cosmopolitanism (Brooks and Waters 2013). Yet for those involved in international student migration, the future is less certain, and a source of considerable anxiety. Sofia, who was affected by the changes in time limits for language schools, was sure that she did not want to return to Venezuela, saying: 'things there are awful .... It's like in Cuba now'. However, she was very unsure about what her life would bring. She said she wanted to go elsewhere, and when we asked her where, said 'I really would like to go to United States. ... I would like but I'm not sure yet .... Or maybe Spain.' Daniel also spoke about this, telling us that 'I don't really know what's going to happen .... So it's just a scary possibility I think'.

Daniel and others expressed their concerns as anxiety and as fear. Lorey suggests that the distinction between the two – between abstract anxiety and concrete fear – is becoming more blurred in an era of increasing precarisation. While personal precariousness is an integral part of the human condition, processes of legal and economic precarisation intensify anxiety and fear. For international students, this is experienced through a lack of ability to plan for or indeed imagine the future. This is also the case for many of those who teach them, since precarisation is not just experienced by students. As Maria said:

> That can be really hard in the short term but also in the long term in terms of making plans and things like that. So it's a real struggle because so many teachers that I know ... are happy to do things like extra Masters programmes for professional development, but they're either not given the opportunity or discouraged from doing it.

Like their international students, many teachers also experience precarity, in 'an industry that doesn't seem to take itself seriously and is not taken seriously by anyone else' (Maria).

Promising precarity

The intersections of legal, economic and personal precarisation and precarity lead to challenging embodied experiences for international students in Dublin. In this situation, the uncertainty that results from temporary legal status, and its consequences for other aspects of students' lives, is often explained away in terms of hope and aspirations. Hope and aspirations take many forms (see Carling and Collins 2018). For international students, they could be related to improved educational or professional qualifications – proficiency in English, or postgraduate training, or relevant work experience. They could also be related to citizenship status, described by Robertson as 'the promise of citizenship' (2015, 942). Hope, in this context, co-exists with anxiety, in what Boccagni and Baldassar describe as an emotional experience for migrants, characterised by 'the simultaneity of attraction and hope for the better life conditions achievable abroad, alongside the anxiety and distress that meeting these expectations entails' (Boccagni and Baldassar 2015, 76).

In our discussion of precarisation and precarity, we have prioritised anxiety and distress. But the embodied experiences of international students encompass positive experiences as well. We want to return to hope and to what Sara Ahmed has called promise. Ahmed focuses on the promise of happiness which also involves 'being intimate with what is not happy' (2010, 31). As Ahmed points out, migrants are often corralled into performing a specific role in order to confirm their belonging. They are, she writes, 'bound by the happiness duty [which] for migrant means telling a certain story about your arrival as good, or the good of your arrival' (2010, 158). We take inspiration from Ahmed's broader characterisation of promise as 'an expression of desire; … an indication of something favourable to come' (2010, 30). While this, like hope, appears to be a future-oriented perspective, it relies also on an orientation towards the past. Inspired by Durkheim, Ahmed insists that 'our history, our arrival, involves moments of fortune and misfortune, [and] hope is an orientation toward such past moments as the relativity of fortune' (2010, 182). Rather than removing anxiety and replacing it with hope or promise, Ahmed argues instead for an intimacy *between* hope and anxiety, a form of 'hopeful anxiety' (2010, 183). This is possible even under conditions of precarisation. As Lorey points out,

> Living and working in precarious conditions, therefore, does not just mean being exposed to the unforeseeable, to insecurity, being able to make long-term plans and being exploitable specifically for this reason. Beyond this, in dealing with contingency, the possibility arises at the same time of being able to leave and start something new: the potentiality of exodus and constituting. (Lorey 2015, 104–105)

The international students we met embodied this potentiality. For some, this was expressed in the good of arrival, as in the case of Joao. As a gay man, he said his decision to move to Dublin was motivated by wanting to be able to fall in love. He said, 'I came to do that, to be able to be a person, the person that I am.' Yet this individualising narrative masks the extent to which Joao relied on communities of solidarity to do this. His move to Dublin was facilitated by financial help from friends and family; he got work in Dublin through Brazilian contacts, and often worked more than permitted hours; he was able to renew his visa despite not having the required level of attendance; and his Irish boyfriend loaned him money so that he could pay for the visa. A few months after we met, he planned to apply for a different visa on the basis of his de facto relationship with his boyfriend, which would allow him to work without restrictions. Therefore, while legal precarisation was creating insecurity for Joao, he was able to constitute alternative experiences through community in place. In fact, for a number of the people we met, the possibility of starting something new was enabled when they were able to change status, most often because of de facto or other relationships.

Another form of potentiality was evident through acts of disobedience (Lorey 2015, 105). These included minor legal transgressions, such as not having the required levels of attendance, working excessive hours, or working informally like Mei, who said

'Chinese people maybe if they have a small job, just need you a couple of hours, they will bring you to there and pay you cash in hand.' For others, precarisation led them to organise and resist. Adriana and Daniel had been working in a voluntary capacity with migrant support organisations. Maria had been working with colleagues in her language school to improve their pay and conditions, and they had just managed to have five paid sick days introduced. When the bakery at which Sofia worked closed without warning, she and her colleagues sought help from other organisations and people, and campaigned for the pay they were owed. As she said, 'It was a bad experience but at the same time it was a good experience because I really met really good people.' The solidarity that emerged through social interaction, both in organising and in everyday lives, led many international students and their teachers to speak with affection for their lives and friends in Dublin. Some people described online communities, for example Facebook groups for Brazilians or Venezuelans in Dublin, as a helpful source of information and support both before and after arrival. Others commented favourably on diversity in Dublin, on the relationships they had been able to develop in the city, and on the ways in which they had been able to make the city navigable. As Paulo told us, 'It's been a great experience to be here.'

Conclusion

International students are an important part of everyday life in Dublin, and their presence has shaped the city in a variety of ways. Despite this, their experiences as residents of Dublin are often obscured. Drawing on in-depth interviews with international students and professionals, and on the work of MRCI, a migrant-supporting NGO, this paper makes the lived experiences of international students in Dublin visible. We found that the concepts of precarisation and precarity – which have legal, economic and personal implications – provide useful insights into the everyday lives of international students in Dublin. We showed the extent of legal precarisation in relation to international student migrants in Ireland, and how this has created hierarchies that range from the more privileged higher education students to the less privileged language students. Data from the MRCI and from our interviews highlighted the embodied effects of legal precarisation on international students in Dublin, and how this translated into economic precarity. The intersection of legal and economic insecurity created difficult conditions, with people caught in the double bind have having to work to pay for study, but needing to study in order to be able to work. This was intensified in Dublin, because of the very high cost of living, particularly housing, in the city. As a consequence, we showed how international students were vulnerable to exploitation – by employers and by landlords. This meant that many worked illegally, in difficult conditions, and often lived in overcrowded accommodation. Paying attention to these experiences shows how everyday life in Dublin rests on the exploitation of vulnerable groups such as international students, who are often forced to tolerate their exploitation out of necessity. This, in turn, affected their sense of personal precariousness. The international students we interviewed expressed this in terms of the barriers they experienced in forming romantic relationships and, more forcefully, in the effects of precarity on their ability to plan or imagine their futures. This is intensified because time spent as a student visa holder does not count towards citizenship in Ireland.

However, we also highlighted the possibilities of precarisation as not just an all-encompassing reality, but also as a site with the promise of 'the small sabotages and resistances of precarious everyday life' (Lorey 2015, 118). We describe this as promising precarity: the lives of international students, as evident in the case of Dublin, are marked by precarity, but these difficulties and anxieties are tempered to some degree by promise, as international students make the city navigable through experiences, relationships and communities. We emphasise precarity because of the specific circumstances that international student migrants encounter, but we recognise how it is co-constituted by promise and/or desire.

Our focus on precarisation, precarity and precariousness – the tripartite division articulated by Lorey – offers an important insight into contemporary migration. Too often, research on migration is fragmented and dichotomised (King 2012). Similarly, research on precarity emphasises work, though the impacts of precarity extend way beyond work to other dimensions of people's lives, shaping their current and future experiences. In this paper, we have considered the everyday lives of international student migrants living in Dublin from the perspective of the precarious. We show the multiscalar intersections of migration and the precarious: specifically the state-level legal and policy changes that frame the process of precarisation; how this leads to economic precarity as an outcome, intensified in the context of Dublin; and how this results in experiences of personal precariousness for migrants living in Dublin, both now and in relation to their future plans. Our emphasis on the precarious, broadly defined, illustrates the complex experiences of international student migrants in Dublin as migrants, as students, as workers, as activists and as social beings, who shape the city by their presence. This complexity also illustrates the possibilities for promise and hopeful anxiety in providing alternatives to governmental precarisation, through the alliances made by those who are framed as merely precarious, but who live alternative, fuller lives.

Disclosure statement

No potential conflict of interest was reported by the author(s).

References

Ahmed, Sara. 2010. *The Promise of Happiness*. Durham: Duke University Press.

Anderson, Bridget. 2010. "Migration, Immigration Controls and the Fashioning of Precarious Workers." *Work, Employment and Society* 24 (2): 300–317.

Beech, Suzanne. 2017. "International Student Mobility: A Critical Overview." In *Vol. 10: Labouring and Learning*, edited by T. Skelton, J. Waters, and T. Abede, 285–303. Singapore: Springer.

Beech, Suzanne. 2018. "Adapting to Change in the Higher Education System: International Student Mobility as a Migration Industry." *Journal of Ethnic and Migration Studies* 44 (4): 610–625.

Boccagni, Paolo, and Loretta Baldassar. 2015. "Emotions on the Move: Mapping the Emergent Field of Emotion and Migration." *Emotion, Space and Society* 16: 73–80.

Brooks, Rachel, and Johanna Waters. 2013. *Student Mobilities, Migration and the Internationalization of Higher Education*. London: Palgrave Macmillan.

Campbell, Iain, Martina Boese, and Joo-Cheong Tham. 2016. "Inhospitable Workplaces? International Students and Paid Work in Food Services." *Australian Journal of Social Issues* 51 (3): 279–298.

Carling, Jørgen, and Francis Collins. 2018. "Aspiration, Desire and Drivers of Migration." *Journal of Ethnic and Migration Studies* 44 (6): 909–926.

Chacko, Elizabeth. 2021. "Emerging Precarity Among International Students in Singapore: Experiences, Understandings and Responses." *Journal of Ethnic and Migration Studies* 47 (20): 4741–4757. doi:10.1080/1369183X.2020.1732618.

Chacko, Elizabeth, and Marie Price. 2021. "(Un)Settled Sojourners in Cities: The Scalar and Temporal Dimensions of Migrant Precarity." *Journal of Ethnic and Migration Studies* 47 (20): 4597–4614. doi:10.1080/1369183X.2020.1731060.

Collins, Francis L. 2018. "Keeping Bodies Moving: Hope, Disruption and the Possibilities of Youth Migration." *Journal of Intercultural Studies* 39 (6): 626–641.

Collins, Francis L., Kong Chong Ho, Mayumi Ishikawa, and Ai-Hsuan Sandra Ma. 2017. "International Student Mobility and After-Study Lives: The Portability and Prospects of Overseas Education in Asia." *Population, Space and Place* 23 (4), doi:10.1002/psp.2029.

Collins, Francis L., and Sergei Shubin. 2015. "Migrant Times Beyond the Life Course: The Temporalities of Foreign English Teachers in South Korea." *Geoforum* 62: 96–104.

Courtois, Aline, and Theresa O'Keefe. 2015. "Precarity in the Ivory Cage: Neoliberalism and Casualisation of Work in the Irish Higher Education Sector." *Journal for Critical Education Policy Studies* 13 (1): 43–66. Accessed 6 July 2017. http://www.jceps.com/archives/2458

Department of Education and Skills. 2010. Investing in Global Relationships: Ireland's International Education Strategy 2010–2015. Accessed 24 May 2017. http://www.educationinireland.com/en/publications/irelandpercentE2percent80percent99s-international-education-strategy-2010-15.html

Department of Education and Skills. 2016. *Irish Educated, Globally Connected: An International Education Strategy for Ireland, 2016*–2020. Accessed 24 May 2017. https://www.education.ie/en/Publications/Policy-Reports/International-Education-Strategy-For-Ireland-2016-2020.pdf

Department of Education and Skills and Department of Justice and Equality. 2014. Regulatory Reform of the International Education Sector and the Student Immigration Regime. Policy Statement. Accessed 10 July 2017. http://www.justice.ie/en/JELR/Pages/publications-immigration-and-asylum?opendocument&start=0&year=2014

Department of Justice and Equality. 2009. "Non-EEA Student Statistics". Accessed 22 August 2017. www.justice.ie/en/JELR/Pages/Ahernpercent20topercent20overhaulpercent20studentpercent20immigration percent20regime

Department of Justice and Equality. 2010. "New Immigration Regime for Full-Time Non-EEA Students". Accessed 27 June 2017. http://www.justice.ie/en/JELR/Pages/Non-EEA-Students

Dunne, Ciarán. 2009. "Host Students' Perspectives of Intercultural Contact in an Irish University." *Journal of Studies in International Education* 13 (2): 222–239.

European Migration Network. 2012. *Immigration of International Students to the EU: EMN Synthesis Report*. Accessed 27 June 2016. http://emn.ie/cat_search_detail.jsp?clog=1&itemID=2547.

Findlay, Allan M., Russell King, Fiona M. Smith, Alistair Geddes, and Ronald Skeldon. 2012. "World Class? An Investigation of Globalisation, Difference and International Student Mobility." *Transactions of the Institute of British Geographers* 37 (1): 118–131.

Finn, Mairéad, and Philip J. O'Connell. 2012. *Immigration of International Students to the EU: Ireland*. Dublin: ESRI.

Fitzgerald, Frances. 2014. Written Answer, Dáil Debates, 17 July 2014. Accessed 27 June 2016. https://www.kildarestreet.com/wrans/?id=2014-07-17a.1608&.

Gebhardt, Dick. 2011. *Peer Review on Developing and Promoting Dublin as an International Student City*. Brussels: Eurocities. Accessed 4 July 2017. http://classof2020.nl/wp-content/uploads/2016/06/Peer-review-on-developing-and-promoting-Dublin-as-an-international-student-city-2011-Eurocities.pdf.

Gilmartin, Mary. 2015. *Ireland and Migration in the Twenty-First Century*. Manchester: Manchester University Press.

Gürüz, Kemal. 2011. *Higher Education and International Student Mobility in the Global Knowledge Economy*. 2nd ed. Albany: State University of New York Press.

HEA. 2016. *Full-Time Enrolments by Domicilary, 2015–2016*. Accessed 4 July 2017. http://hea.ie/statistics-archive/

INIS. 2013. Statistics on Visas for Non-EEA students. Accessed 4 July 2017. http://www.inis.gov.ie/en/INIS/Pages/Statisticspercent20onpercent20Visaspercent20forpercent20Non-EEApercent20Students

INIS. 2017. Interim List of Eligible Providers, 14 March 2017. Accessed 4 July 2017. http://www.inis.gov.ie/en/INIS/Pages/Interimpercent20Listpercent20ofpercent20Eligiblepercent20Programmespercent20-percent20ILEP.

Kehm, Barbara M., and Ulrich Techler. 2007. "Research on Internationalization in Higher Education." *Journal of Studies in International Education* 11 (3/4): 260–273.

King, Russell. 2012. "Geography and Migration Studies: Retrospect and Prospect." *Population, Space and Place* 18 (2): 134–153.

King, Russell, and Parvati Raghuram. 2013. "International Student Migration: Mapping the Field and New Research Agendas." *Population, Space and Place* 19: 127–137.

Kitchin, Rob, Rory Hearne, and Cian O'Callaghan. 2015. *Housing in Ireland: From Crisis to Crisis.* NIRSA Working Paper No. 77. Maynooth: NIRSA. Accessed 7 July 2017. https://www.maynoothuniversity.ie/social-sciences-institute/working-papers.

Lewis, Hannah, Peter Dwyer, Stuart Hodkinson, and Louise Waite. 2015. "Hyper-Precarious Lives: Migrants, Work and Forced Labour in the Global North." *Progress in Human Geography* 39 (5): 580–600.

Lorey, Isabell. 2015. *States of Insecurity: Government of the Precarious.* London: Verso.

Madge, Clare, Parvati Raghuram, and Patricia Noxolo. 2015. "Conceptualising International Education: From International Student to International Study." *Progress in Human Geography* 39 (6): 681–701.

Marrow, Helen B. 2013. "In Ireland 'Latin Americans are Kind of Cool': Evaluating a National Context of Reception with a Transnational Lens." *Ethnicities* 13 (3): 645–666.

Mavroudi, Elizabeth, and Adam Warren. 2013. "Highly Skilled Migration and the Negotiation of Immigration Policy: Non-EEA Postgraduate Students and Academic Staff at English Universities." *Geoforum* 44: 261–270.

McPhee, Siobhán. 2016. "'Finding Their Way': The Negotiation of the City by Low-Skilled Service Sector Migrant Workers in Dublin." *Urban Geography* 37 (3): 396–415.

MRCI. 2012a. *Who Cares? The Experiences of Migrant Care Workers in Ireland.* Dublin: MRCI. Accessed 7 July 2017. http://www.mrci.ie/wp-content/uploads/2012/12/Who-Cares-The-experience-of-Migrant-Care-Workers-in-Ireland-Nov-2012.pdf.

MRCI. 2012b. *Part of the Family: The Experiences of Au Pairs in Ireland.* Dublin: MRCI. Accessed 7 July 2017. http://www.mrci.ie/wp-content/uploads/2012/10/PartofTheFamily.pdf.

MRCI. 2015a. *All Work and Low Pay: The Experiences of Migrants Working in Ireland.* Dublin: MRCI. Accessed 7 July 2017. http://www.mrci.ie/wp-content/uploads/2015/11/MRCI-All-Work-and-Low-Pay.pdf.

MRCI. 2015b. *Migrant Workers in the Home Care Sector: Preparing for the Elder Boom in Ireland.* Dublin: MRCI. Accessed 7 July 2017. http://www.mrci.ie/wp-content/uploads/2015/09/Migrant-Workers-in-the-Home-Care-Sector-Preparing-for-the-Elder-Boom-in-Ireland.pdf.

Murphy-Lejeune, Elizabeth. 2002. *Student Mobility and Narrative in Europe: The New Strangers.* London: Routledge.

O'Connor, Sinéad. 2017. "Problematising Strategic Internationalisation: Tensions and Conflicts Between International Student Recruitment and Integration Policy in Ireland." *Globalisation, Societies and Education*, doi:10/1080/14767724.2017.1413979.

OECD. 2013. *Education Indicators in Focus.* 2013/05 (July). Accessed 24 May 2017. http://www.oecd.org/edu/skills-beyond-school/educationindicatorsinfocus.htm

O'Reilly, Aileen, Dermot Ryan, and Tina Hickey. 2010. "The Psychological Well-Being and Sociocultural Adaptation of Short-Term International Students in Ireland." *Journal of College Student Development* 51 (5): 584–598.

Pan, Darcy. 2011. "Student Visas, Undocumented Labour, and the Boundaries of Legality: Chinese Migration and English as a Foreign Language Education in the Republic of Ireland." *Social Anthropology* 19 (3): 268–287.

Park, Joseph Sung-Yul. 2011. "The Promise of English: Linguistic Capital and the Neoliberal Worker in the South Korean Job Market." *International Journal of Bilingual Education and Bilingualism* 14 (4): 443–455.
Prazeres, Laura. 2013. "International and Intra-National Student Mobility: Trends, Motivations and Identity." *Geography Compass* 7 (11): 804–820.
Puar, Jasbir. 2012. "Precarity Talk: A Virtual Roundtable with Lauren Berlant, Judith Butler, Bojana Cvejić, Isabell Lorey, Jasbir Puar, and Ana Vujanović." *TDR/The Drama Review* 56 (4): 163–177.
Raghuram, Parvati. 2013. "Theorising the Spaces of Student Migration." *Population, Space and Place* 19 (2): 138–154.
Robertson, Shanthi. 2013. *Transnational Student-Migrants and the State*. Basingstoke: Palgrave Macmillan.
Robertson, Shanthi. 2015. "Contractualization, Depoliticization and the Limits of Solidarity: Noncitizens in Contemporary Australia." *Citizenship Studies* 19 (8): 936–950.
Robertson, Shanthi. 2016. "Student-Workers and Tourist-Workers as Urban Labour: Temporalities and Identities in the Australian Cosmopolitan City." *Journal of Ethnic and Migration Studies* 42 (14): 2272–2288. doi:10.1080/1369183X.2016.1205808.
Robertson, Shanti, and Elaine Lynn-Ee Ho. 2016. "Temporalities, Materialities and Connecting Locales: Migration and Mobility in Asia-Pacific Cities." *Journal of Ethnic and Migration Studies* 42 (14): 2263–2271. doi:10.1080/1369183X.2016.1205804.
Sá, Creso M., and Emma Sabzalieva. 2018. "The Politics of the Great Brain Race: Public Policy and International Student Recruitment in Australia, Canada, England and the USA." *Higher Education* 75 (2): 231–253.
Sheridan, Vera. 2011. "A Holistic Approach to International Students, Institutional Habitus and Academic Literacies in an Irish Third Level Institution." *Higher Education* 62 (2): 129–140.
Smith, Aoife. 2015. "Part of the Family? Experiences of Au Pairs in Ireland." In *Au Pairs' Lives in Global Context: Sisters or Servants?*, edited by Rosie Cox, 170–186. Basingstoke: Hampshire: Palgrave Macmillan.
Standing, Guy. 2014. *The Precariat: The New Dangerous Class*. 2nd ed. London: Bloomsbury Academic.
Thomas, Susan. 2017. "The Precarious Path of Student Migrants: Education, Debt, and Transnational Migration Among Indian Youth." *Journal of Ethnic and Migration Studies*, doi:10.1080/1369183X.2017.1286970.
Van Mol, Christof. 2014. *Intra-European Student Mobility in International Higher Education Circuits: Europe on the Move*. London: Palgrave Macmillan.
Van Mol, Christof, and Christiane Timmerman. 2014. "Should I Stay or Should I Go? An Analysis of the Determinants of Intra-European Student Mobility." *Population, Space and Place* 20 (5): 465–479.
Waters, Johanna. 2009. "Transnational Geographies of Academic Distinction: The Role of Social Capital in the Recognition and Evaluation of 'Overseas' Credentials." *Globalisation, Societies and Education* 7 (2): 113–129.
Wilken, Lisanne, and Mette Ginnerskov Dahlberg. 2017. "Between International Student Mobility and Work Migration: Experiences of Students From EU's Newer Member States in Denmark." *Journal of Ethnic and Migration Studies* 43 (8): 1347–1361.
Wills, Jane, Kavita Datta, Yara Evans, Joanna Herbert, Jon May, and Cathy McIlwaine. 2010. *Global Cities at Work: New Migrant Divisions of Labour*. London: Pluto Press.

Emerging precarity among international students in Singapore: experiences, understandings and responses

Elizabeth Chacko

ABSTRACT

In this paper, I explore precarity as experienced by international students studying in the honours college of a public university in the city–state of Singapore. Precarity for this group emanates from the intersection of their temporary migrant status, the country's changing immigration and economic development policies and public opinion about international students in the country. Through interviews and focus group discussions, I examine the life trajectories and aspirations of this group, how they cope with precarity and the strategies they used to minimise their perceived precariousness. I use the term 'emerging precarity' to underscore the temporal nature of students' precarity that arises as they are about to graduate. At this juncture, precarity is heightened by the removal of resources, the ending of their visa status as students and changing policies regarding their ability to stay on and work in the country after earning a degree. Students in this study found ways to counter the effects of precarity and underscore their potential as future workers, long-term residents and possibly future citizens by building their store of human capital and asserting that their understanding of Singaporean values and cultures made them 'locals', on par with the native-born in the workplace.

Introduction

In 2017, over 5.3 million students were enrolled in institutions of tertiary education outside their country of citizenship compared to 2 million in 2000 (UNESCO 2019). Student mobility across international borders for education is a rising trend (Bhandari and Blumenthal 2011) and the number of post-secondary students enrolled in institutions abroad is projected to further grow to 6.4 million by 2025 (OECD 2009). International students move across international borders to complete a programme or degree in another country, to spend time abroad as part of an organised programme of study or even to participate in short stays for language education, summer schools or international field trips (Brooks and Waters 2013; King and Raghuram 2013). In addition to international education being an important revenue-earning sector[1], governments also recognise the potential for university students with desired human capital to become future workers, permanent residents and citizens. In a global economy where knowledge, information and technology are at a premium, international students with skills sets in these areas are among the favoured migrants (Ziguras and Law 2006). Thus, growing numbers of international students may also be considered temporary migrants whose sojourn in the receiving country though limited by visas, may be extended if their skill sets match the needs of the country's economy.

International students already in university programmes are also considered more likely to understand the cultural mores of the destination countries as they become immersed in national and local cultures, preparing them to move somewhat seamlessly from the university to the work place. Additionally, these students bring with them knowledge of customs and practices of their home countries and are often comfortable in multiple cultures and languages. They could thus act as effective bridges between countries and cultures, an added bonus for future international business transactions and collaborations (Waters 2007).

While countries in Anglo-America and Western Europe are the preferred destinations for international students, new knowledge hubs that challenge their hegemony in higher education have emerged in the Asia-Pacific region (Borjesson 2017; Collins et al. 2017; Jöns and Hoyler 2013). One such hub is the city–state of Singapore, which like other countries that are destinations for tertiary education, is engaged in a global competition for international students and talent (Ng 2011, 2013). Singapore provides a particularly salient case study as a country that has woven the recruitment, nurturing and in-country placement of talented international students into its plan for continued modernisation and development. Like many of the economically developed countries that are significant centres for international education, Singapore is characterised by declining birth rates and an ageing population (OECD 2017). Hence, the recruitment of young people at the cusp of their work lives is an added incentive as they could join the country's workforce, stabilise or increase the country's population and potentially contribute to its economic development for several decades.

This study examines how precarity emerges over time and towards the end of the international students' undergraduate career, and how it is experienced and manifested physically, socially, economically and psychologically. Precarity may be defined as having an uncertain existence due to one or more factors such as job insecurity, unreliability or lack of living wages as well as limited material, social and other entitlements (Standing 2014; Schierup and Jorgensen 2016; Vosko 2010). I use international students as a case study to understand the precarity of these temporary migrants who are located at the intersection of migrant aspirations, employment prospects and socio-cultural integration in the cities in which they live for purposes of higher education and possibly, work. I also investigate how students cope with uncertainty and precarity and how they position themselves to address some of the concerns arising from their temporary status and improve their attractiveness as future workers and continued residents.

Precarity for temporary migrants and international students

Guy Standing (2014) defined the precariat as a group that is characterised by various forms of insecurity in employment, steady living wages, and restricted access to civil, socio-cultural, economic and political rights. Most of the emphasis of studies on the precariat and precarious labour has been on labour rights and conditions, particularly for those in jobs where they may be fired at will, have little by way of a safety net and in which remuneration is low and uncertain. Lorey (2015) provided a more nuanced understanding of the precarious, distinguishing between precariousness, precarity and precarisation. According to her, precariousness is an existential state, a common form of human existence; precarity creates differentiations within this state, leading to segmentation and hierarchies, while precarisation can be understood as a form of governance that relies on the destabilisation of employment. Other authors have noted that precarity does not only refer to uncertainty and irregularity of work and low wages but includes limited access to health care, housing, education, cultural and social benefits and a path to permanent stay (Goldring and Landolt 2011; Vosko 2010; Schierup and Jorgensen 2016).

Globalisation and immigration regimes are implicated in the creation of the precariat (Anderson 2010). Indeed, precarity often signifies a state of uncertainty, dependency and powerlessness that is forged in the crucible of neoliberalism. While low-skilled workers with temporary or uncertain legal status are among the most vulnerable groups and form a sizeable part of the precariat, white-collar workers and high-skilled job seekers are not exempt (Chacko and Price 2021). Wang, Li and Deng (2017) found that highly educated internal migrants in Beijing experienced precarity that stemmed from lack of access to affordable housing, a problem that was linked to the country's household registration system (hukou) which controlled access to public housing and even job opportunities.

Jordan (2017) noted that cities are progressively becoming spaces of insidious precarity in areas such as housing and employment security. Global cities in particular are identified as having concentrations of economic/work precarity (Coe 2013; Wills et al. 2010). High-skilled migrants usually have greater agency in determining their migration trajectories than their low-skilled counterparts, but they are plagued by some of the same issues that cause precarity, especially if their legal status is tenuous or temporary. Countries and employers may vary in their definition of 'high skill', often factoring not just educational qualifications but also occupational and linguistic fluency in determining admission patterns for immigrants (Block 2016).

As Goldring, Berinstein and Bernhard (2009: 245) note, '... The concept of precarious status reflects insecurities associated with policies designed to ... curb the overall number of permanent immigrants on the part of states of immigration, and the tendency to make citizens increasingly individually responsible for their existence.' In her study of immigrant Asian Indian IT professionals in Canada, Maitra (2015: 195) demonstrated that as this white-collar group worked with India-based recruitment agencies in the hope of finding IT-related employment in developed countries, they were converted into '... a globally circulating and precarious workforce subjected to multiple insecurities of severe regulations and flexible work patterns of the recruitment agencies.'

The irregularity that characterises precarious work has ramifications for wages and benefits for temporary skilled migrants. Lowell and Avato (2014) through their analysis of data from the National Survey of College Graduates in the United States found that holders of H-1B visas (which include those who were once international students) earned considerably less than natives with the same credentials. Lewchuck et al. (2015) highlighted the lack of stable employment among educated, high-skilled and well-paid workers on limited-term visas in Canada who were engaged in sectors such as health and finance, noting that high wages did not necessarily compensate for lack of job stability.

In a study that focused on migrant nurses, the authors demonstrated that persons brought to Australia under a visa programme for temporary skilled workers had restricted social entitlements and that the structural constraints that emanated from the nurses' position as temporary residents exposed them to exploitation, a consequence of their weakening financial status and dependence on employers and agents (Boese and Macdonald 2017).

Inequalities in international academic mobility offer opportunities as well as constraints that affect outcomes for these students (Bilecen and Van Mol 2017). For international students in tertiary education who hoped to gain work experience or find a job in the countries where they are studying, uncertainty following graduation is the norm. Martin (2017) explains how their visa status and racism factor into how Chinese students are steered towards precarious and underpaid employment in Chinese restaurants in Australia's Chinatowns, leading to an experience of being stuck in place with few avenues for employment mobility.

Robertson (2013, 2015) observed that like their low-skilled counterparts, international students may be more vulnerable to labour exploitation on account of their visa status and the ambiguity surrounding their ability to obtain a work permit when they complete their courses of study. Maury (2017) noted that precarity often emanated from the overlap of legal status as student-migrant as well as a migrant worker for international students who worked in low paying jobs while studying. In some situations, these intersecting and overlapping statuses converted this population into a flexible work force that was forced to be constantly on the move between home, work and educational institution.

Students may also hope to stay on in the destination country for a while to earn money to pay off debts incurred for their studies abroad (Thomas 2017). International students like other migrants on limited-term visas have to navigate ephemeral opportunities in the workforce as they negotiate the shifting terrain of policies related to temporary workers and prospects that emerge or dry up with shifts in supply and demand. In doing so they often experience multiple layers of precarity that emanate from legal, economic and personal issues (Gilmartin, Coppari and Phelan 2021).

Singapore as a destination for international students

Singapore's emphasis on attracting international students to study in its universities aligns with its position as an important global city in Asia but also speaks of its high-skilled labour needs. Since the 1960s, the country has transformed itself from one that relied on low-skilled labour in industries such as garment manufacturing and electronics assembly to one with a knowledge-based economy (Kwong et al. 2001). Singapore's economy has continued to grow and expand into new areas such as research and development, biomedical sciences, technology and finance. As globalisation intensified, there was an increasing need for skilled labour, which was seen as essential to generate revenue and increase prosperity. However, the country's low birth rate, which has continued to fall well below replacement level and its ageing population meant that there was insufficient local labour with skill sets to meet the demands of an evolving and growing economy.

Since the 1980s, Singapore has had a history of actively recruiting promising students as well as professionals in fields that are deemed critical for its evolving economy. In the early decades of these programmes, the country also had in place policies that allowed high-skilled students to apply for permanent residency, setting them on an early path towards citizenship (Yang 2016). In the late 1980s, the Singaporean government decided to bring in foreign talents (skilled labour) to augment the country's native labour force. The country used various strategies to create a deep pool of high-skilled personnel for the financial, manufacturing, medical and service sectors for which the country is known today.

In 1988, the then Minister for Home Affairs announced that foreign talents would be used to supplement the local workforce and to boost the economy with the 'skills, enterprise and drive' of 'high calibre and trained people'. In keeping with this policy, the Government of Singapore instituted the Immigration Affairs Committee (IMAC) in 1989 to recruit skilled workers and professionals to work in Singapore. Bureaucratic hurdles were removed and efforts were made to attract foreign talents to work in the country both as temporary visitors and likely permanent residents and citizens. By recruiting foreign talent from the Asia-Pacific region with a focus on those of Chinese and Indian heritage, the Singaporean government simultaneously attempted to keep the ethnic mix of the country stable, hoping to pre-empt the rise of inter-ethnic tensions that could arise if new ethnic populations were brought into the country.

In 2002 the government put into action a plan to make Singapore a 'Global Schoolhouse' (Collins et al. 2014; Sidhu, Ho and Yeoh 2011), a destination for fee-paying international students from pre-school through graduate school. The Singaporean government hoped to capture a larger share of the global education market, attracting 150,000 full-fee-paying international students (40,000 undergraduates) by 2015 and growing Education's share in the national economy from 1.9% to 3.5% (Ministry of Trade and Industry 2002).

The government also continued to woo and fund international students from Asia who showed exceptional promise and who could become members of Singapore's highly skilled work force (Collins et al. 2014). In particular, it wanted the best students in science and engineering who had a strong affiliation with Asia and a good understanding of Asian history, cultures and development (Sidhu, Ho and Yeoh 2011). The Agency for Science, Technology and Research (A*STAR) is a public sector organisation that was created in 1991 to foster scientific research and groom talent for Singapore's knowledge-based economy. A*STAR underwrites the education abroad of select Singaporean citizens at reputed universities in the United States and Europe with the intention that these funded students will join Singapore's burgeoning science and technology industries (Olds 2007).

In 2001, A*STAR established its overseas National Science Scholarships programme as part of the government's plan to develop human capital. International students who showed an aptitude for STEM disciplines were identified while still in middle school and supported through scholarships and nurtured by the Singaporean Government as part of the country's long-term plans to grow its skilled labour force (Yang 2016). However, these and other policies were to change in light of protests by native Singaporeans in the 2000s and especially after 2010, when natives who were constrained in their use of physical demonstrations and writings to express dissent, took to social media and other online venues to communicate their dissatisfaction with immigration policies that privileged 'foreign talent'.

Singapore's education system is a part of its plan for modernisation, economic growth and higher productivity. The country's human resource strategy is to invest in education and to keep pace with and meet the demands of a global knowledge-driven economy (Lee 2008). International students were also supported by government-funded scholarship programmes other than A*STAR. Established universities in Singapore began to deploy 'talent scouts' to visit middle and high schools in neighbouring countries of Asia, offering scholarships to students wishing to study mathematics, science and engineering in particular. These scholarships often carry bonds, requiring awardees to work in Singapore after graduation. Although drawn from a number of Asian countries, the majority of these students were from China (Yeoh and Lin 2013).

Funded international students in STEM fields were attracted to Singapore's premier public universities, such as Nanyang Technological University and the National University of Singapore. The steady rise of these universities in ranking among world and Asian universities since 2010 is a matter of pride for the country. Currently, each of these two universities ranks among the top five Asian universities and one or the other takes top position according to the QS World University Rankings (2019).

For undergraduates, government scholarships for selected students were worth between S$18,000 and S$25,000 per year and covered tuition and accommodation. Under the terms of the scholarship, these international students were required to work in a Singapore-based company for up to six years after getting their degree. In 2005, it was revealed that the government had awarded at least 2000 scholarships each year to overseas students, worth up to S$3.6 million (Singapore Parliamentary Report 2005).

Singaporeans feared that the flow of foreign students particularly to its premium public universities was at the expense of educational and job opportunities for the native-born (Koh 2003). Among the issues raised in Internet fora by discontented citizens in the months leading to the highly politicised 2011 elections in Singapore were the widening gap between the rich and the poor, high housing prices and immigration laws that privileged foreigners over natives for sought-after positions in Singapore's best universities as well as in employment. Not surprisingly, the processes by which international students could become permanent residents of Singapore have become more difficult over time. The Employment Pass Eligibility Certificate (EPEC) Scheme, introduced by Singapore's Ministry of Manpower in 1992, which allowed the holder of the certificate to stay in Singapore for up to two years and search for a job, was discontinued in late 2011.

Before 2011, international students with needed skills who were studying in the country's top universities were invited to apply for Permanent Resident status on receiving a job offer. As a permanent resident of Singapore, the foreign talent could sponsor his or her parents for residency. Now, it is very unlikely that an international student could hope to advance towards permanent residency on entering the Singaporean work force. Currently, after a student has completed the course of study and obtained a diploma s/he would require a work pass initiated by an employer and approved by the Ministry of Manpower to stay on in the country and work (Ministry of Manpower 2018).

Although the dominant People's Action Party (PAP) that had been in power since independence in 1965 won the 2011 election, the dissatisfaction of the citizenry was evident (Mydans 2011). Possibly in response to citizens' concerns, in his National Day Rally speech in 2011, Prime Minister Lee Hsien Loong announced that the government would keep the number of international students in Singapore's universities steady while increasing the share of native Singaporeans by14,000 by 2015 (Tan 2011). Public reaction to students from China (especially those on government scholarships), often referred to as 'PRC scholars' turned hostile in 2011 and especially after a student from the People's Republic of China studying at a prestigious university in Singapore made insulting remarks in 2012 about Singapore and Singaporeans on social media. In response, native Singaporeans questioned the motives and loyalty of PRC scholars studying in Singapore, viewing them as opportunists who were using government funding and the country as a stepping stone towards upward socio-economic mobility elsewhere (Yeoh and Lin 2013).

By 2012, there were approximately 84,000 international students in Singapore, the bulk of whom (~70%) were in programmes in tertiary education, while the sector's share in the GDP had increased to 3.2%. The government also announced a shift in the Global Schoolhouse initiative from an emphasis on numbers and GDP share to a focus on the quality of education and its relevance to the economy, both to develop industry-relevant human capital and to attract, develop and retain high-skilled individuals as the global competition for talent intensified (Parliament Questions and Answers 2012). International students in Singapore's universities were therefore faced with the challenge of making life decisions in an environment fraught with instability and change.

Subsequently, the number of international students in the country's top universities declined. For example, at the National University of Singapore, the share of international students in the student body fell from 23.3% in 2013 to 17.3% in 2017 (Seah and Png 2018). Nonetheless, international students continue to play a critical role in the government's plan to use its acclaimed institutions of higher education to foster modernisation, build cultural, economic and social capital and raise the profile of Singapore as a regional and global hub of innovation (Collins et al. 2014; Sidhu, Ho and Yeoh 2011).

Methods and research participants

This study primarily draws on interviews conducted in English with 32 international students of Chinese and Indian ethnicity who were in the third or fourth year of study at the undergraduate honours college of a leading public university in Singapore. I also conducted two focus group discussions with a subset of this population that was majoring in a STEM field. I used a snowball approach to identify potential interviewees. Carried out in 2013 and 2014, the interviews, which lasted 1–1.5 h explored why the students had decided to study in Singapore, their goals and aspirations, experiences of academic learning and social relations on campus, and their integration into campus life and the city. I also explored the issues participants faced as international students, their strategies to overcome problems and how they positioned themselves as future workers and possibly, permanent residents. The interviews and discussions were recorded, transcribed and analysed for common themes to understand how students' experience as temporary migrants fit with theoretical understandings of precarity, vulnerability and integration.

The interviews and focus group discussions were conducted in a residential college on campus. During focus groups, the interactions between participants had a synergistic effect (Cameron 2010) as students responded to observations and comments made by fellow discussants. Each focus group discussion took about two hours. One focus group was comprised entirely of students (five males, one female) who hailed from the People's Republic of China, a major source country for international students at the university. All six students in this focus group were the only children of their parents, a consequence of China's one-child policy for several decades. They lived in the same student dormitory and a subset of the group even shared a suite.

The second focus group comprised of students (four males, three females) of Indian and Chinese ethnicity. The ethnic Chinese students in this group hailed from Taiwan, Indonesia and Malaysia, which, in addition to Mainland China are significant origin countries for ethnic Chinese students in Singapore. Most of the students had joined the university after getting their high school diplomas from their home countries. A few of the students who were Chinese nationals had been in Singapore since middle school, having secured scholarships from middle through high school and again for their bachelor's degree from the Singapore government.

Changing policies, uncertainty and emerging precarity

Precarity for the international students in this study arose out of specific economic considerations such as demand and supply and Singaporean government policies related to the employment of non-natives. Ongoing social and economic change, as well as perceived threats to natives' economic prospects and cultural values increased the possibility of a defensive reinforcement of boundaries that separated native-born and foreigners on the basis of culture, nativity and identities even in institutions of higher education.

The international students in this study reported that Singapore's top universities were selected by their parents as ideal places to obtain an undergraduate degree because the parents felt that the education these youths received in Singapore would be of a high quality, imparted in English, and would well prepare them for a career in any part of the world. The ability to study in a country with a rising profile in the Asia-Pacific region and indeed the world, with highly ranked universities in a setting open to employing talented international students once they had completed their degrees were additional incentives.

Parents of the students in this study were reportedly heartened by the fact that the native Singaporean population was composed largely of ethnic Chinese and ethnic Indians as they felt that cultural dissimilarities would be few and could be easily bridged. Parents preferred to send their wards to a Singaporean university over one in Anglo-America or even Australia because Singapore was not too distant from their countries and visits home were more affordable. Particularly for parents of the female students in the study, an understanding that Singapore was a safe place with very low levels of crime and violence was a bonus.

International students reported that as their tenure as undergraduates came to a close, they recognised the tenuous nature of their continued stay in Singapore as their legal status of being on a student visa would end and that the future was very uncertain. It was at this point in their period as student-migrants that they began to experience an emerging precarity. While excelling academically had been their focus during the first few years in college, labour market uncertainty upon graduation appeared as a source of stress and worry during the final years, even for students on scholarships that allowed/required them to work in Singapore:

> I'm kind of stressed. I'm not sure what I will do after I graduate. I need to get a job soon. But either way, I have to hang around here for a while. (4th year A*STAR engineering student, citizen of the PRC)

Asymmetries due to differentials of nativity, legal status, power, access to resources and other factors were keenly felt by international students as they experienced emerging precarity. These students expected the process whereby they became firmly embedded and accepted in Singaporean society to begin when they acquired a work permit. Those with bonds knew that they would have to find a job soon after graduation and many final year students were anxious because it was getting increasingly difficult to find a job through campus interviews. Students in the focus groups reported that on speaking to recent alumni, they discovered that most alumni had found jobs through networking and knowing the right people. This was perceived to place non-native students at a distinct disadvantage, as they did not have a network of family and friends in Singapore to assist them in their job searches.

Fourth year international students who were on Singapore government scholarships that covered tuition and provided a stipend for living expenses were worried that following graduation and the termination of the stipend they would be short on funds particularly for rent as non-subsidised housing in Singapore was expensive. Anxiety stemming from possible future financial and employment precarity had severe effects on the subjective well-being of the international students and often manifested psychosomatically. Many reported losing sleep due to worry, feeling constantly under strain and worried that they would not be able to surmount the problems they would face upon graduation if they could not find employment right away. Julian, a 4th year engineering student from Taiwan noted that had been breaking out into hives and that medical tests indicated that the problem could not be attributed to allergies, and the likely cause was psychological distress.

Some of the anxiety at this juncture in their lives stemmed from the students' perceived obligations to their parents. They knew that they were a critical link in the transnational strategy adopted by their parents, who put aside their desire to keep their offspring in the motherland close to the nuclear family, so that those in the next generation could lead socially and economically upwardly mobile transnational lives (Yeoh et al. 2005). The inability to find a suitable employment post-graduation was viewed by students in this study as more than personal disappointment – it was experienced as a failure to fulfil their filial duties and as letting down the family. Students in their fourth year who were approaching graduation met parents' questions about the future with dread as they often did not have anything positive to report by way of employment. Yi-Peng, who studied Computer Science said,

> It's natural for them (his parents) to want to know what is going on, but I feel very anxious because I don't know what's in store. Having them ask again and again, every time we talk is depressing. I feel badly to tell them not to ask. And with cell phones, there's only so much you can do to avoid the calls and questions … I want to do right by them. They would like me to get a job here in Singapore. I would like that too.

The students in science and engineering felt that there were fewer opportunities for them beyond continuing to engage in research in an economy that was geared towards high-skilled services rather than industry. They believed that with their newly minted Bachelor's degrees they were more likely to get 'generalist' kinds of jobs that did not match their training rather than those that required particular skill sets. They were also concerned about the increasing competition that they would have to face both from other international students and native-born students. Their response to precarisation was to make strategic decisions to enhance their value-creating qualities, often by offering to work with professors in research labs and by creating a strong research profile while still undergraduates.

Experiences of cultural precarity and international students' resilience

As Anderson (2010) observed, immigration and visa requirements can delay and even halt migrants' involvement in social and other networks that could aid settlement and integration into the receiving society. Student experiences in the wider community outside of campus may be constrained by visa status, resources, fluency in the cultures and language of the host country and limited avenues for inclusion (Chacko and Sojo 2016; Yeoh, Foong and Ho 2014) inhibiting their integration into the city in which they dwell. According to Hainmueller and Hopkins (2015) immigrants with a high socio-economic status (such as highly skilled temporary migrants and some international students) are more likely to be accepted by natives than those who are poorer. But this kind of acceptance is not always problem-free. Even among high-skilled immigrants with a high socio-economic status, phenotypes, accents and cultural differences may set them apart from the mainstream society to which they may feel they belong (Chacko 2015).

Ellerman (2019) underscores the important of intersectionality along axes of inclusion and exclusion in creating a 'politics of belonging' that is often (re)produced by immigration policy. Additionally, insider/outsider demarcations are reinforced through socio-cultural and spatial exclusions. However, belonging needs to be considered as existing along a continuum rather than as a discrete quality that is either present or absent (Block 2016). Nowicka (2018) uses the term 'cultural precarity' to highlight the importance of belonging in understanding qualities of precarity, noting that cultural precarity is not restricted to populations that belong to races and religions that are different than those of the majority group but can be experienced within ethno-racially similar groups that have dissimilar languages and nationalities.

A study on global competitiveness conducted by the Economic Intelligence Unit of *The Economist* ranked Singapore the third most competitive city in the world after New York and London (Economic Intelligence Unit 2012). A city's ability to attract and retain global talent was considered a critical factor in achieving a high score in global competitiveness. And indeed, an important reason international students reported that they came to Singapore was because they recognised its rising eminence in Asia and the world not just in education, but also in its burgeoning finance, biomedical and IT enterprises. When questioned about their attachment to Singapore and their degree of comfort in spaces within it, international students noted that unlike low-skilled temporary labour migrants, they did not feel economically or spatially excluded from places in the city–state. However, they sometimes felt limited in their ability to fully participate in the symbolic and discursive life of the city. Native Singaporeans often positioned themselves as authentic citizens who are loyal to the state and therefore more deserving of resources, in contrast to the perceived otherness and opportunism of the foreign talents (Yang 2016).

Since Singapore became independent in 1965, the government has attempted to forge a sense of national identity among Singaporeans. The government initially rallied its citizens around hard work and economic development and later incorporated 'Asian values' as an intrinsic part of national Singaporean identity (Ortmann 2009). Nevertheless, the students

I spoke with were ambivalent about whether their status as Asians and denizens of Singapore was valued or carried much weight, as they felt that they were still set apart from native Singaporeans using other identity measures.

Focus group discussants and interviewees pointed out that insider–outsider distinctions remained with international students irrespective of the length of their tenure in Singapore, resulting in ambiguous articulations of belonging. Temporariness of status sometimes led to angst that went beyond economic imperatives and spilled into cultural realms. Uncertainties of stay sometimes led to ambivalent feelings and a hesitation to develop emotional ties or roots in Singapore. Some students who experienced cultural precarity felt that it was best to be guarded in their acculturation and not become too attached to the city–state even though their plan was to stay on and work there and ultimately become permanent residents:

> I feel it's kind of dangerous for me to fully assimilate myself to the culture here. I'm not sure I can stay so I have to keep a distance … Because I feel that it is quite difficult for people to have two strong cultural identities, and to me, it's like you have to choose one primary one over the other. So for me, I have been thinking that I am a very authentic Chinese, and retain very close and intimate cultural and ties with my friends and family back in China […] But I also feel that I understand Singaporeans and Singaporean culture. Can I be an authentic Chinese and also an authentic Singaporean? Should I even try? (Wei, PRC Chinese A*STAR scholarship student majoring in physics)

A 22-year old who came to Singapore from the PRC when she was in Secondary 3 (9th grade) had this to say:

> I have spent a lot of my life here, so I feel a sense of familiarity. But I don't think I am Singaporean-Singaporean. I have friends that tell me, 'Eh, you speak like a Singaporean.' I may speak like a Singaporean but people know that I am Chinese. I don't think I am accepted here the way I am in China.

The international students in this study were imbricated in complex socio-economic, cultural, ideological networks across different spaces within Singapore. While insiderness may be produced through membership in the community of students and scholars on a university campus, and even through a common ethno-racial identity, according to the focus group discussants the students' outsider status was continually reinforced. Racism resulting from phenotype was not likely to affect international students of Chinese or Indian ethnicity studying in Singapore since the largest demographic and politically powerful group in the country comprises of ethnic Chinese, and Indians form a significant ethnic group in the country. However, their 'very China' embodied appearances and their socio-cultural behaviours often set them apart from native Singaporeans (Yang 2014).

However, insider/outsider demarcations were frequently drawn using cultural differences between natives and foreigners within these ethnic groups. Such delineations were keenly felt in the matter of language, accents and other dissimilarities, creating a form of cultural precarity that which made it difficult for even ethnic Chinese and Indian international students to meld into Singaporean society. Some indicators of difference were only evident to those who were familiar with cultural norms that were peculiar to Singapore, such as naming practices. Li, an engineering major who is from the PRC and came to Singapore as a high school student said:

> I was teased because of my name, which has two syllables, while most Singaporean Chinese names have three syllables. I suppose that is a giveaway. I feel that others can still detect that I was not born in Singapore and think that I can never be really Singaporean.

However, students in this study found ways to disrupt populist narratives and underscore their ability to integrate and ultimately become valuable members of the country. Fluency and accent were considered critical markers of identity. Speaking English with a Singaporean accent and being able to converse in Singlish (an English-based creole language that is used colloquially in Singapore) were considered important signs of integration into Singaporean society and creating a sense of belonging that also helped ease social anxieties:

> After living here for so long, yes. I feel a connection to the people here, to the society. I feel that I could fit in here, but that also depends on perspective. Some people think that I'm a Singaporean because I behave like one and sound like one. I feel at first I stood out mostly because of my accent, so I tried very hard to change my accent and to speak Singlish so that I can fit in better. (Raj, Indian student majoring in Biology)

For students who had entered Singapore's educational system in middle or high school, navigating the various high-stakes examinations were markers of experiences shared with native Singaporean classmates. This shared 'suffering' produced a sense of camaraderie with native students, and also added to the students' sense of belonging to Singapore. Students offered these processes as experiences that prepared them to be fully folded and integrated into Singaporean society as future citizens. Yongbao, a Chinese student who studied in Singapore since he was in 8th grade noted:

> Going through the PSLE and A-level examinations was stressful but also a bonding experience. I think it is important for (male) international students who are planning to stay on here to go through life in that sequence (secondary school to post-secondary school to National Service to University). You have to go through the whole journey to feel really absorbed into society and feel really Singaporean. It gives you a lot of common things that you can relate to - you can talk about secondary school, about army, about university. You are no longer an outsider simply looking in.

Campus was the place where students felt most at home, having lived in college dormitories throughout their tenure as undergraduates. The pressures to excel academically if the student wished to keep his or her scholarship or be absorbed into the labour force often meant that international students (particularly those on scholarships), were almost single-mindedly focused on academics, forgoing many of the social pleasures of college life. However, participation in co- and extracurricular activities was required by the university especially if students wished to live on campus, as was the case for all the international students in this study.

In their third and fourth years, many of the international students felt they needed to focus more on their studies so that they could continue to perform at the top of their class, but had to engage in mandatory extracurricular activities. They were often torn between wanting to focus more on their studies and build human capital that could be advantageous when seeking employment and wishing that they could have better work-life balance and more social activities and play in their lives.

Additionally, unlike in universities in the United States where a residential experience on campus is customary, native college students in Singapore may be 'day scholars' who live at home with their families and commute to the university for classes on a daily basis. While studying in junior college and at the university, the international students in this study lived in hostels, which facilitated interactions with fellow international students rather than natives. Therefore, there were fewer opportunities for the international students to form strong relationships with Singaporean peers:

> All the people staying [in the student hostels] were the same like me ... We were from different places in China, India, Indonesia, Vietnam, Malaysia, all kinds of places, Thailand ... Most of the people who stayed in hostels were foreigners and I became friends with them. I don't have many close friends who are Singaporean. (Prasad, Student from India majoring in mathematics)

Nonetheless, co-presence and mingling in spaces on university campuses and in the city allowed international students to realise and act on relational affinities. Educational experiences that were shared with native Singaporean students were offered as important in creating friendships and integrating students better. Often friendships with native students were forged through academic group projects, school events and co-and extra-curricular activities. Students joined co-curricular activities that aligned with their interests and to meet people with similar passions. These shared experiences and resulting friendships with native Singaporean students greatly added to the immigrant students' sense of integration and belonging to Singapore and helped diminish feelings of social and cultural precarity.

Young international students in this study who were nearing graduation reconciled their uncertain legal status in Singaporean society and their position as residents of the city for extended periods of time by offering 'local' as a social identity. 'Local' had come to have a distinct meaning for this group, denoting those who had experienced prolonged stay in the city–state. A local was not merely familiar with Singapore but was someone who had an intimate understanding of spaces within the city and was adept at navigating them. International students who were 'locals' also believed they had an in-depth understanding of the Singaporean way of life and Singaporean culture.

A student from India emphasised the difference between being considered a local and being a Singaporean. To him, 'Singaporean' denoted being a native or at least being a naturalised citizen, while being a local meant someone who was attuned to life in Singapore: 'We treat ourselves as part of the society after living here for so long. But we consider ourselves as local, not as a Singaporean, as we feel we belong here.'

Using 'local' as a spatial identity that was not necessarily connected to legal status, allowed international students to redraw and redefine the lines between natives and foreigners in a more inclusive manner. International students offered having local experience and knowledge as core qualities that demonstrated that they were not permanent outsiders who could not be incorporated into Singaporean society. Students' identity as a 'locals' drew on residential longevity varying from four to eight years in Singapore but was also linked to aspirations at the individual level to become a talent working in a high-skilled occupation and as a part of a community that was more firmly connected to the state as a permanent resident. In their minds, being local gave these international students an advantage and greater legitimacy as future long-term residents and citizens, thereby decreasing their perceived precarity.

Conclusion

This article links to this special issue's theme of the spatial, scalar and temporal precarities faced by temporary migrants by exploring the mutual effects international students and cities have on each other. As temporary migrants, students understood that the uncertainty that characterised their post-degree professional futures and consequent precarity was shaped by complex political and economic systems that were beyond their control. Academic and employment goals were the main drivers for these students who aimed to obtain a tertiary degree from a Singaporean university. Temporal precarity for international students in Singapore escalated over the years as the state's policies regarding employment and permanent residency became increasingly restrictive. This precarity that was baked into state policy was further intensified for students as they approached graduation if they were not able to find employment.

Student migrants' sense of belonging to the city–state was shaped by responses to them by native Singaporeans and by invisible boundaries that were etched by clear or subtle cultural differences even when natives and migrants shared a race/ethnicity. The students in this study challenged stereotypes about the inherent inability of foreign talent to become truly Singaporean. They tried to better blend into Singaporean society by learning to speak Singlish and by adopting mannerisms of Singaporeans.

The city–state of Singapore offered itself to international students simultaneously as an empowering and changeable space. Students underscored the role of Singapore as a global cosmopolitan city, which necessitated a narrative of openness and multiculturalism that could run contrary to localised anxieties regarding foreign talent being incapable of integrating into Singaporean society due to their alien cultures.

Although free to move about the city as they chose, international students sometimes felt unwelcome due to anti-migrant discourses that wrote them out of socially constructed spaces of belonging. These temporary migrants also recognised that despite spending their college years in Singapore, they may not get the opportunity to stay on and work in the city and ultimately become permanent residents and citizens. Although not subject to race-based exclusionary practices, language and naming were important lenses through which students' experience of Singapore and places within it could be discerned. The international students reactions to socio-cultural exclusion were to offer counter narratives that explained their positions in relation to existing social structures. They used creative strategies to blend into Singaporean society and minimise their foreignness, which they hoped would decrease their precarity and assist them in plans to work in the country post-graduation. They positioned themselves spatially within the regime of migration control by using the term 'local' as an identity to characterise their familiarity with the city and their knowledge of Singaporean cultural practices and professed values, a familiarity that was built over time as they learned to navigate the city and its spaces.

Note

1. International students in U.S. colleges and universities contributed USD 44.7 billion to the United States economy during the 2018–2019 academic year (IIE 2019).

Disclosure statement

No potential conflict of interest was reported by the author(s).

References

Anderson, Bridget. 2010. "Migration, Immigration Controls and the Fashioning of Precarious Workers." *Work, Employment and Society* 24 (2): 300–317.

Bhandari, Rajika, and Peggy Blumenthal. 2011. *International Students and Global Mobility in Higher Education: National Trends and New Directions*. New York: Palgrave Macmillan.

Bilecen, Basak, and Christof Van Mol. 2017. "Introduction: International Academic Mobility and Inequalities." *Journal of Ethnic and Migration Studies* 43 (8): 1241–1255.

Block, Laura. 2016. *Policy Frames on Spousal Migration in Germany: Regulating Membership, Regulating the Family*. Berlin: Springer Verlag.

Boese, Martina, and Kate Macdonald. 2017. "Restricted Entitlement for Skilled Temporary Migrants: The Limits of Migrant Consent." *Journal of Ethnic and Migration Studies* 43 (9): 1472–1489.

Börjesson, Mikael. 2017. "The Global Space of International Students in 2010." *Journal of Ethnic and Migration Studies* 43 (8): 1256–1275.

Brooks, Rachel, and Johanna Waters. 2013. *Student Mobilities, Migration and the Internationalization of Higher Education*. London: Palgrave Macmillan.

Cameron, Jenny. 2010. "Focusing on the Focus Group." In *Qualitative Research Methods in Human Geography*. 3rd ed., edited by Iain Hay, 152–172. Toronto: Oxford University Press.

Chacko, Elizabeth. 2015. "Hybrid Sensibilities: Highly Skilled Asian Indians Negotiating Identity in Private, Semi-Private, and Public Spaces of Washington, DC." *Journal of Cultural Geography* 32 (1): 115–128.

Chacko, Elizabeth, and Marie Price. 2021. "(Un)settled Sojourners in Cities: The Scalar and Temporal Dimensions of Migrant Precarity." *Journal of Ethnic and Migration Studies* 47 (20): 4597–4614. doi:10.1080/1369183X.2020.1731060.

Chacko, Elizabeth, and Gloriana Sojo. 2016. "Spaces of Integration: International Students in a Global City." In *Race, Ethnicity and Place in a Changing America*. Vol. 3., edited by J. W. Frazier, E. L. Tettey-Fio, and N. F. Henry, 335–343. Albany: SUNY Press. Chapter 22 in.

Coe, Neil. 2013. "Geographies of Production III: Making Space for Labour." *Progress in Human Geography* 37 (2): 271–284.

Collins, Francis L., Kong Chong Ho, Mayumi Ishikawa, and Ai-Hsuan Sandra Ma. 2017. "International Student Mobility and After-Study Lives: the Portability and Prospects of Overseas Education in Asia." *Population, Space and Place* 23 (4), doi:10.1002/psp.2029.

Collins, Francis L., Ravinder Sidhu, Nick Lewis, and Brenda S.A. Yeoh. 2014. "Mobility and Desire: International Students and Asian Regionalism in Aspirational Singapore." *Discourse: Studies in the Cultural Politics of Education*, 35(5): 661–676.

Economic Intelligence Unit. 2012. *Hotspots: Benchmarking Global City Competitiveness*. London: The Economist.

Ellerman, Antje. 2019. "Discrimination in Migration and Citizenship." *Journal of Ethnic and Migration Studies*. doi:10.1080/1369183X.2018.1561053.

Gilmartin, Mary, Pablo Rojas Coppari, and Dean Phelan. 2021. "Promising Precarity: The Lives of Dublin's International Students." *Journal of Ethnic and Migration Studies* 47 (20): 4723–4740. doi:10.1080/1369183X.2020.1732617.

Goldring, Luin, Carolina Berinstein, and Judith K. Bernhard. 2009. "Institutionalizing Precarious Migratory Status in Canada." *Citizenship Studies* 13 (3): 239–265.

Goldring, Luin, and Patricia Landolt. 2011. "Caught in the Work-Citizenship Matrix: The Lasting Effects of Precarious Legal Status on Work for Toronto Immigrants." *Globalizations* 8 (3): 325–341.

Hainmueller, Jens, and Daniel J. Hopkins. 2015. "The Hidden American Immigration Consensus: A Conjoint Analysis of Attitudes Towards Immigrants." *American Journal of Political Science* 59 (3): 529–548.

Institute of International Education (IIE). 2019. "Open Doors 2019." https://www.iie.org/Research-and-Insights/Open-Doors/Open-Doors-2019-Media-Information.
Jöns, Heike, and Michael Hoyler. 2013. "Global Geographies of Higher Education: The Perspective of World University Rankings." *Geoforum: Journal of Physical, Human, and Regional Geosciences* 46: 45–59.
Jordan, Lucy. 2017. "Introduction: Understanding Migrants' Economic Precarity in Global Cities." *Urban Geography* 38 (10): 1455–1458.
King, Russell, and Parvati Raghuram. 2013. "International Student Migration: Mapping the Field and New Research Agendas." *Population, Space and Place* 19: 127–137.
Koh, Aaron. 2003. "Global Flows of Foreign Talent: Identity Anxieties in Singapore's Ethnoscape." *SOJOURN: Journal of Social Issues in Southeast Asia* 18: 230–256. doi:10.1355/SJ18-2C.
Kwong, Kai-Sun, Chau Leung-Chuen, Francis T. Lui, and Larry D. Qiu. 2001. *Industrial Development in Singapore, Taiwan and South Korea*. Singapore: World Scientific Publishing Company.
Lee, Sing-Kong. 2008. *Toward a Better Future: Education and Training for Economic Development in Singapore Since 1965*. Washington, DC: The World Bank.
Lewchuck, Wayne, Michelynn Laflèche, Stephanie Procyk, Charlene Cook, Diane Dyson, Luin Goldring, and Karen Lior. 2015. *The Precarity Penalty: the Impact of Employment Precarity on Individuals, Households and Communities – And What to do About it*. Ottawa, Ontario: Canadian Electronic Library.
Lorey, Isabell. 2015. *State of Insecurity: Government of the Precarious*. Brooklyn, NY: Verso.
Lowell, B. Lindsay, and Johanna Avato. 2014. "The Wages of Skilled Temporary Migrants: Effects of Visa Pathways and Job Portability." *International Migration* 52 (3): 85–98.
Maitra, Srabani. 2015. "The Making of the 'Precarious': Examining Indian Immigrant IT Workers in Canada and Their Transnational Networks with Body Shops in India." *Globalisation, Societies and Education* 13 (2): 194–209.
Martin, Fran. 2017. "Rethinking Network Capital: Hospitality Work and Parallel Trading Among Chinese Students in Melbourne." *Mobilities* 12 (6): 890–907.
Maury, Olivia. 2017. "Student-Migrant-Workers: Temporal Aspects of Precarious Work and Life in Finland." *Nordic Journal of Migration Research* 7 (4): 224–232.
Ministry of Manpower. 2018. Work Passes and Permits. Ministry or Manpower, Singapore. Accessed October 2, 2018. http://www.mom.gov.sg/passes-and-permits.
Ministry of Trade and Industry. 2002. *Panel Recommends Global Schoolhouse Concept for Singapore to Capture Bigger Slice of US$2.2 Trillion World Education Market*. Singapore: Ministry of Trade and Industry.
Mydans, Seth. 2011. "Vote Forces Singapore's Leader to Reconsider Style." *New York Times, Asia Pacific Edition*, May 8.
Ng, Pak Tee. 2011. "Singapore's Response to the Global War for Talent: Politics and Education." *International Journal of Educational Development* 31 (3): 262–268.
Ng, Pak Tee. 2013. "The Global War for Talent: Responses and Challenges in the Singapore Higher Education System." *Journal of Higher Education Policy and Management* 35 (3): 280–292.
Nowicka, Magdalena. 2018. "Cultural Precarity: Migrants' Positionalities in the Light of Current Anti-Immigrant Populism in Europe." *Journal of Intercultural Studies* 39 (5): 527–542.
OECD. 2009. *Higher Education to 2030, Volume 2: Globalisation*. Paris: OECD Publishing.
OECD. 2017. *Education at a Glance 2017: OECD Indicators*. Paris: OECD Publishing. https://doi.org/10.1787/eag-2017-en.
Olds, Kris. 2007. "Global Assemblage: Singapore, Foreign Universities, and the Construction of a "Global Education Hub." *World Development* 35 (6): 959–975.
Ortmann, Stephan. 2009. "Singapore: The Politics of Inventing National Identity." *Journal of Current Southeast Asian Affairs* 28 (4): 23–46.
QS World University Rankings. 2019. https://www.topuniversities.com/university-rankings/world-university-rankings/2019
Robertson, Shanthi. 2013. *Transnational Student-Migrants and the State*. Basingstoke: Palgrave Macmillan.

Robertson, Shanthi. 2015. "Contractualization, Depoliticization and the Limits of Solidarity: Noncitizens in Contemporary Australia." *Citizenship Studies* 19 (8): 936–950.
Schierup, Carl-Ulrik, and Martin Bak Jorgensen. 2016. "An Introduction to the Special Issue. Politics of Precarity: Migrant Conditions, Struggles and Experiences." *Critical Sociology* 42 (7-9): 947–958.
Seah, Kelvin, and Ivan Png. 2018. "Time for Singapore Universities to Admit More International Students." *TODAY*, January 29. Accessed April 1, 2018. https://www.todayonline.com/daily-focus/education/time-singapore-universities-admit-more-international-students.
Sidhu, Ravindar, K. C. Ho, and Brenda Yeoh. 2011. "Emerging Education Hubs: The Case of Singapore." *Higher Education* 61 (1): 23–40.
Singapore Parliamentary Report. 2005. February 28, Volume 79, col 762.
Standing, Guy. 2014. *The Precariat: The New Dangerous Class*. 2nd ed. London: Bloomsbury Academic.
Tan, Emilia. 2011. "Singapore: New 'cap' on Foreign Students." *University World News*, August 21, Issue No: 185. http://www.universityworldnews.com/article.php?story=20110819174750326.
Thomas, Susan. 2017. "The Precarious Path of Student Migrants: Education, Debt, and Transnational Migration Among Indian Youth." *Journal of Ethnic and Migration Studies* 43 (11): 1873–1889.
UNESCO. 2019. "International Students – Migration Data Portal." https://migrationdataportal.org/themes/international-students.
Vosko, Leah. 2010. *Managing the Margins: Gender, Citizenship, and the International Regulation of Precarious Employment*. Oxford: Oxford University Press.
Wang, Hao, Wei Li, and Yu Deng. 2017. "Precarity Among Highly Educated Migrants: College Graduates in Beijing, China." *Urban Geography* 38 (10): 1497–1516.
Waters, Johanna. 2007. "Roundabout Routes and Sanctuary Schools': The Role of Situated Educational Practices and Habitus in the Creation of Transnational Professionals." *Global Networks* 7 (4): 477–497.
Wills, Jane, Kavita Datta, Yara Evans, Joanna Herbert, Jon May, and Cathy McIlwaine. 2010. *Global Cities at Work: new Migrant Divisions of Labour*. London: Pluto Press.
Yang, Peidong. 2014. "A Phenomenology of Being "Very China": An Ethnographic Report on the Self-Formation Experiences of Mainland Chinese Undergraduate "Foreign Talents" in Singapore." *Asian Journal of Social Science* 42 (3-4): 233–261.
Yang, Peidong. 2016. *International Mobility and Educational Desire: Chinese Foreign Talent Students in Singapore*. New York: Palgrave Macmillan.
Yeoh, Brenda S., M. Foong, & Ho K. C. 2014. "International Students and the Politics of Language Among "Globalising Universities" in Asia." *Knowledge Cultures* 2 (4): 64–89.
Yeoh, Brenda S.A., Shirlena Huang, and Theodora Lam. 2005. "Transnationalizing the 'Asian' Family: Imaginaries, Intimacies and Strategic Intents." *Global Networks: A Journal of Transnational Affairs* 5 (4): 307–315.
Yeoh, Brenda S.A., and Lin Weiqiang. 2013. "Chinese Migration to Singapore: Discourses and Discontents in a Globalizing Nation-State." *Asian and Pacific Migration Journal* 22 (1): 31–53.
Ziguras, Christopher, and Siew Fang Law. 2006. "Recruiting International Students as Skilled Immigrants: The Global 'Skills Race' as Viewed from Australia and Malaysia." *Globalisation, Societies, and Education* 4: 59–76.

The ordinary lives and uneven precarity of the DACAmented: visualising migrant precarity in metropolitan Washington

Marie Price and Giancarla Rojas

ABSTRACT

In many countries, undocumented immigrant youth experience differential socio-legal considerations because of their real and perceived vulnerability. Deferred Action for Childhood Arrivals (DACA) is an example of a relatively new 'temporary' and 'skilled' migrant category in the United States created for undocumented youth in 2012 and rescinded 5 years later with a new administration. Nearly 700,000 immigrants still have DACA as of 2019. To visualise the place-specific and day-to-day experiences of being DACAmented, we used a photo solicitation approach with college students living in Metropolitan Washington DC. The value of this method is discussed with regard to appreciating the importance of protected places, scalar uncertainties, and the shifting socio-legal frameworks that immigrant youth contend within an urban immigrant gateway. The research underscores that those with DACA experience spatially uneven and oscillating precarity over time and yet the 'ordinariness' of their daily lives is a political expression of belonging. The possibility that this status could completely disappear in 2020 heightens the overall precarity for this group. This case study is indicative of broader trends towards the creation of temporary socio-legal structures for undocumented youth that can either heighten or lessen their precarity over time and across scales.

Among contemporary flows of irregular and temporary immigrants, there are significant numbers of children and youth. Because of the particular vulnerability of immigrant youth, local and national governments as well as civil society have created socio-legal processes to respond to the needs, merits and vulnerabilities of younger migrants (Gonzales, Terriquez, and Ruszczyk 2014; Hellgren 2014; Menjívar and Parreira 2019; Ruszczyk 2019; Blue et al. 2021). This study examines one such temporary program in the United States, the Deferred Action for Childhood Arrivals (DACA)[1], established by executive order in August 2012 by President Barack Obama and rescinded by President Donald Trump in 2017/2018. It then examines the everyday experience of having DACA in a particular place, the suburbs of Metropolitan Washington DC, with the intent to better understand oscillations in precarity and the ordinariness of daily life through a photo solicitation methodology.

Being 'DACAmented[2]' provides a temporary quasi-legal status with the benefits of authorisation to work, an ability to obtain a driver's license and, in some states, to be eligible for in-state college tuition (Gonzales, Terriquez, and Ruszczyk 2014). Plus, the immediate threat of deportation is diminished. Most DACA holders work and/or seek higher education. From 2012 until early 2017, over 887,000 individuals applied for DACA and by March 2017 788,000 had been approved (Capps, Fix, and Zong 2017, 2). In September 2017, President Donald Trump announced that he would rescind DACA, and in March 2018, the program was rescinded.[3] Because of the continuing of DACA renewals, as of 30 June 2019, there were still 660,880 DACA recipients in the United States (USCIS 2019). The overall declines are explained by the fact that no new people are added, some decide not to renew or are declined renewal, and others adjust their immigration status and no longer need DACA.

The DACA program began a 'normalisation' process for undocumented youth who mostly came to the United States as children, studied in primary and secondary schools, and in most ways fit into U.S. society, often having limited memory of their origin countries. As a report from the Migration Policy Institute notes, 'DACA is unique among immigration policies in its focus on educational attainment as a condition for eligibility' (Hooker, McHugh, and Mathay 2015, 9). After all, to qualify for DACA, applicants had to obtain a high school education using the English language, and some 18% of DACA holders had enrolled in college (Zong et al. 2017). Zong's study found that 55% of DACA holders were employed, and the rest were in school (either secondary and college). One in three of those who were studying was also working.

This research examines the experiences of DACA holders who are currently in college and living in the Virginia suburbs of metropolitan Washington, DC. The authors, an academic and a former-DACA holder working for an immigrant advocacy organisation, were interested in visualising the daily lives of DACAmented youth enrolled in college as a window to understand this latest class of temporary and skilled migrant and their everyday lives in the Washington DC suburbs. Although most DACA holders have been in the United States since early childhood, their temporariness stems from the uncertainty of their status rather than any prescribed length of stay. The skill level comes from that the fact that study participants are currently in college, hold DACA, and hope to work as professionals upon graduation.

The specifics of DACA are unique to the U.S. experience, but many countries wrestle with policies to address undocumented and unaccompanied minors and whether or not these populations should be regularised and/or temporarily permitted to stay (Menjívar and Parreira 2019). DACA was a stop-gap measure to address the realities of the 1.5 generation of undocumented youth who grew up in the United States without authorisation but are culturally and socially American (Rumbaut 2004; Gonzales 2015). Yet DACA is the representative of expanding categories of temporariness employed in many countries that allow migrants (both regular and irregular) to fill labour needs while precluding permanent residence (Boese and Macdonald 2016). In the United States, categories of temporary migrants have expanded in the last three decades to include: H1-B Visas, Temporary Protected Status (TPS), and Deferred Enforcement Departure (DED) (Blue et al., 2021). Along with DACA, such categories may confer legal non-immigrant status but do not provide a path to permanence, resulting in an unstable situation that can be suddenly overturned, as the Trump Administration demonstrated.

To understand the scalar and temporal aspects of having DACA, this study employs a spatial and visual approach. Spatially, our concern is with the lived experience of youth with DACA who grew up in the ethnically diverse and immigrant-rich suburbs of Northern Virginia, where the expectation for high school students is to attend university (Violand-Sanchez and Price 2017). It is also an area near the nation's capital and far from the US–Mexican border; for many years the undocumented population here grew but felt relatively safe from persecution or removal (Walker and Leitner 2011). This setting shaped the attitudes of the DACAmented as well as the community around them in public schools and colleges. To capture the daily lives and limits through images and landscapes, we turned to a participatory photo collection and discussion format modeled in Photo Voice and asked participants to visualise their lives with and without DACA through photographs.

Scale and the specificity of the place greatly impact migrant experiences of inclusion or exclusion, and this is especially true for the DACAmented. As noted by Gonzalez, compared to their parents, the DACAmented

> relationship with their community and their sense of place and belonging grow out of deeper, more intimate and local experiences. Thus these young people are perhaps more vulnerable to the effects of a dysfunctional immigration system that marks them as insiders and outsiders. (Gonzales 2015, xx–xxi).

Since the livelihoods of temporary migrants mostly play out in neighbourhoods, municipalities, and cities, it is important to understand the particular circumstances of the metropolitan Washington suburbs, a settlement area that has not received much attention with regards to the DACAmented population (Bjorklund 2018).

What follows is a literature review that focuses on the scalar and temporal dimensions of precarity that undocumented youth experience in cities. We understand precarity not as a constant experience, but one that is triggered in particular settings and under different socio-legal contexts. Conceptually we contrast *precarity* with the *ordinariness* of the daily routines of work and study that our participants shared, particularly under the 'master status' that DACA provides. We then turn to a discussion of the value of visual data in terms of understanding the experience of temporary migrants and what can be learned from it. Before outlining the methodology used, we include a brief summary of the immigrant context in Metropolitan Washington. After the findings are presented, we return to our discussion of precarity and the value and challenges of adopting a visual approach to understanding the everyday lives of undocumented youth living under heightened socio-legal precarity.

Literature review

Migrant precarity in this special issue is characterised by livelihoods that are temporary, uncertain, exploitive, and restrictive in terms of mobility and benefits (Chacko and Price 2021). While migrants often experience precarity (Anderson 2010; Robertson 2015; Hira-Friesen 2018; Wang, Li, and Deng 2017; Strauss and McGrath 2017) undocumented children and youth may experience extreme precarity and new forms of vulnerability, especially when migrating without a parent (Menjívar and Parreira 2019; Allsopp and Chase 2019; Blue et al, 2021). Yet as minors, children and youth are often treated differently by receiving states, and they may be able to regularise their status with legal assistance. Ironically, there is a stark difference in potential services and statuses available to those same migrants once they turn 18 and are considered 'adult'. The phenomenon of 'disappearing' from bureaucratic processes when young people turn 18 is well known, especially in countries with active detention and deportation regimes such as Norway, Sweden, the UK, and the US (Allsopp and Chase 2019, 299). At the same, there are powerful examples from diverse cities (such as Los Angeles, Stockholm, Amsterdam, Paris, or Barcelona) of civil society organising and coordinating to secure rights and reduce the precarity of undocumented populations, especially youth (Hellgren 2014; Mensink 2019; Ruszczyk 2019; Terriquez and Lin 2019).

As Roberto Gonzales (2011) argued in his influential essay 'Learning to be Illegal' undocumented youth in the United States are protected during their school years because of federal legislation that assures access to public education regardless of legal status. It is with the milestones of youth such as seeking a driver's license or paid employment that young people learn about illegality as a way of life. Gonzales observes 'the transition to illegality brings with it a period of disorientation, whereby undocumented youth confront legal limitations and their implications and engage in a process of retooling and reorienting themselves for new adult lives' (Gonzales 2011, 606). For undocumented youth in many countries, before they become adult their daily lives may be relatively protected while in school; it is when they age-out of that environment that their precarity intensifies.

Fear of detention and deportation is assumed to be a major source of precarity for undocumented populations. Yet this fear is spatially and temporally uneven, rather than a constant concern. In a recent study of undocumented youth in California, the researchers conclude that 'enforcement mechanisms function as structural triggers, sparking fear of deportation in particular instances' (Enriquez and Millán 2019, 15). Undocumented youth were conscious of inhabiting protected spaces (schools and homes) and moving through more vulnerable ones (public work sites or using mass transportation) as well as the gendered and racial profiles that make Latino men more vulnerable to removal. The same authors also noted that the most valued aspect of having DACA was work authorisation and the ability to obtain a driver's license. Deportation protection was a tertiary impact mentioned by only a handful of participants. The intention of DACA was to reduce the fear of deportation for undocumented youth, yet the program's greater value to recipients was employment authorisation (reducing economic precarity) and securing driver's licenses (improving physical mobility and thus reducing social precarity).

Ordinariness as a response to precarity

Going to work, driving a car, or attending college are ordinary acts for youth growing up in suburban America. These acts matter because as everyday practices located in particular communities they are indicative of political belonging. Political geographers have employed the idea of 'ordinary' to analyse the complexities of citizenship and how the spatiality of laws and norms are unevenly embedded in daily life (Staeheli et al. 2012). In their article 'Dreaming the Ordinary', the authors note that

> something that seems so ordinary for thousands of American high school graduates each year – going to a publicly funded university in the state of their residence – is in fact extra-ordinary for thousands who cannot attend … .It seems unfair because something that has become an expectation as a social right of citizenship for American teenagers is not available to those who are citizens in all but legal status. (Staeheli et al. 2012, 629)

The powerful advocacy networks that Dreamers (undocumented youth) in the United States have harnessed is fuelled by this sense of fairness, as both experiencing social inclusion through education and daily life experiences in their youth but then experiencing profound exclusion once leaving the relative security of high school or graduating from college (see Nicholls 2013; Pulvirenti and Padilla-Rodríguez 2015; Vargas 2018). Ordinariness can thus be viewed as an act of *prefigurative politics* in which boundaries are blurred between political goals and means and that allow activists live out the change they would like to see rather than just demand the change (Mensink 2019). Mensink bases his study on political movements to support undocumented migrants in Amsterdam, but he makes the general argument that 'leading a more normal life is already (partly) enacted in the organisation of a movement itself' (Mensink 2019, 6).

Similarly, Patricia Ehrkamp's work (2005) on the complex local and transnational attachments of Turkish migrants in a neighbourhood in Durisburg, Germany explores how daily practices (both material and symbolic) become acts of place-making and political belonging even when *de jure* citizenship is contested (Ehrkamp 2005). We concur with the observation that 'citizenship is located in multiple sites, some of which are material places, some of which are symbolic, and some of which are institutional' (Staeheli et al. 2012, 630). In our work with DACA holders, they regularly affirm their 'right' to be here and that they belong. That said, even among high-achieving students with robust family and community support systems, the uncertainty of the DACA program functions as a 'master status' that interferes with daily life, education and career plans (Terriquez 2015; Enriquez 2017). To capture the conflict inherent in both ordinariness and precarity for the DACAmented, we turn briefly to the value of visualisation.

Ordinary visualisations

While images are often used to depict the precarious lives of temporary migrants (Kendall 2012), it is less common that these same migrants document and visualise their own experiences. The exercise of visualisation of life 'with' and 'without' DACA became a way of exploring and sharing this transitional moment. Inspired by the Photo Voice methodology that has been used by other geographers (Schuch et al. 2014), the approach was developed to use participatory photography as a tool for social change and awareness. For the participants, the aim was to enhance their photographic and communication skills so they could draw attention to the daily reality of their lives and to underscore the ordinary aspects of how distinct places and landscapes are imbued with meaning, meaning that suddenly shifts in the intensity of precarity depending upon situational context and timing. It is difficult to visualise life with or without a particular legal status – taking such an abstract concept and expressing it photographically has, to our knowledge, not been done before.

Yet approaching migrant experiences visually affirms what Knowles et al. have argued that 'geography, as we practice it, is a visual way of knowing' (2014, 9). The value of photographs taken by our participants of meaningful places and objects also shares in Rebecca Solnit's observation of 'human psyches as landscapes' (2013, 25) that have texture, specificity and emotional value. These same landscapes can also be imbued with fear as geographer Yi-Fu Tuan explored in his influential monograph (2013). Fear is a multi-sided emotion with immigrants fearing exclusionary practices, racism, and expulsion, while native-born residents expressing fear of 'strange people crowding into their city' (Tuan 2013, 168). But fear is also extremely sensitive to scalar and temporal factors, something we will illuminate to better appreciate migrant precarity.

Capital city and suburban gateway

Metropolitan Washington DC became a significant immigrant destination in the 1990s (Singer 2004). Today, it is a metropolitan area where 22.6 percent of its 6 million residents are immigrants. The nation's capital draws immigrants from across the globe, placing it into the ranks of hyperdiverse or super diverse immigrant gateways (Friedman et al. 2005; Price and Benton-Short 2007; Nicholls and Uitermark 2016). The vast majority of the foreign born are from Latin America (39.9%) and Asia (36.2%), yet there are significant numbers of immigrants from Africa (14.5%) and Europe (8.4%).

The majority of newcomers to the capital region settle in the suburbs of Maryland and Virginia, with less than 10 percent in the District of Columbia. In the close-in suburbs, generally speaking, there were more jobs, access to excellent public education, and older affordable housing stock (Price and Singer 2008). Roughly half of the metropolitan area's immigrant population resides in the Northern Virginia counties of Arlington, Alexandria, Fairfax, Prince William and Loudoun. These suburban counties are ethnically diverse, well-educated and have some of the highest household incomes in the country; the participants in this study were all from the Northern Virginia suburbs which have a mixed record of inclusionary and exclusionary immigrant policies (Walker and Leitner 2011). Yet because these destinations are relatively new, many of the institutional support systems present in the established immigrant gateway are still developing.

In terms of scalar considerations, Metropolitan Washington includes portions of three states (Virginia, Maryland and West Virginia) along with all of the District of Columbia. The complex geography that the DACAmented, and undocumented youth in general, encounter when trying to access higher education is keenly observed in this metro area that is home to 12,480 DACA recipients (Svajlenka 2019). In the District of Columbia, undocumented youth (with or without DACA) who have graduated from District high schools are eligible for in-state tuition and financial aid or tuition assistance at the one public university in the District. In Maryland, as a result of a statewide referendum in 2012, undocumented students (with or without DACA) who graduate from Maryland high schools are eligible for in-state tuition but must go to community college first. Yet in Virginia, only DACA recipients are eligible for in-state tuition, other undocumented youth must pay out-of-state tuition. Finally in West Virginia, a jurisdiction in the metropolitan area with the fewest number of immigrants, there are no tuition equity policies for undocumented youth. In all these jurisdictions, DACA provides work authorisation, which is true throughout the United States. Thus, depending on where undocumented youth resides in the metropolitan area, there are divergent opportunity structures that influence the choice to go and remain in college.

Methodology

In the spring of 2017 when participants engaged in this study, the DACA program was still accepting new applicants but everyone was mindful of potential policy changes under consideration in the then-new Trump Administration. Those who volunteered for the study were all DACAmented college students (two men and four women) who had their own motivations. Most notable was their desire to be part of a research experience that was both personal and immediate. They were intrigued by the challenge to visualise their daily experiences of ordinariness and exclusion as the fate of DACA was being publicly debated. Moreover, the workshop setting allowed for socialising and building connections among college students facing similar issues. This can be both empowering and also reduce the social isolation resulting from the fear of deportation of family members or disruption of career aspirations due to legal status (Wong et al. 2017; Jones and Nichols 2017).

This methodological approach is grounded in concerns with positionality and efforts were made to reduce some of the inherent power imbalances between researchers and participants (Chacko 2004). 'Positionality marks the social situatedness of individual subjects with particular sociospatial contexts and relations to others that shape their knowledge, views, subjectivity, identity, imaginary, and conditions of existence' (Leitner and Ehrkamp 2006, 1616). As a research team, our identities and subjectivities are inextricably tied to our shared desire to reduce the precarity of immigrant youth through advocacy and research (Leitner and Strunk 2014). One of the authors is a young Latina DREAMer who recently graduated from college and works for an immigrant advocacy organisation; she secured legal permanent residence through marriage to a U.S. citizen and thus no longer has DACA. Having experienced first-hand the daily exclusions and precarity of being undocumented, finding ways to communicate the ordinariness of such life experiences is a motivation for this study. The other author is a white university professor and immigration scholar who was born in the United States and thus has no direct experience with the daily precarities of being undocumented. Her motivations are tied to her long-standing research about the mixed embeddedness of immigrants in localities and the intersectionality of human capital, ethnicity, race, gender and legal status in the experience of inclusion/exclusion over space, scale, and time. As a research team, their mix of experiences, backgrounds, ethnicities and ages facilitated trust among the participants, especially one of the researchers had shared their experiences and was relatively close in age. But the researchers did have many privileges, notably that of citizenship, so certain power imbalances were inevitable despite our sensitivities.

Students met to discuss the project and to share their views about life with DACA. They concluded that they would take pictures of daily life with DACA and how their lives might change if DACA were eliminated; the later proved harder to do. The ground rules were that no photos would include undocumented people who could be identified and photos would not be taken if they made people feel uncomfortable. They also agreed to not post any of their images on social media without the consent of the group. The goal was for each student to create 20 images over a three-week period, but in practice, the average was closer to 15 with a total of 90 images. Most of the pictures were taken over the three-week period, but students also inserted older photos that signified their life with or without DACA.

The most important part of the exercise was three weeks later when the group convened to share and discuss their photos in a 4-h workshop that was recorded and transcribed. Images were printed and spread out on a table. Each participant shared their images and many wrote captions. The group discussed each image and ultimately the pictures were sorted into themes. Particular images were weighted for their emotional importance. The value of the focus group methodology came forward as images could be assessed in terms of the themes they conveyed as well as the relative power or meaning of an image. Eventually, eight themes were developed from grouping the images; these themes were *school, work, freedom, transportation, fear, hope, differentiated time, and home*. Not everyone had the same favourite meaningful image but a small group of images rose to the top among the participants that captured their DACA status and what life without DACA might mean.

In addition to our qualitative data from a small group of students, survey results taken in 2018 from 111 undocumented students affiliated with the Dream Project were provided to us. The Dream Project is a not-for-profit organisation in Virginia that supports undocumented youths' access to college through mentoring and scholarships. All the study participants were affiliated with this organisation and participated in the survey. Responses to seven statements on a Likert scale were used to understand shifts in attitudes about college, career paths and overall fears with the rescinding of the DACA program.

Findings

At the beginning of the project, before photos were taken, students discussed the meaning of DACA to them and what it would mean if it disappeared. One of the older participants recounted going to college before DACA existed so there was a continuum of the DACA-mented experience from pre-DACA to life with DACA. For all these college students DACA was a highly valued asset. There are the obvious attributes such as eligibility to work or obtain a driver's license. And, in the case of Virginia, students who graduate from Virginia high schools with DACA are eligible for in-state college tuition, which reduces costs by two-thirds. But there are the intangible qualities of DACA such as 'a door opening' so that 'you can do the things that your parents brought you here to do'. DACA makes life in the city less scary, at least for the youth who have it. But it also draws a sharp contrast with the fear that their undocumented parents live with. Although each group member expressed appreciation for having access to DACA, they also expressed living in a temporary limbo status. As one youth described it, 'having DACA is like being given a little taste of candy. It is good but it is not enough.'

Similarly, all of the participants in the study were conscious of the possibility of having the DACA program eliminated. Losing even this temporary status means loss of work authorisation, no longer having a social security number or driver's license, and being blocked from various programs – in short, a return to the shadows. They were also keenly aware of the psychological challenges of the mental stress of living with fear of deportation on a daily basis, as has been documented (Roche et al. 2018).[4]

To understand the scalar and spatial dimensions of precarity for the DACAmented we took the categories that were created and considered how they informed our spatial understandings and the emotional qualities given to those spaces. Since all the participants were students, there were many photos of *school* and studying and such activities were viewed positively. The images ranged from exterior shots of buildings, to details of lab set-ups, to late nights of studying for exams (Figure 1). These images were remarkable in their ordinariness and could have been taken by any student anywhere. Of the photos taken, students liked best an exterior image of a main campus building at Northern Virginia Community College that looked contemporary, substantial and invitingly illuminated. Schools, like home, were seen as positive and hopeful spaces with minimal precarity.

As young students with career aspirations, attending college opened a door to opportunities that their parents could not imagine. The favourite image by far (Figure 2) among the participants was of a DACAmented student in cap and gown hugging a grandmother at a graduation ceremony. There is not only the joy of the event but a family accomplishment that is generational in the making. For the DACAmented, college success is typically viewed as the deferred success of parents and grandparents. Figure 2 was captioned with 'I want to dedicate all of my accomplishments to my supportive family.'

Mobility and transportation at multiple scales came through in the photographs, and there were clear positive associates with DACA and vulnerabilities without it. Walking, driving, waiting for a bus, being stuck in traffic are all daily scenes in a congested metropolitan area. As DACA holders, all of the study participants are licensed drivers, a status

Figure 1. The everyday routines of college students in familiar and low-precarity settings in school and studying at home.

Figure 2. A DACAmented student graduating was highly rated for it positive emotional value in the focus group. It was captioned 'I want to dedicate all of my accomplishments to my supportive family.'

that most of their parents do not have. And the ability to drive was embraced. As Miguel explained:

> Every time I hang out with my Dad, I drive. He takes the risk of driving without a license when I'm not around. But when we are together, I always drive because I have a license and the proper documents.

Driving without a license is fraught with risk, as even being pulled over for a minor infraction can lead to a chain of events ending in deportation. Access to a driver's license is one of the major advantages of having DACA. And losing this right is a sudden escalation into precarity. One student presented a photo of a bus stop and said without DACA students would resort to BMW, which is Bus, Metro, Walk (Figure 3). 'If I didn't have DACA I would not be able to drive. I would use public transportation or just walk to get to places.' If life with DACA provided more freedom to experience new places, life without DACA collapsed down to just 'do what you have to do and then go home.'

Beyond driving, participants found multi-scalar mobility with their status travelling greater distances and even crossing international boundaries. Two images were from aeroplane windows showing the landscape of Honduras (Figure 4). During the Obama administration, youth with DACA could get permission to travel back to their origin countries

Figure 3. Mobility with and without DACA.

for special circumstances. One participant was able to return to Honduras to reunite with a grandmother who raised her. 'DACA has provided a lot for me. Being able to go back to my country and see my grandma after 10 years was definitely a good thing.' Others expressed new freedoms to travel. 'The freedom to run as long or as far as I want' was the caption for a picture of a summer meadow with mountains in the distance taken during a road trip in New England. Others talked about expanding their mobility away from home, school and work, and trying new things like going to a concert in another city. One student joked, 'before DACA I couldn't even go to the park.'

The image that best symbolised life without DACA is Figure 5, showing the light of day coming through a partially opened door. The sense of options narrowing and increased anxiety about leaving the safety of home encapsulates a new sense of fear. One participant remarked that she used to feel safe living a block away from the police station but now she doesn't because she fears that the police are working with ICE (Immigration and Customs Enforcement) the agency responsible for deportations. Since 2017 with the inauguration of the Trump Administration, familiar localities are experienced with greater trepidation and daily mobilities are restricted. One student explained it this way,

> When I was showing my mom the pictures, with everything going on after the election, I think my mom and I have only left our house two times to go out and do things like take a walk or see something new. If you don't have to leave your house, then you don't do it, especially for security wise.

For the DACAmented greater mobility is a cherished benefit, but recent anti-immigrant policies have increased fear. The loss of DACA would significantly restrict mobility.

Figure 4. With DACA, a participant was able to go back to Honduras and see a grandmother after 10 years of separation. For the participants DACA meant increased and multi-scalar mobility.

The ordinariness of work and associated aspirations of a middle-class lifestyle were well represented. Figure 6 shows photos of employment in low-skilled jobs such as housekeeping, or wearing dark work shoes for restaurant work at Applebee's. One image showed a woman in a uniform looking at an expensive Michael Kors purse through a display window at a mall. The image 'suggests that it is something she would like to have but may never be able to afford.' Another student took a photo from a rooftop of an apartment building where she works as a nanny in the afternoons. The panorama shows the Washington DC skyline with the monuments and the Capitol dome, 'this is the view I want for my future.' Work is essential to their success and dreams for the future, yet only one set of images tried to imagine what work life would look like without DACA.

Figure 5. Without DACA illustrated by daylight coming in a partially opened door. This image represents a narrowing of options and increased anxiety about leaving home.

One student did a series of images of her room with huge numbers on her computer denoting the time. She said 'these pictures are about waiting and that uncertainty of DACA or No DACA, hiding in one's room and waiting. It is a safe place but maybe it is also a kind of cage' (Figure 7). In the series of six photos (two are shown), with DACA the bed is made, and the room is empty in the middle of the day because the student is working. Without DACA the bedroom is messy, at all different hours of the day, the student is asleep, on the Internet, only leaving for a short period of time. The setting appears more like a cage than a place of retreat yet it is also an ordinary middle-class room, occupied by one young adult, with a large Apple computer marking time. In visualising daily life without DACA the student saw *time* itself was being differentiated into life with or without DACA.

Since all of the students were Latinx immigrants, they had varying degrees of remembering a home somewhere else in Latin America. They also shared a mixed sense of identity, of being American and being something else. The most popular image of all the photos taken was Figure 8, which suggests an American identity shared with an identity to an origin country. It shows a samponia (a traditional instrument from the Andes) and an American flag hanging on the wall of an apartment in Metropolitan Washington. As

Figure 6. Images of work which show the low status jobs that many students have as well as their aspirations for skilled employment and more resoures.

one student explained looking at the picture 'I think home. Even though you are here, you try to make it feel like you are back there.' Students felt that this image might best summarise the DACA experience for someone who doesn't know anything about being DACAmented. It represents cultural mixing that gives one a sense of belonging as well as an actual home – in this case in the United States.

Overall, the students felt that the Washington Metropolitan area, and Northern Virginia in particular, was a safe space for undocumented people. Far from the US/Mexican border with a large and diverse immigrant community, the area seemed immune from the work place raids and ICE checkpoints seen in other parts of the country, although this was never entirely true. With the election of Donald Trump in November 2016, that sense of security waned. As one student remarked:

> In the Burke area, in the Northern Virginia, we don't see the risk as much as those living maybe in Arizona or California because we are living 'in the shadows' and we are hidden. But then we are starting to see cases of ICE raiding Annandale, Manassas, and Faulkner County. And so we are getting out of that safety net. We thought we were hidden and good, but we are seeing cases all over the country now, so you don't feel as safe as you used to. For a long time my parents didn't really worry because we were not in those places. It is getting worse and worse as the Trump administration is hiring more ICE officials.

When considering the time, in particular, the students wrestled with their oscillating precarity as the protections DACA afforded came into sharp relief, as well as the possibility that such protections may not be there in the future. Consequently, this shaped the way

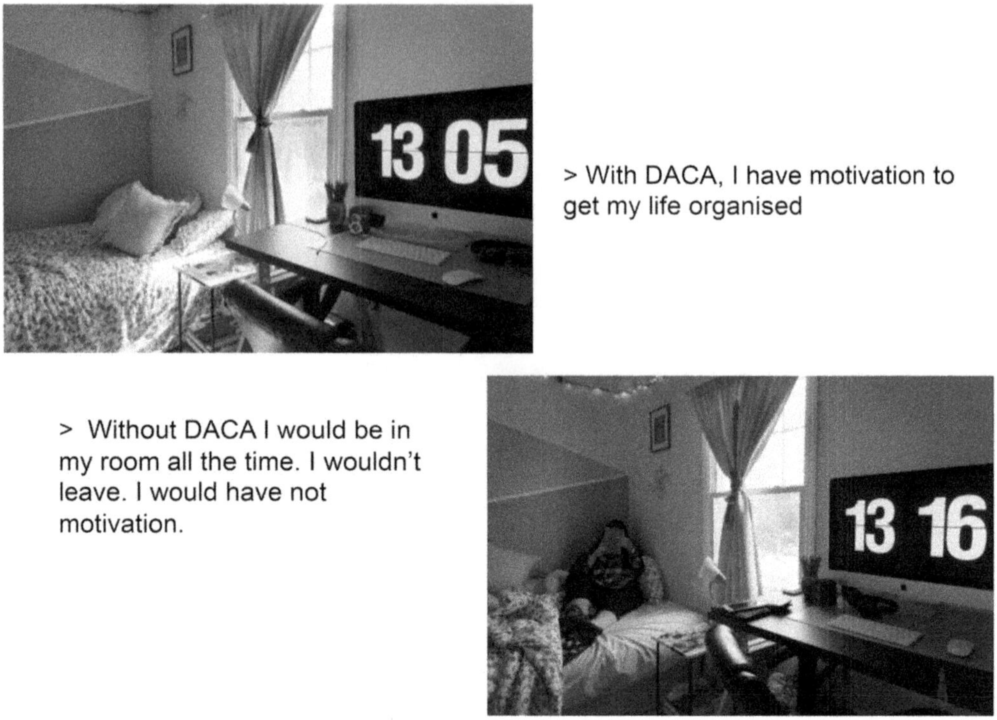

Figure 7. Daily life with and without DACA.

they thought about the differential experience of time. When asked to summarise the lessons learned from the entire process of taking pictures and discussing them with the group, one student remarked, 'it made me put everything into perspective and think about how my life really is different with DACA.'

Those with DACA know that their status is precarious but they all expressed greater concern for their undocumented relatives, especially parents, and how they moved through their daily lives. One student shared:

> My mom was working six days a week, now she is working four days a week because she did not want to expose herself. If I didn't have DACA, then I would be in the same situation, not working or going out much.

Another worried about his mom not being able to defend herself due to limited English language skills, saying 'you always see those videos of people being discriminatory towards people who can't speak the language. I don't know if that will happen but if it does I want to be there.'

Later, as the group reflected on gaps in the images, students noted there was only one image of food – a one photo of two steaming bowls of pho soup from a Vietnamese restaurant. This led to a discussion about food insecurity and undocumented status. On the positive side, the picture signified one can come home and if they see nothing in their fridge they can go out and try something new: an expression of freedom and mobility. But later, another student noted that many undocumented families do not have enough

Figure 8. 'We are American and we have ties to our home countries. This picture makes me feel like home.' The image was the favourite one of all the participants, in part because it suggested belonging to American and their home countries.

money to afford reliable meals, a point that the families themselves don't talk about. Or, the food that is purchased is microwaveable food that is quick and easy, rather than buying something organic and fresh. Even in the relatively affluent suburbs of Northern Virginia, an image of food led to an extended discussion of how mixed immigration statuses created more or less precarious relationships and experiences with food.

The rescinding of DACA happened in March 2018, after this photo solicitation exercise. To better understand the impact of this event the Dream Project shared with us their administrative survey data about student attitudes given the political changes. Of

111 undocumented youth surveyed (both in college and recent graduates), 98 percent strongly agreed or agreed with the statement 'the current political situation is difficult for dreamers in higher education.' While acknowledgement of the obstacles is obvious to nearly everyone, there is still considerable resilience and optimism. When the current college students responded to the prompt 'I often feel depressed and doubt my ability to graduate' only 44 percent strongly agreed or agreed with it. Moreover, 90 percent of these same students agreed or strongly agreed with the statement 'I am a resilient person.'

Discussion and conclusion

When we began this project, we envisioned that this methodology would allow us to assemble a collection of evocative images that would help people understand the daily lives and limits of being DACAmented. The images, however, were remarkable in their ordinariness, many of which could have been taken by suburban college students anywhere in the United States. We contend this ordinariness underscores a sense of belonging, a *de facto* citizenship, that offers insight into the lived experiences of those with DACA. As Staeheli et al. observe:

> The conceptualization of citizenship as ordinary trains our analytical lens on the ways in which laws and social norms are entwined with the routine practices and experiences of daily lives, as citizens—and other political subjects—negotiate exclusion and marginalization. (2012, 630)

Images gathered through photo solicitation collectively captured the ordinary experiences of undocumented youth working, commuting, and studying in an immigrant gateway city. A casual viewer might not notice anything special or unique about these lives, and certainly not see them as irregular in any legal sense. Yet in the process of documenting daily lives and sharing these micro geographies and landscapes, the scalar and temporal oscillations in individual precarity become more obvious.

The participants found the exercise challenging and also revealing. It encouraged them to think more broadly and concretely about how they benefitted from DACA. Since this exercise occurred in the spring of 2017, there are no new DACA holders now, but individuals who have DACA can continue to renew their status, which these students have done. For the DACAmented there is always the sharp contrast between their lives and the limits of their family members who live with the even greater precarity of irregular or undocumented status. They felt the greatest anxiety for their parents who often did not have the language skills of their children and were often at risk of deportation due to driving without proper licensing. As DACAmented college students, their sense of fear, anxiety and precarity varied but all admitted experiencing more anxiety and fear since the election of Donald Trump.

From the perspective of the researchers, we found the most insight from the discussion of the photographs, the captions created, and the grouping into themes that captured the range of experiences. At first, we were surprised to see so many images concerning transportation and studying. But then again, this takes up much of the daily lives of the participants. We were also reminded of the deeper anxiety that this particular temporary status of uncertain duration imposes upon our participants. The notion of DACA or even illegality as a 'master status' that shapes one's daily decision making also came through as we discussed and organised the photographs. Despite the uncertainty, we found that students felt a sense of belonging affiliated with protected spaces such as schools, neighbourhoods and places of work. And while they did not have citizenship, they strongly felt they belonged in the American immigrant story and were empowered by and some even participated in political activism.

We had hoped that this photo solicitation might lead to a virtual or actual exhibit of images that might enhance public understanding of the lives of the DACAmented. Yet, the images themselves were not especially dramatic and did not tell a story on their own. This was due in part to the limitations put on the process to not take identifiable photos of undocumented people and the abstract nature of the prompt. The process, however, of taking, sorting and discussing the images did lead to a deeper understanding of both the ordinariness of lives with DACA, the spatial unevenness of how precarity is experienced through daily movements, and the psychological pressures that living with heightened precarity places on people. Thus as a methodology for understanding the lived experience of temporariness it was revealing.

The revelations were not all negative. Having DACA ushered in new freedoms of mobility and experiences that were cherished and represented in the photographs – especially the chance to return to Central America to visit a grandmother. The openings that DACA provides are contrasted with the closings feared should DACA be eliminated entirely. With DACA there is bigness in the world; without it, space compresses to small and uncomfortable dimensions, likened by one of the study participants to a cave.

At a conceptual level, this project seeks to understand the scalar and temporal dimensions of life with DACA in metropolitan Washington DC. In terms of scale, students focused on the intimate scale of the home and the classroom as feeling more secure. Moving between those spaces, however, could bring different levels of vulnerability. With DACA, students' movements throughout the world increased, in some cases resulting in cross continental or international travel. Yet, students also responded to a rise in anti-immigrant sentiment by reducing their mobility, sticking close to home, avoiding new and even familiar spaces.

As a case study, Metropolitan Washington includes jurisdictions in three states as well as the District of Columbia, each of which has slightly different policies towards undocumented youth. This variegated policy landscape within one metropolitan area means that particular places are extremely important in shaping opportunities structures. Just as Blue et al. (2021) show the vagaries of asylum processing of unaccompanied minor children across cities in the United States, similar patterns of inclusion and exclusion are evident in state and local policies and resources available for the undocumented in general and undocumented youth in particular.

In terms of the temporal dimensions of precarity, the election of Donald Trump and his decision in 2017 to rescind DACA marked a sharp break in the meaning of being DACA-mented. While the fate of DACA as of this writing is being considered by the U.S. Supreme Court, all of the study participants are either still in school or have graduated. They are able to work, study, and drive with their current status. But the heightened precarity of their situation is obvious. Unless the U.S. Congress acts and creates laws that offer a DACA-like status or even a path to permanent residency, it is difficult to make long-term plans. Ironically, in their life experience and outlook, these young people act and live like college students anywhere and they are resilient. They aspire to careers as teachers, lawyers, and physician assistants. But they are situated in political and legal discourses, that cast them as (un)settled sojourners with no claim to permanence. This permanent temporariness is an all too familiar status that many skilled migrants and undocumented youth face in cities around the world.

Notes

1. To be eligible for DACA, an undocumented youth had to arrive the US before the age of 16 by 15 June 2007; also, a person must have a high school education or its equivalent, or have served in the military. Applying for DACA requires completing a background check, no criminal record, and a $495 processing fee in order to receive status for two years, which is renewable for the same fee.
2. This is a colloquial term used by students with DACA and is a reference to the term documented, which implies a legal status.
3. Challenges by federal courts forced the Trump administration to continue renewing DACA applications but no new ones are being accepted. In November 2019, the U.S. Supreme Court heard testimony regarding the termination of the DACA program, they will likely release their opinion in June 2020.
4. All the study participants still have DACA because of court challenges, but no new DACA applications have been processed since the fall of 2017.

Disclosure statement

No potential conflict of interest was reported by the author(s).

References

Allsopp, Jennifer, and Elaine Chase. 2019. "Best Interests, Durable Solutions and Belonging: Policy Discourses Shaping the Futures of Unaccompanied Migrant and Refugee Minors Coming of age in Europe." *Journal of Ethnic and Migration Studies* 45 (2): 293–311.

Anderson, Bridget. 2010. "Migration, Immigration Controls and the Fashioning of Precarious Workers." *Work, Employment and Society* 24 (2): 300–317.

Bjorklund, Peter, Jr. 2018. "Undocumented Students in Higher Education: A Review of The Literature, 2001 to 2016." *Review of Educational Research* 88 (5): 631–670.

Blue, Sarah A., Alisa Hartsell, Rebecca Torres, and Paul Flynn. 2021. "The Uneven Geography of Asylum and Humanitarian Relief: Place-based Precarity for Central American Migrant Youth in the United States Judicial System." *Journal of Ethnic and Migration Studies* 47 (20): 4631–4650. doi:10.1080/1369183X.2020.1732588.

Boese, Martina, and Kate Macdonald. 2016. "Restricted Entitlement for Skilled Temporary Migrants: The Limits of Migrant Consent." *Journal of Ethnic and Migration Studies*. doi:10.1080/1369183X.2016.1237869

Capps, Randy, Michael Fix, and Jie Zong. 2017. "The Education and Work Profiles of the DACA Population." Migration Policy Institute Issue Brief.

Chacko, Elizabeth. 2004. "Positionality and Praxis: Fieldwork Experiences in Rural India." *Singapore Journal of Tropical Geography* 25 (1): 51–63.

Chacko, Elizabeth, and Marie Price. 2021. "(Un)Settled Sojourners in Cities: The Scalar and Temporal Dimensions of Migrant Precarity." *Journal of Ethnic and Migration Studies* 47 (20): 4597–4614. doi:10.1080/1369183X.2020.1731060.

Ehrkamp, Patricia. 2005. "Placing Identities: Transnational Practices of Local Attachments of Turkish Immigrants in Germany." *Journal of Ethnic and Migration Studies* 31 (2): 345–364.

Enriquez, Laura E. 2017. "A 'Master Status' or the 'Final Straw'? Assessing the Role of Immigration Status in Latino Undocumented Youths' Pathways out of School." *Journal of Ethnic and Migration Studies* 43 (9): 1526–1543.

Enriquez, Laura E., and Daniel Millán. 2019. "Situational Triggers and Protective Locations: Conceptualizing the Salience of Deportability in Everyday Life." *Journal of Ethnic and Migration Studies*. doi:10.1080/1369183X.2019.1694877.

Friedman, Samantha, Audrey Singer, Marie Price, and Ivan Cheung. 2005. "Race, Immigrants and Residence: A New Racial Geography of Washington, DC." *Geographical Review* 95 (2): 210–230.

Gonzales, Roberto G. 2011. "Learning to be Illegal: Undocumented Youth and Shifting Legal Contexts in the Transition to Adulthood." *American Sociological Review* 76: 602–619.

Gonzales, Roberto G. 2015. *Lives in Limbo: Undocumented and Coming of Age in America*. Berkeley: University of California Press.

Gonzales, Roberto G, Veronica Terriquez, and Stephen P. Ruszczyk. 2014. "Becoming DACAmented: Assessing the Short-Term Benefits of Deferred Action for Childhood Arrivals (DACA)." *American Behavioral Scientist* 58 (14): 1852–1872.

Hellgren, Zenia. 2014. "Negotiating the Boundaries of Social Membership: Undocumented Migrant Claims-Making in Sweden and Spain." *Journal of Ethnic and Migration Studies* 40 (8): 1175–1191.

Hira-Friesen, Parvinder. 2018. "Immigrants and Precarious Work in Canada: Trends, 2006–2012." *Journal of International Migration and Integration* 19 (1): 35–57.

Hooker, Sarah, Margie McHugh, and Angelo Mathay. 2015. Lesson from the Local Level: DACA's Implementation and Impact on Education and Training Success. Report from the Migration Policy Institute National Center on Immigration and Integration Policy. 53.

Jones, Terry-Ann, and Laura Nichols. 2017. *Undocumented and in College: Studies and Institutions in a Climate of National Hostility*. New York: Fordham University Press.

Kendall, David. 2012. "Always let the Road Decide: South Asian Labourers Along the Highways of Dubai, UAE: a Photographic Essay." *South Asian Diaspora* 4 (1): 45–55.

Knowles, A. K., Tim Cole, and Alberto Giordano. 2014. *Geographies of the Holocaust*. Bloomington: Indiana University Press.

Leitner, Helga, and Patricia Ehrkamp. 2006. "Transnationalism and Migrants' Imaginings of Citizenship." *Environment and Planning A* 38: 1615–1632.

Leitner, Helga, and Christopher Strunk. 2014. "Space of Immigrant Advocacy and Liberal Democratic Citizenship." *Annals of the Association of American Geographers* 104 (2): 348–356.

Menjívar, Cecilia, and Krista M Parreira. 2019. "Undocumented and Unaccompanied: Children of Migration in the European Union and the United States." *Journal of Ethnic and Migration Studies* 45 (2): 197–217.

Mensink, Sander. 2019. "Prefiguration, Strategic Interaction and Political Belonging in Undocumented Migrant and Solidarity Movements." *Journal of Ethnic and Migration Studies*. doi:10.1080/1369183X.2018.1561251

Nicholls, Walter J. 2013. *The DREAMers: How the Undocumented Youth Movement Transformed the Immigrant Rights Debate*. Redwood City, CA: Stanford University Press.

Nicholls, Walter J, and Justus Uitermark. 2016. "Migrant Cities: Place, Power, and Voice in an era of Superdiversity." *Journal of Ethnic and Migration Studies* 42 (6): 877–892.

Price, Marie, and Lisa Benton-Short. 2007. "Immigrants and World Cities: From the Hyper-Diverse to the Bypassed." *GeoJournal* 68 (2-3): 103–117.

Price, Marie, and Audrey Singer. 2008. "Edge Gateways: Suburbs, Immigrants and the Politics of Reception in Metropolitan Washington." In *Twenty-First Century Immigrant Gateways: Immigrant Incorporation in Suburban America*, edited by Audrey Singer, Caroline Bretell, and Susan Hardwick, 137–168. Washington, DC: Brookings Institution.

Pulvirenti, Emma Sepúlveda, and Ivón Padilla-Rodríguez. 2015. *The Country I Call Home: Stories of Growing Up a Citizen in Every Way but One*. Reno: University of Nevada.

Robertson, Shanthi. 2015. "Contractualization, Depoliticization and the Limits of Solidarity: Noncitizens in Contemporary Australia." *Citizenship Studies* 19 (8): 936–950.

Roche, Kathleen M, Elizabeth Vaquera, Rebecca White, and Maria Ivonne Rivera. 2018. "Impacts of Immigration Actions and News and the Psychological Distress of U.S. Latino Parents Raising Adolescents." *Journal of Adolescent Health* 62: 525–531.

Rumbaut, Rubén G. 2004. "Ages, Life Stages, and Generational Cohorts: Decomposing the Immigrant First and Second Generations in the United States." *International Migration Review* 38 (3): 1160–1205.

Ruszczyk, Stephen P. 2019. "Non-state Actors in the Regularization of Undocumented Youths: the Role of the 'Education Without Borders Network' in Paris." *Journal of Ethnic and Migration Studies* 45 (15): 3023–3040.

Schuch, Johanna Claire, Brisa Urquieta de Hernandez, Lacy Williams, Heather A. Smith, Janni Sorensen, Owen J. Furuseth, and Michael F. Dulin. 2014. *Progress in Community Health Partnerships: Research, Education and Action* 8 (2): 197–205.

Singer, Audrey. 2004. *The Rise of new Immigrant Gateways*. Washington, DC: Center for Urban and Metropolitan Policy, Brookings Institute.

Solnit, Rebecca. 2013. *The Faraway Nearby*. New York: Penguin Books.

Staeheli, Lynn A., Patricia Ehrkamp, Helga Leitner, and Caroline R. Nagel. 2012. "Dreaming the Ordinary: Daily Life and the Complex Geographies of Citizenship." *Progress in Human Geography* 36 (5): 628–644.

Strauss, Kendra, and Siobhán McGrath. 2017. "Temporary Migration, Precarious Employment and Unfree Labour Relations: Exploring the 'Continuum of Exploitation' in Canada's Temporary Foreign Worker Program." *Geoforum; Journal of Physical, Human, and Regional Geosciences* 78: 199–208.

Svajlenka, Nicole Prchal. 2019. "What We Know About DACA Recipients, By Metropolitan Area." Center for American Progress. https://www.americanprogress.org/issues/immigration/news/2019/09/23/474653/know-daca-recipients-metropolitan-area/.

Terriquez, Veronica. 2015. "Dreams Delayed: Barriers to Degree Completion among Undocumented Community College Students." *Journal of Ethnic and Migration Studies* 41 (8): 1302–1323.

Terriquez, Veronica, and May Lin. 2019. "Yesterday They March, Today They Mobilized the Vote: a Developmental Model for Civic Leadership among the Children of Migrants." *Journal of Ethnic and Migration Studies*. doi:10.1080/1369183X.2018.1556457.

Tuan, Yi-Fu. 2013. *Landscapes of Fear*. Minneapolis: University of Minnesota Press.

USCIS. 2019. Approximate Active DACA Recipients Demographics.

Vargas, Jose Antonio. 2018. *Dear America: Notes of an Undocumented Citizen*. New York: Harper Collins.

Violand-Sanchez, Emma, and Marie Price. 2017. "Mentoring and Retaining College-Bound Dreamers: Establishing the Dream Project, a Non-Profit Organization in Virginia." In *Teachers as Allies: Transformative Practices for Teaching Dreamers and Undocumented Students*, edited by S. Wong, E. Sanchez Gosnell, A. M. Foerster Luu, and L. Dodson, 98–107. New York: Teachers College Press.

Walker, Kyle, and Helga Leitner. 2011. "The Variegated Landscape of Local Immigration Policies in the United States." *Urban Geography* 32: 1–23.

Wang, Hao, Wei Li, and Yu Deng. 2017. "Precarity among Highly Educated Migrants: College Graduates in Beijing, China." *Urban Geography* 38 (10): 1497–1516.

Wong, S., E. Sanchez Gosnell, A. M. Foerster Luu, and L. Dodson. 2017. *Teachers as Allies: Transformative Practices for Teaching Dreamers and Undocumented Students*. New York: Teachers College Press.

Zong, Jie, Ariel G. Ruiz Soto, Jeanne Batalova, Julia Gelatt, and Randy Capps. 2017. "A Profile of Current DACA Recipients by Education, Industry and Occupation." Migration Policy Institute Fact Sheet.

Index

Note: Figures are indicated by italics. Tables are indicated by bold. Endnotes are indicated by the page number followed by "n" and the endnote number e.g., 20n1 refers to endnote 1 on page 20.

For Product Safety Concerns and Information please contact our EU
representative GPSR@taylorandfrancis.com
Taylor & Francis Verlag GmbH, Kaufingerstraße 24, 80331 München, Germany

www.ingramcontent.com/pod-product-compliance
Ingram Content Group UK Ltd.
Pitfield, Milton Keynes, MK11 3LW, UK
UKHW020205200926
475702UK00004B/620
* 9 7 8 1 0 3 2 4 3 3 8 1 3 *